ZZ
EC12
E60
1991

DOCUMENTS OFFICIELS

MAY 2 6 1992

GOVERNMENT
PUBLICATIONS

ENERGY POLICIES

HUNGARY

NO RETURN

1991 SURVEY

MAY 26 1992
MAI

INTERNATIONAL ENERGY AGENCY
2, RUE ANDRÉ-PASCAL, 75775 PARIS CEDEX 16, FRANCE

The International Energy Agency (IEA) is an autonomous body which was established in November 1974 within the framework of the Organisation for Economic Co-operation and Development (OECD) to implement an international energy programme.

It carries out a comprehensive programme of energy co-operation among twenty-one* of the OECD's twenty-four Member countries. The basic aims of the IEA are:

- i) co-operation among IEA participating countries to reduce excessive dependence on oil through energy conservation, development of alternative energy sources and energy research and development;

- ii) an information system on the international oil market as well as consultation with oil companies;

- iii) co-operation with oil producing and other oil consuming countries with a view to developing a stable international energy trade as well as the rational management and use of world energy resources in the interest of all countries;

- iv) a plan to prepare Participating Countries against the risk of a major disruption of oil supplies and to share available oil in the event of an emergency.

* IEA Participating Countries are: Australia, Austria, Belgium, Canada, Denmark, Germany, Greece, Ireland, Italy, Japan, Luxembourg, the Netherlands, New Zealand, Norway, Portugal, Spain, Sweden, Switzerland, Turkey, United Kingdom, United States. The Commission of the European Communities takes part in the work of the IEA.

ORGANISATION FOR ECONOMIC CO-OPERATION AND DEVELOPMENT

Pursuant to Article 1 of the Convention signed in Paris on 14th December 1960, and which came into force on 30th September 1961, the Organisation for Economic Co-operation and Development (OECD) shall promote policies designed:

- to achieve the highest sustainable economic growth and employment and a rising standard of living in Member countries, while maintaining financial stability, and thus to contribute to the development of the world economy;
- to contribute to sound economic expansion in Member as well as non-member countries in the process of economic development; and
- to contribute to the expansion of world trade on a multilateral, non-discriminatory basis in accordance with international obligations.

The original Member countries of the OECD are Austria, Belgium, Canada, Denmark, France, Germany, Greece, Iceland, Ireland, Italy, Luxembourg, the Netherlands, Norway, Portugal, Spain, Sweden, Switzerland, Turkey, the United Kingdom and the United States. The following countries became Members subsequently through accession at the dates indicated hereafter: Japan (28th April 1964), Finland (28th January 1969), Australia (7th June 1971) and New Zealand (29th May 1973). The Commission of the European Communities takes part in the work of the OECD (Article 13 of the OECD Convention). Yugoslavia takes part in some of the work of the OECD (agreement of 28th October 1961).

© OECD/IEA, 1992
Application for permission to reproduce or translate
all or part of this publication should be made to:
Head of Publications Service, OECD
2, rue André-Pascal, 75775 PARIS CEDEX 16, France

Foreword

Since 1990 the Government of Hungary has been committed to a process of transition towards a market economy following earlier attempts at partial economic reform. During 1991 major progress was made in reorientating the energy sector particularly in pricing reform and in the restructuring of industry. The pace of implementing reforms is now extremely rapid and from the last quarter of 1991 through 1992 all of the the principal energy enterprises will begin operating under new structures. Their performance will demonstrate the extent to which the reforms described in this report are succeeding, and indicate where further change is required.

Detailed examination of the energy sector was undertaken by the IEA during the summer and early autumn of 1991. The main findings are presented in this survey. The report assesses long term energy policies, examines the development of energy supply and demand and discusses the energy outlook and the impact of economic reform on the energy sector. The energy supply industries are reviewed in turn. Particular attention is paid to restructuring of the energy sector industries and to the development of frameworks of relations between government and industry appropriate to a market economy. The report offers recommendations aimed at indicating the key energy issues to be resolved to ensure the success of the transition.

This survey of energy policies in Hungary is the second of a series of reports on non-member countries to be published by the IEA. The report is the result of a growing programme of co-operation between the IEA and Hungary. Collaboration in its preparation proved extremely fruitful and the support provided by the Hungarian Government was exceptionally full and open.

Table of Contents

List of Figures

Annex I

List of Tables

Introduction

An IEA review team visited Hungary to prepare this survey of energy policies in Hungary from 24th June 1991 to 5th July 1991 and again between 18th and 20th September 1991. Discussions were held with government policy makers, leaders of industry and other groups of people concerned with energy and related matters, such as environmental protection. The team greatly appreciates the general attitude of openness and willingness to co-operate shown by everyone it met in discussing policy matters and obtaining firsthand experience of existing conditions during a number of site visits.

The starting point for the team's examination of energy policy was the Ministry of Industry and Trade's paper Hungarian Energy Policy - June 1991, a policy paper approved by the Government in June 1991. Policy and structural change in Hungary's energy sectors are developing rapidly and the team witnessed remarkable progress in the focus of policies between its first visit and the conclusion of the review process in the autumn of 1991. Many more significant developments are certain to unfold during 1992. The members of the review team were:

Dr Jan Geerlings,
Team leader, formerly Deputy Director General of Energy in the Ministry of Economic Affairs, the Netherlands.

Stephen Perkins,
International Energy Agency, Non-Member Countries Division.

Erich Unterwurzacher,
International Energy Agency, Energy Conservation and Efficiency Division.

Guy Caruso,
Director, Energy Emergency Policy and Evaluation, Department of Energy, United States.

Pierre Girouard,
Nuclear Development Division, Nuclear Energy Agency of the OECD.

Richard Hamilton,
The World Bank, Central European Department.

Les Webber,
Business Development, Northridge Petroleum Marketing Inc., Canada.

Professor Nigel Lucas,
ERL Energy Limited and Imperial College, United Kingdom.

Statistical support was provided by:

Kyran O'Sullivan,
International Energy Agency, Energy Statistics Division.

During its stay in Hungary the team had discussions with representatives of the following organisations (our apologies are extended to any groups that we have omitted from the list by mistake):

Ministry of Industry and Trade, MOIT;
Ministry of Finance;
Ministry of International Economic Relations;
Ministry of Environment and Regional Development;
Ministry of Transport, Telecommunications and Water Management;
Ministry of the Interior;
Ministry of Labour;
Ministry of Welfare;

Members of Parliament;
Budapest City Municipality;
State Energy and Energy Safety Authority, AEEF;

Energy Efficiency Office, EHI (part of AEEF);
Central Bureau of Statistics;
National Atomic Energy Commission;
State Property Agency, SPA;

Hungarian National Oil and Gas Trust, OKGT, now the Hungarian Oil and Gas Corporation, MOL;
DKV Refinery Százhalombatta (part of MOL);
Gas and Oil Transporting Company, GOV (part of MOL);
Petroleum Trading Company, ÁFOR (part of MOL);
Shell Interag Company Ltd.;
Agip Hungaria Rt.;
Mineralimpex;
Budapest Gas Works;

Hungarian Electricity Board, MVMT;
Paks Nuclear Power Plant (part of MVMT);
Ajka Power Station (part of MVMT);
Gagarin Power Station (part of MVMT);
Miskolc Power Distribution Company;

Mininvest;
Coal Mining Restructuring Centre, SZÉSZEK;

Central Institute for Mining Development;
Veszprém Coal Mining Company;
Borsod Coal Mining Company;
Mátraalja Coal Mining Company;

National Technical Development Committee, OMFB;
Institute for Electrical Power Research, VEIKI;
Energy Management Institute, EGI;
Eróterv Engineering Consultants;
Technical University of Budapest;
ORMAT Turbines Ltd.;

Regional Environmental Centre for Central and Eastern Europe;
Representatives of several environmental organisations;
District Heating Works of Budapest;
Association of District Heating Distributors
Institute for Transport Sciences;
Representatives of enterprise.

The team wishes to put on record its gratitude for the time that all concerned, despite the other heavy pressures on them, readily gave to participation in discussions and for the way in which its many questions were answered.

CRITICAL POLICY ISSUES

Strategic, Economic and Political Developments

Strategic Considerations

Hungary has a population of 10.6 million and a land area of 93 000 square kilometres, with a population density of 114 inhabitants/km². Around one fifth of the population lives in Budapest, the capital. Elevation varies between 100 and 1 000 metres above sea level and the largest part of the country is rather flat — the Pannonian or Great Plain. The river Danube, flowing through Budapest, links the country with the Black Sea and in the near future will be connected to the North Sea via the Rhine-Main-Danube Canal. Road and rail networks, pipelines for oil and gas, and the high voltage electricity grid are well developed and of significant potential strategic value for regional energy trade. Hungary's domestic energy production — oil, gas, nuclear power, very low calorific coal and lignite — covers around half of primary energy requirements (52% in 1990). Hungary thus depends on imports for approximately half of its primary energy supplies. Domestic production has peaked, and energy consumption will probably increase in the future, so import dependence will in all likelihood also increase. In addition Hungarian nuclear power production is dependent on foreign enrichment and processing facilities, currently in the former USSR, though uranium ore sufficient for domestic requirements is mined within the country. (Treating nuclear power production dependent on foreign facilities unconventionally as "imported energy", as is frequently the case in Hungarian literature, yields an import dependence ratio for 1990 of around 60% of total primary energy supply).

The country is landlocked, with a small internal market. It borders Austria, the Czech and Slovak Federal Republic (CSFR), the former USSR, Romania and Yugoslavia. Principally because of former alliances, Hungary's main supplier of hydrocarbons and electricity is the former USSR. The combination of large imports from a single supplier and the country's landlocked situation creates special difficulties. The only sea link of significant capacity for fuel imports is the Adria pipeline running through former Yugoslavia and on to the CSFR from the Adriatic terminal at Krk Island. The pipeline was operated at around 70% capacity between mid-1990 and mid-1991 to compensate for a sharp drop in the supply of oil from the former USSR.

In view of economic and political uncertainties in the former USSR and Yugoslavia, significant uncertainty applies to imported energy supplies both with respect to the operation of the Adria pipeline and to the future availability of gas, oil and electricity from the former USSR. Much attention is being given to developing infrastructural links with or through OECD Member countries. Providing access through such links to large supplies of oil, electricity or as yet unsold natural gas will inevitably take time and require major investments. In the interim, domestic coal production is of strategic value and developing hydrocarbon storage facilities will be important in improving supply security.

Economic and Political Reform

Since 1968, when major revision of the central planning system was begun, Hungary has been experimenting with economic reforms to establish a market based economy. A modern tax system (introduced in 1988), liberalisation of trade (1991), encouragement of direct foreign investment, legislation permitting joint stock companies (1988), and a two-tier banking system including

Figure 1

MAJOR IMPORT AND TRANSIT FLOWS OF OIL, GAS AND ELECTRICITY IN 1990

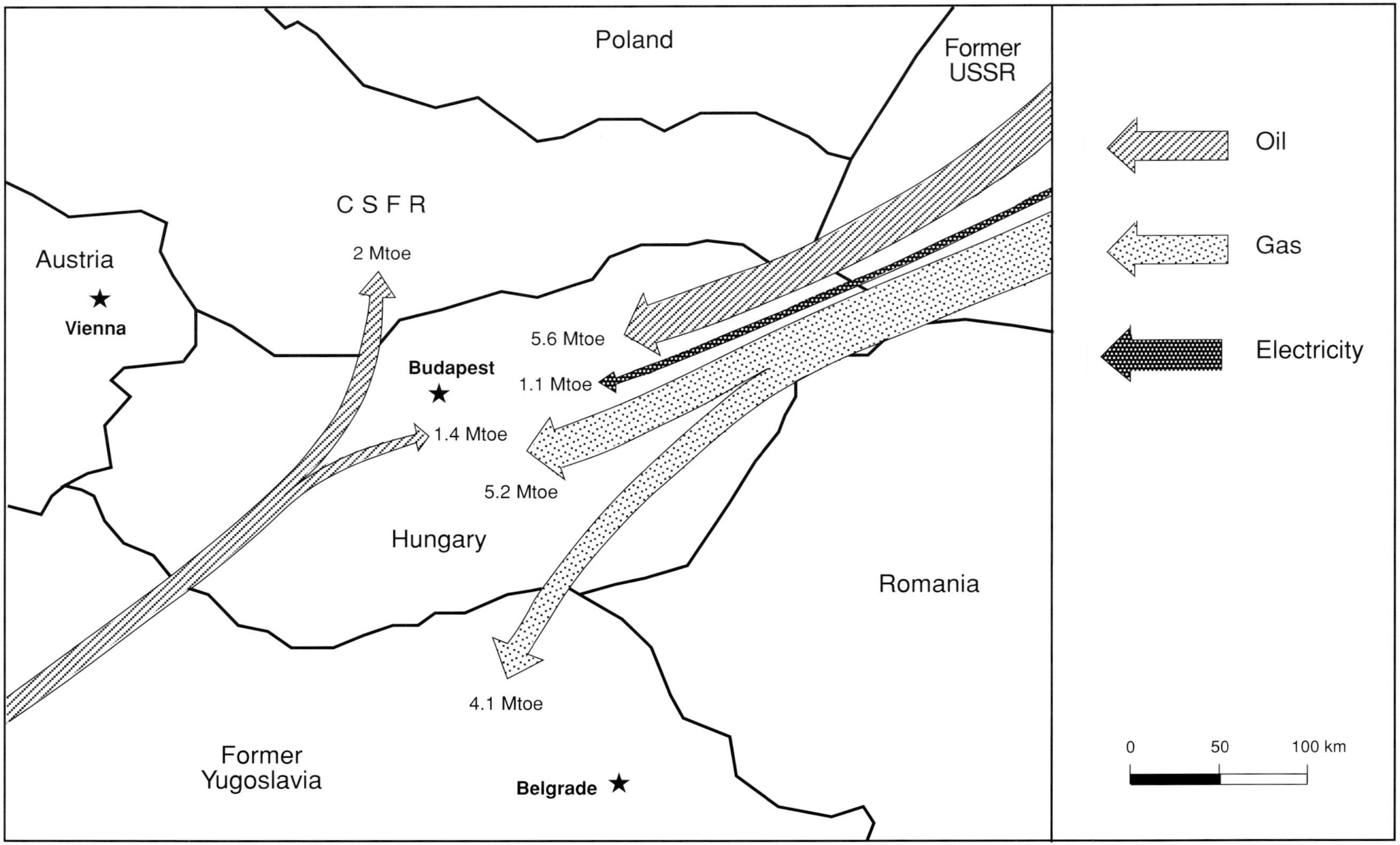

the National Bank of Hungary and commercial banks have been established. During the late 1980s, however, real per capita GDP declined, and in 1989 the current account deficit rose sharply to 5.2% of GDP, undermining Hungary's access to international financial markets. In response, the Government took measures to tighten monetary and fiscal policy. Pressures for political reforms led to Hungary's first free multi-party elections in April 1990, the coming to power of a non-Communist coalition Government in mid-1990 and acceleration of the pace of economic reforms.

The current account deficit was eliminated in 1990 and growth of 9.5% in exports to the convertible currency area indicated that economic restructuring away from exports to CMEA countries was under way. There was also strong growth in direct foreign investment in Hungary. However, real GDP fell by 5% in 1990, partly because of a 27% decline in rouble exports. Inflation was 29%, unemployment doubled to 2% and Hungary's gross convertible currency debt remains high — $21 billion or 65% of GDP at the end of 1990, about 200% of projected 1991 convertible currency exports. Economic output was expected to have declined again in 1991. Current projections indicate a very small increase in GDP in 1992 and larger increases in subsequent years. (For further information on general economic developments refer to *OECD Economic Survey of Hungary,* Paris 1991).

The Government's current structural reform programme is designed to complete the transition to a competitive market economy. It comprises four main components:

- reduction of the role of the state through private sector development and measures to reduce the role of the state budget in redistributing resources through taxes and subsidies;

- intensification of competition through further import and domestic price liberalisation, break-up of highly concentrated market structures and promotion of small and medium-sized enterprises;

- financial system reform;

- further development of an adequate social safety net.

International and bilateral agencies are providing loans to support Hungary's reforms.

Since 1989 reform of the policy making process has been systematic, and it continues to unfold. Single party control has been replaced by a multi-party system, currently under a coalition Government. The organisation of ministries has undergone a series of changes, the role of regional government institutions has been largely suspended and the 3 000 municipalities have been assigned increased competence. Further alterations in the organisation of government can be expected. Such profound changes have inevitably led to a situation in which the legislative and regulatory machinery, already overburdened by the economic transition, suffers from a lack of experience. It will take some time before a satisfactorily transparent framework of responsibilities emerges. Some resistance and delay in adapting to change is also inevitable. This is demonstrated to some extent through continuing government influence on prices in areas where they have officially been liberalised. At the same time the shortcomings of former policy making procedures have led to a general distrust of government planning. Flexible and responsive planning must, however, remain a responsibility of government and in this respect clear definitions of the limits and responsibilities of government are required. In the energy sector separation of the functions of ownership, regulation and management is particularly urgent. Increased attention will have to be given to the setting of clear objectives, to effective monitoring of developments supported by an appropriate system of data collection and to clear accountability in policy making.

Energy Issues

Government Energy Policy Objectives

The Hungarian Government began working on a new energy policy in 1989. Though this has been an extremely difficult task, the main policy objectives are clear. They are stated in the Ministry of Industry and Trade's policy paper *Hungarian Energy Policy — June 1991.* At the beginning of the paper the Ministry lists its objectives:

- eliminating one-sided energy import dependence — which results in economic dependence — and realising opportunities to diversify imports;

- improving energy efficiency, partly through encouraging energy conservation, and partly through influencing the restructuring of production;

- establishing market conditions in energy supply, and developing liberalised prices that reflect international values;

- giving priority to low capital cost solutions and economic means of supply, and to the creation of a flexible energy system, responsive to demand;

- giving due consideration to environmental protection priorities in the energy sector;

- involving the public in decisions connected with the development of energy systems that have an impact on the whole society, and making all efforts to reach social consensus;

- developing new organisational and control systems appropriate to a market economy and curtailing monopoly powers;

- limiting state intervention to a justified and necessary level[1].

This statement of objectives addresses the main problems facing the Hungarian Government in the energy sector in a balanced way and can be fully subscribed to by the IEA. To further the achievement of these objectives it is recommended that additional attention be given to the following general points:

- clarifying the framework of government responsibilities in the energy and energy related sectors, with the objective of making the responsibilities of each ministry, and their interrelations, more transparent;

- strengthening the process of decision making relating to the restructuring of these sectors, not least in government itself;

- ensuring that government and industry work closer together in decision making, especially in the areas of pricing and restructuring. Central government and industry each need to work closely with local government and consumer representatives in this respect, too;

- ensuring that the public is sufficiently informed of developments in energy policy. This is important in maximising commitment to the implementation of policy, as there are frequently significant costs associated with the changes that restructuring implies.

Institutional Arrangements

Energy policy is primarily the responsibility of the Ministry of Industry and Trade (MOIT). The Ministry has four divisions — energy, trade, economic affairs and industrial policy — each headed by an under-secretary of state. Within the Energy Division there are three departments: Energy Policy, Energy Supply and Environmental Protection and Safety. The Energy Policy Department's responsibilities include policy formulation and international co-operation. Price control is the responsibility of the Energy Supply Department. The Environmental Protection and Safety Department is responsible for all sectors of industry. The organisation of the Ministry is outlined in Figure 2. In addition, there are a number of commissioners, or special advisers to the Minister.

A number of other ministries and government agencies have responsibilities regarding the energy sector. The Ministry of Finance is responsible for policy concerning taxation, and ultimately for budgetary allocations to energy sector industries. It is also responsible for the liquidation of enterprises, in particular the coal mining companies that have filed for financial liquidation. The Ministry of International Economic Relations is responsible for duties on imports and exports of energy carriers and was formerly responsible for all import-export companies, including the one importing oil and natural gas. The Ministry continues to be involved in negotiating framework agreements with the former USSR for imports of electricity and hydrocarbons. However, with the liberalisation of oil trade in Hungary, and changes in the organisation of Soviet trade, the Ministry's future role would appear uncertain.

The Ministry of Environmental Protection and Regional Development has joint responsibility with MOIT for environmental protection in the energy sector. The Ministry of the Interior has responsibility for local government, which is expected to play an increasingly important role in the distribution of electricity, natural gas and district heating. The State Property Agency (SPA) is responsible for the implementation of the privatisation of selected companies, and though at the time of this review it had not handled the privatisation of any energy sector companies, it may be given regulatory responsibilities for all privatisation in the future. The SPA reports to a Minister without Portfolio. The Ministry of Labour is responsible for labour and employment policy including employment services, job creation and retraining programmes at national and regional levels. The Ministry of Welfare is responsible for social policy, including social security (though unemployment benefits are administered by the Ministry of Labour). As such it has a key interest in the future of the mining industry. Where a

---

1.   The full paper from which these points are adapted is included in this report as Annex I.

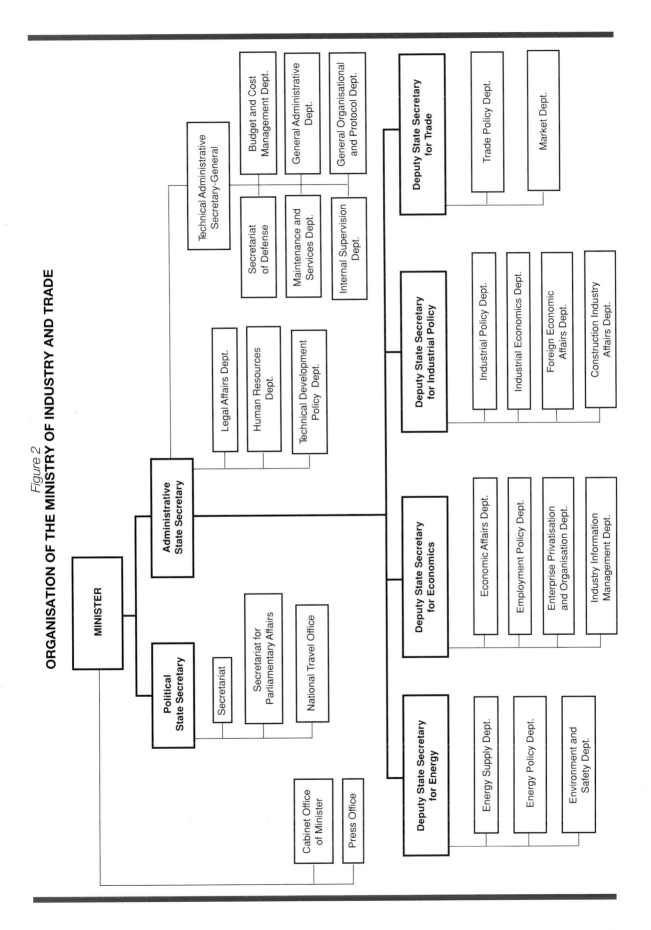

Figure 2

ORGANISATION OF THE MINISTRY OF INDUSTRY AND TRADE

policy document has implications for more than one agency of government, the initiating agency is obliged to seek agreement with the others concerned before presenting proposals to cabinet.

Some rationalisation of government responsibilities for energy sector industries would appear desirable. Some responsibilities are the result of past organisational relationships that are no longer relevant. Responsibilities in the field of energy efficiency need to be more clearly defined. The division of responsibilities for energy imports between MOIT and the Ministry of International Economic Relations may no longer be appropriate. Any reorganisation should be based on a statement of energy policy and directed at ensuring its efficient implementation. Indecision over the role of municipal governments, particularly with regard to revenue raising and policy co-ordination, introduces additional uncertainty into the Government's restructuring and privatisation plans.

MOIT is understood to be reorganising arrangements for the formulation and implementation of energy policy. This reorganisation should be directed at enhancing the implementation of policy set out in the Ministry's paper *Hungarian Energy Policy — June 1991,* and the opportunity could be used to balance resources to reflect the requirements of market based systems. The Energy Division has a total staff of 67 and a professional staff of 51; the ratio of support staff to professional staff appears to be too low to be efficient. A review of staffing in the Ministry would seem appropriate, to assess actual needs and examine ways in which efficiency could be improved, taking into account the development of any independent regulatory agencies. Finally, a review of the mechanisms for liaison within the Ministry and between it and other ministries is recommended. Responsibilities in this respect need clarification and mechanisms for co-ordination need strengthening, although full credit should be given for the establishment of the current procedures.

Ownership, Restructuring and Regulatory Issues

In keeping with the Government's goal of breaking up highly concentrated economic structures, plans exist for the restructuring of all the major energy enterprises. The electricity trust, MVMT, and the former oil and gas trust, OKGT, are being reorganised into joint stock companies. Services peripheral to their core businesses are being separated into independent companies in the first stage of restructuring. In the coal mining industry reorganisation is accompanied by financial bankruptcy procedures for some mining companies. The key objectives of restructuring in the early stages must be to increase management effectiveness and improve transparency and accountability in terms of economic performance. Introduction of competition into energy markets is an important but distinct objective of restructuring, and the priority that should be accorded it varies among the energy supply sectors.

Accounting practice is central to the effectiveness and accountability of management, and the Government's progress in reforming accounting procedures is welcome. A new accounting law modelled on practice in western European countries goes into effect on 1st January 1992. Its success should be kept under review, and further measures (such as provision for training) undertaken if necessary. Principles of cost accounting are not widely enough understood or followed in the energy supply and distribution industries generally. This results in significant uncertainty in establishing costs and undertaking project assessments.

Government policy on privatisation allows for four categories of enterprise:

- Some entities will remain entirely in state ownership.

- Most government owned enterprises are to be privatised without limitation.

- In a small number of cases where enterprises are judged to be of some strategic importance a minimum 51% share is to be retained exclusively for Hungarian nationals; examples include vehicle manufacturing and the national airline, Malev.

- For industries of great strategic importance a minimum 51% share will be reserved for central government ownership.

This last category includes the electricity supply industry; oil production, trading and refining; and natural gas production, import and transmission, though not regional gas distribution or coal mining. In November 1991, the Dorog coal mine became the first energy sector industry to be privatised. The non-core service companies separated from energy enterprises are likely to be other early candidates for privatisation. Restructuring and privatisation are two distinct processes, and the distinction should be clearly maintained for restructuring to be fully effective and the success of privatisation maximised. Clear statements of policy differentiating the objectives of restructuring and of privatisation may be required to make explicit the rationale for changes in the structure and operations of energy industries.

Local government is expected to play an increasingly important role in the ownership of energy sector industries. Ownership of district heating companies is to be transferred to municipal governments. The Budapest gas distribution company is owned by the city government and municipalities are likely to reassume some role in the ownership of other regional gas distribution companies. Local authorities may also play a role in the ownership of electricity distribution systems. The authority, structure and responsibilities of local government generally are undergoing systematic transformation, and though the progress made so far in defining the responsibilities of municipal and regional government authorities is welcome, legislation to provide further clarification is urgently required.

The separation of ownership, management and regulatory functions will be central to the success of the restructuring of the Hungarian economy, particularly in the energy sector, where the Government is expected to retain a role in ownership of a number of industries, at least in the short term. The scope and limitations of the rights, privileges and duties established by the new forms of ownership must be made explicitly clear. The objectives of creating a market oriented business environment and improving the effectiveness of management imply that the exercise of control by government over state owned enterprises should be minimised. Control should be limited to measures such as the setting of financial performance criteria to be met by management. Intervention in management decisions is likely to reintroduce some of the limitations experienced under the central planning system. The Government should further assess the framework necessary for separating ownership, regulatory and management functions. The experience of OECD Member countries may prove instructive in this regard.

Regulation, necessary where markets are significantly monopolistic in character, may be best achieved by an organisation independent of direct government control. This is particularly true in Hungary, where direct government regulation in the past largely failed to be effective in the long term. Where regulation is judged necessary, specific proposals as to the nature, composition, powers and responsibilities of the regulatory organisation should be developed at the earliest

possible opportunity, in order to minimise uncertainties in the industries concerned. Above all, implementation of regulations should be transparent. Uncertainty as to the nature of regulatory arrangements is a disincentive to investment. The experience of OECD Member countries may also prove useful in this regard.

Energy Pricing, Taxation and Subsidies

One of the main principles set out in *Hungarian Energy Policy — June 1991* is the development of liberalised prices that reflect international values. In conformity with this principle, the Government has made very large increases in energy prices since 1989, particularly for household consumers, for whom prices of coal, district heating and electricity (in Budapest) were less than one-third of estimated economic costs in 1989.

The Government removed formal control over petroleum product prices — except for liquid petroleum gas (LPG) — as of 1st January 1991. It has, in addition, made a commitment to the World Bank to remove controls on other energy prices in two stages. During 1991 coal, firewood and LPG prices are to be liberalised. By mid-1992 the Government has agreed to eliminate all household energy subsidies from the state budget, transfer authority for setting district heating prices to local governments and implement agreed new tariff structures for electricity and natural gas. Where central government is to continue administering energy prices — electricity and natural gas — those prices are to reflect economic costs fully. The same should apply to district heating prices, which are administered by local government.

Thus, assuming that liberalised prices for energy carriers will be set by suppliers to cover their costs, and if local governments do not subsidise district heating prices, all energy prices should be at least at the economic cost level by mid-1992. (Some prices would be above this level because of sales taxes on gasoline and diesel oil and import taxes on all imported energy). This will require further large increases in prices, especially to households for electricity, district heating and gas, before mid-1992. It also implies the elimination of subsidies for gas supplied to the fertiliser industry. These actions merit full support since they provide the basis for economically efficient energy markets, yield prices that give correct incentives for energy conservation — which in turn will have beneficial environmental effects — and reduce demand on government resources. It follows that any financial assistance judged necessary to compensate specific groups of consumers for price rises should be provided in the form of direct support, not through price management of any kind. Specific recommendations on pricing are given later in the report.

Research and Development

The proportion of GDP spent on R&D in Hungary was around 1.7% until recently, compared to around 3% on average in OECD Member countries. There is an extensive network of R&D institutions, including 51 independent research institutes financed from the state budget and attached to the Academy of Science, 18 state owned self financing research institutes and many research units in universities and private enterprise.

The National Committee for Technological Development (OMFB) was established in 1962 to prepare and implement government R&D policy. The funds managed by OMFB, which are substantial, are obtained from a 4.5% tax on industrial profit. The tax, paid in monthly instalments, is projected to raise about forints (Ft) 10 billion[1] in 1991. Of this, Ft 1.8 billion is allocated to the Academy of Sciences, Ft 1 billion goes to higher education and Ft 2 billion is allocated for miscellaneous expenditure by the parliament (in 1990 this allocation was used to reduce the current account deficit). The remaining Ft 6 billion will be managed by OMFB, with Ft 1 billion allocated for infrastructure such as libraries, universities and information technology.

Starting in 1991, financing of research proposals by OMFB can take place only through competitive bidding. No formal priorities have been set for government R&D, but some priority tasks have been indicated by OMFB, including the introduction of energy efficient technology and the use of new and renewable energy sources. The competition is managed by the Board of Technical Experts of OMFB, whose 15 members are appointed by the Prime Minister. The board is responsible for the call for proposals, evaluation, award of contracts and publication of results. The board asks independent experts to assist in the evaluation of proposals.

This programme has proceeded slowly. By mid-1991 only Ft 300 million of the Ft 6 billion budget for 1991 had been disbursed and by September the figure was only Ft 1.5 billion. This has caused severe problems for the research institutes, as they depend on orderly funding to maintain financial equilibrium. One reason for the slow disbursement is the onerous procedure of evaluation, but there is also some sign that OMFB regrets the introduction of the competitive system.

Total dependence on the competitive system has serious flaws. It does not allow government to fund certain essential programmes such as nuclear safety. Moreover it is difficult for OMFB to mount well structured R&D programmes because even if the offer of proposals covers the desired area there are certain to be overlap, omission and incongruities in timing. It is likely, for these reasons, that the system will be changed.

Other energy R&D is undertaken by the electricity board (MVMT), the oil and gas corporation (MOL) and the large engineering companies. MVMT entrusts the largest part of its R&D to the Institute for Electrical Power Research, Villamos Energia Ipari Kutató Intézet (VEIKI). VEIKI is independent of MVMT and works for it and other customers on contract. MVMT's budget for research in 1990 was Ft 436 million, most of which was spent at VEIKI. MOL spent Ft 700-800 million on R&D in 1990 in its in-house research institutes, and within research institutes attached to its constituent companies. No complete statement of energy R&D expenditures is yet available from the Hungarian Government.

Priorities for the use of national funds for energy R&D should be established by government with reference to the priorities of national energy policy. Management of the funds should follow the customer contractor principle with as direct a relationship as is feasible between the commissioning agency and the contractor. Nuclear safety research should be managed by the National Atomic Energy Commission and research supporting energy policy decisions should be handled by MOIT.

The remaining funds can be disbursed by OMFB in line with multi-year programmes defined by OMFB according to government established priorities. The competitive system might well be retained for this purpose. The present single committee for scrutiny of all OMFB-sponsored R&D could be replaced by advisory panels for each programme. The need to keep good scientists and effective research institutions in the country should be taken into account in OMFB's funding decisions.

---

1.   On average in 1991, $1 was about equal to Ft75.

Energy Supply and Demand

Structure

Data on the supply of energy in Hungary (production and imports) between 1973 and 1990 are presented in Table 1. Overall indigenous energy production increased in 1973-1988 as a whole. Then in 1989 and 1990 it declined sharply with the acceleration of Hungary's economic transition and associated losses of markets in former CMEA member countries and the fall in economic output. Coal production declined consistently throughout the period, representing 16% of total primary energy supply (TPES) in 1990 against 34% in 1973. The production of oil remained small but stable (7% of TPES in 1990) and gas production peaked in 1985, when it represented 19% of TPES (13% in 1990). Nuclear power production at the Paks power station began in 1983 and is now constant, representing 13% of TPES in 1990. Net energy imports have risen sharply over the period. The net dependence on imports increased from 38% in 1973 to 49% in 1990.

TPES peaked in 1987 at 31.8 Mtoe, then decreased about 3% per year to 1990, when it was back at the 1977 level. In 1991 a further and probably much sharper drop in energy consumption took place in response to increased energy prices and a further decline in economic output.

The primary fuel supply pattern is illustrated in Figure 3. There are significant differences between Hungary and western Europe, reflecting previous, centrally planned economic conditions in Hungary. This is particularly true for oil, which has a low share, primarily as a result of low demand in the transport sector. Oil accounts for only 29% of TPES in Hungary against 44% in OECD Europe.

Data detailing sectoral end-use energy consumption in Hungary are not presented in this report for the period before 1989. While such data are in fact available, their usefulness is limited because the methodology is dissimilar to that generally employed in market economies. For instance, in market economies all consumption of fuels for transport comes under the heading "transport", including diesel oil used by industrial vehicle fleets and gasoline consumed in the cars of private motorists. In Hungarian statistics, however, these were classified as industrial and residential use, respectively. Again, in market economies primary fuels for steam raising in industrial enterprises are recorded under the fuel input headings for each branch of industry. This has not been the case in Hungarian statistics, where fuel inputs for steam raising in

---

Table 1
Evolution of Primary Energy Supply
(Mtoe)

	1973	1975	1980	1985	1989	1990
Indigenous production	14.56	14.27	15.12	16.95	16.69	14.64
Coal	7.98	7.34	6.94	6.28	5.30	4.46
Crude oil	1.99	2.00	2.03	1.96	1.91	1.88
Natural gas	4.03	4.31	5.09	5.84	4.72	3.81
Nuclear	-	-	-	1.68	3.62	3.57
Other (incl. NGLs)	0.56	0.62	1.06	1.19	1.14	0.92
Imports	9.62	11.68	15.36	15.35	16.23	15.49
Exports	0.72	0.57	1.30	1.76	2.25	1.69
Stock building	0.04	-0.44	-0.45	-0.43	-0.27	-0.15
TPES	**23.50**	**24.94**	**28.73**	**30.11**	**30.40**	**28.29**

Source: AEEF.

Table 2
Energy Balance, 1990
(Thousand toe)

	Coal+ Other Solids	Crude Oil	Oil Prods.	Natural Gas	Nuclear Power	Hydro+ Others	Elec- tricity	Heat	TOTAL
Indigenous Production	4 733	2 261	244	3 812	3 578	15	-	-	14 644
Imports	1 433	6 286*	1 621	5 191*	-	-	957	-	15 489
Exports	-37	-	-1 636	-20	-	-	-	-	-1 693
Stock Changes	485	-544	-20	-69	-	-	-	-	-148
TPES	**6 614**	**8 003**	**210**	**8 915**	**3 578**	**15**	**957**	**-**	**28 293**
Petroleum Refineries	-	-7 995	7 957	-	-	-	-	-	-37
Public Electricity	-2 241	-	-227	-809	-3 578	-15	2 209	-	-4 663
Electricity Autoproducers	-9	-	-4	-13	-	-	7	-	-18
CHP Plants	-164	-	-87	-212	-	-	228	151	-85
District Heating	-721	-	-313	-1 500	-	-	-	1 995	-539
Other Transformation	40	-	-117	-	-	-	-	-	-77
Own Use	-129	-1	-322	-207	-	-	-390	-492	-1 541
Distribution Losses	-9	-8	-5	-249	-	-	-355	-130	-757
TFC	**3 381**	**-**	**7 093**	**5 924**	**-**	**-**	**2 655**	**1 523**	**20 577**
TOTAL INDUSTRY	**877**	**-**	**1 603**	**3 166**	**-**	**-**	**1 131**	**406**	**7 182**
Iron and Steel	664	-	102	422	-	-	148	99	1 435
Chemical	0	-	744	950	-	-	240	227	2 162
(of which: Feedstocks)	-	-	603	550	-	-	-	-	1 153
Non-Ferrous Metals	76	-	119	96	-	-	152	11	454
Non-Metallic Minerals	99	-	155	704	-	-	95	0	1 054
Transport Equip.+Machinery	14	-	97	316	-	-	129	27	582
Mining and Quarrying	1	-	17	5	-	-	30	2	55
Food and Tobacco	18	-	199	445	-	-	131	6	798
Paper, Pulp and Printing	-	-	48	101	-	-	48	16	212
Wood and Wood Products	0	-	1	3	-	-	18	1	24
Construction	2	-	39	11	-	-	33	2	86
Textiles and Leather	0	-	1	98	-	-	70	15	184
Non-Specified Industry	1	-	81	17	-	-	38	0	137
TOTAL TRANSPORT	**1**	**-**	**2 883**	**0**	**-**	**-**	**95**	**2**	**2 981**
Air	-	-	161	-	-	-	-	-	161
Road	-	-	2 546	0	-	-	-	-	2 546
Rail	1	-	167	-	-	-	95	2	265
Internal Navigation	-	-	9	-	-	-	-	-	9
TOTAL OTHER SECTORS	**2 503**	**-**	**2 383**	**2 758**	**-**	**-**	**1 430**	**1 116**	**10 189**
Agriculture	75	-	677	242	-	-	150	-	1 145
Commerce+Public Services	191	-	361	785	-	-	439	285	2 061
Residential	2 179	-	1 163	1 580	-	-	790	830	6 543
Non-Specified Other	58	-	182	151	-	-	51	-	441
NON-ENERGY USE	**-**	**-**	**225**	**-**	**-**	**-**	**-**	**-**	**225**
MEMO ITEMS									
Electricity Generated (GWh)	*8 295*	*-*	*1 361*	*4 846*	*13 731*	*178*	*-*	*-*	*28 411*
Public	*8 152*	*-*	*1 016*	*4 386*	*13 731*	*178*	*-*	*-*	*27 463*
Autoproducers	*143*	*-*	*345*	*460*	*-*	*-*	*-*	*-*	*948*

* Excluding transit.

Source: AEEF.

Figure 3
Structure of TPES by Fuel Type, 1989

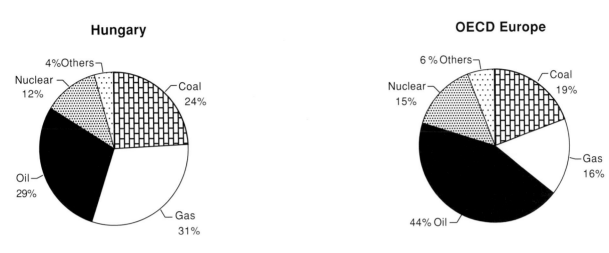

Sources: Energy Balances of OECD Countries 1980-1989, Paris: OECD, 1991; and AEEF.

Figure 4
Structure of Energy End-Use by Sector, 1989

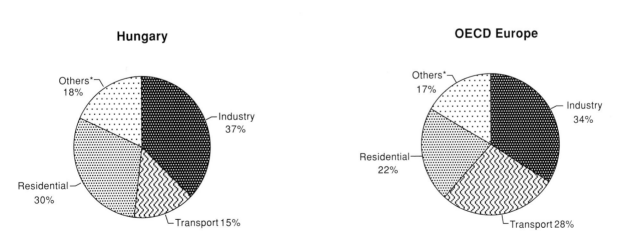

* Includes commercial and public sectors, agriculture and non-energy uses.
Sources: Energy Balances of OECD Countries 1980-1989, Paris: OECD, 1991; and AEEF.

industry have been recorded in the category "energy transformation" and transferred to the "heat" column of the energy balance. Final consumption was then recorded by industrial branch under the "heat" heading. These methodological problems do not, of course, apply to energy production or imports. The energy balance for 1990 (Table 2) together with the balances for 1989 to 2010 (Annex II) have been adjusted by the Hungarian authorities to accord with the practice in market economies.

Reflecting conditions in formerly planned economies, the structure of Hungarian energy demand is substantially different from that of OECD countries. Figure 4 illustrates for Hungary and OECD Europe the shares of total final consumption (TFC) in the main end-use sectors: industry, transport, residential and others. Consumption in the transport sector is considerably lower in Hungary than in western European countries and the proportions of industrial and residential sector consumption are

Table 3
GDP of Hungary (billion 1981 forints)

Year	GDP	Growth (%)
1989	863	-0.2
1990	812	-5.9
1991	768	-5.4
1992	769	0.1
1993	791	2.8
1994	820	3.7
1995	845	3.1
2000	973	2.8 (1995-2000)
2005	1 186	4.0 (2000-2005)
2010	1 489	4.7 (2005-2010)

Note: These GDP projections were used in the preparation of the energy balances and statistics included in Annex II, but differ from the projections described in the paper *Hungarian Energy Policy — June 1991* (Annex I).

Source: AEEF.

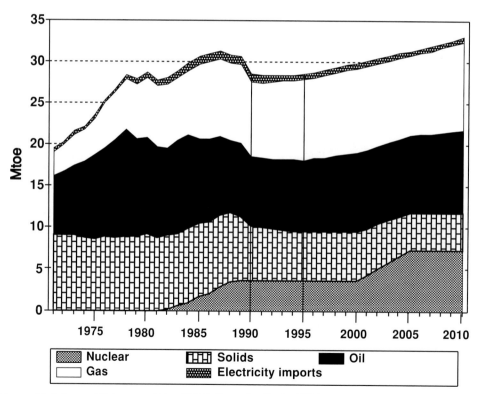

Figure 5
TPES by Fuel, 1971-2010
(if nuclear power generation is expanded)

Legend: Nuclear, Solids, Oil, Gas, Electricity imports

Sources: *Energy Statistics and Balances of Non-OECD Countries,* Paris: OECD, 1991; and AEEF.

correspondingly larger. An end-use structure similar to those in OECD countries is expected to emerge once the economic transition is accomplished. Industrial restructuring, economic growth and efficiency improvements will ultimately reduce the share of industrial energy use in TFC. Increased disposable incomes imply substantial growth in energy demand in the transport sector to meet increased mobility requirements.

Outlook

The Hungarian Government provided detailed energy balances for 1989 and 1990 and projected balances for 1995, 2000, 2005 and 2010 (Figures 5, 6 and 7, Table 2 and Annex II). The projections are based on the GDP growth assumptions shown in Table 3. They also incorporate the effects of substantial restructuring of large energy intensive industries. For the period

after 2000 two variants are presented, one involving new nuclear power capacity, the other involving a new baseload lignite power station. In Figures 5 and 6 balances for the periods between the years for which forecasts were provided are shown as linear projections. Although a linear trend is also displayed for the period between 1990 and 1995, a further fall in TPES is actually expected in 1991. The point at which TPES ultimately begins to increase again remains uncertain.

The forecasts show a decline in energy demand from 30.4 Mtoe in 1989 to 28.3 Mtoe in 1995, primarily as a result of reduced economic growth and industrial energy demand. From 1995 onwards, energy demand growth of about 1% per year is projected and total energy demand is estimated to rise to 29.6 Mtoe in 2000 and 32.8-33.2 Mtoe in 2010. The Government's estimates imply that energy intensity (TPES per unit of GDP) will fall by 14% from 1989 to 2000 and by a

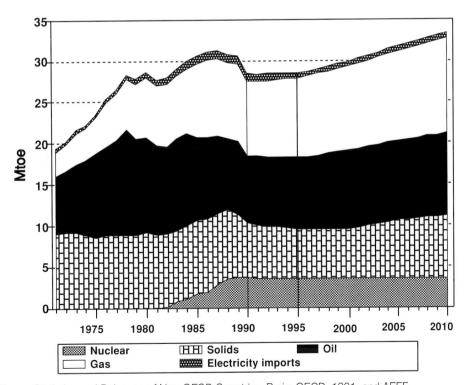

Figure 6
TPES by Fuel, 1971-2010
(if lignite power generation is expanded)

Sources: *Energy Statistics and Balances of Non-OECD Countries,* Paris: OECD, 1991; and AEEF.

Table 4
Projected Primary Energy Balances
(Mtoe)

	1989	1995	2000	2005		2010	
				Nuclear	Lignite	Nuclear	Lignite
Indigenous production	16.69	14.25	12.78	14.37	13.06	13.11	12.38
Coal	5.30	3.78	3.92	2.50	4.97	2.15	5.20
Other solids	0.32	0.29	0.26	0.26	0.26	0.24	0.24
Oil	2.72	2.45	1.86	1.45	1.45	1.03	1.03
Natural gas	4.72	4.20	3.21	2.85	2.85	2.38	2.38
Nuclear	3.62	3.52	3.52	7.30	3.52	7.30	3.52
Hydroelectric	0.01	0.01	0.01	0.01	0.01	0.01	0.01
Net imports	13.98	14.01	16.84	16.74	18.47	19.70	20.82
Coal	2.17	1.82	1.71	1.79	1.79	2.13	2.13
Other solids	-0.02	-	-	-	-	-	-
Oil	6.07	6.20	7.63	7.74	8.17	8.79	8.91
Natural Gas	4.82	5.45	6.96	6.67	7.97	8.24	9.24
Electricity	0.95	0.54	0.54	0.54	0.54	0.54	0.54
TPES	**30.40**	**28.26**	**29.62**	**31.11**	**31.83**	**32.81**	**33.20**
Coal	7.37	5.60	5.63	4.29	6.76	4.28	7.33
Other solids	0.30	0.29	0.26	0.26	0.26	0.24	0.24
Oil	8.79	8.65	9.49	9.19	9.62	9.82	9.94
Natural gas	9.36	9.65	10.17	9.52	10.82	10.62	11.62
Nuclear	3.62	3.52	3.52	7.30	3.52	7.30	3.52
Hydroelectric	0.01	0.01	0.01	0.01	0.01	0.01	0.01
Electricity imports	0.95	0.54	0.54	0.54	0.54	0.54	0.54
Shares of TPES							
Coal	24%	20%	19%	14%	21%	13%	22%
Other solids	1%	1%	1%	1%	1%	1%	1%
Oil	30%	31%	32%	30%	30%	30%	30%
Natural gas	31%	34%	34%	31%	34%	32%	35%
Nuclear	12%	12%	12%	23%	11%	22%	11%
Hydroelectric	0%	0%	0%	0%	0%	0%	0%
Electricity imports	3%	2%	2%	2%	2%	2%	2%

Source: AEEF.

further 27% from 2000 to 2010. This rate of improvement in energy efficiency is plausible up to 2000, given Hungary's high current energy intensity relative to western Europe, the likely impact of recent large increases in energy prices, expected industrial restructuring and the fact that comparable achievements have been realised in some OECD countries. However, the effects of restructuring and raising prices to economic cost levels are likely to have run their course by 2000, so doubts arise as to whether energy intensity will improve as projected from 2000 to 2010.

The expected energy intensity improvement stems in large part from the projected fall of 38% in industrial energy consumption, from 8.24 Mtoe in 1989 to 5.14 Mtoe in 1995, followed by increases to 5.27 Mtoe in 2000 and 5.95 Mtoe in 2010. Particularly large reductions in energy demand are expected to result from restructuring of large energy intensive industries (iron and steel, non-ferrous metals, petrochemicals and chemicals). These reductions are partially offset by increases in demand in other industries. For the transport sector, however, experience in western Europe and the Government's own predictions of increases in the number of vehicles suggest that demand will grow more rapidly than the 1.8% per year projected to 2010.

Alternative scenarios based on different rates of growth in economic output presented in Hungarian Energy Policy — June 1991 show only slight differences in the TPES growth rate. This is due to the underlying assumption that at higher rates of economic growth, accelerated turnover of capital equipment and a more rapid restructuring of the economy will result in increased efficiency improvements, sufficient to offset the pressure on energy demand. Such effects can indeed be expected but their potential significance remains to be determined. Economic restructuring together with more market oriented energy pricing will result in patterns of energy growth very different from extrapolations of past trends. This

makes forecasting difficult, with major uncertainties both in the effects of price reform on sectoral energy consumption, and in the evolution of demand by sector thereafter. In these circumstances, it would be more useful to develop scenarios to test a wider range parameters.

The changes forecast in electricity consumption in the projected balances (Annex II), corresponding to the "moderately optimistic" scenario (described in Annex I), seem rather modest. Total electricity demand is forecast to grow by only 1.2% per year, from 40.7 TWh in 1989 to 43.8 TWh in 2000 and 52.1 TWh in 2010. In the past, electricity demand has consistently grown faster than GDP both in Hungary and in OECD Europe. Industrial restructuring and adjustment of prices to economic levels will undoubtedly limit growth in electricity demand during the 1990s, and the

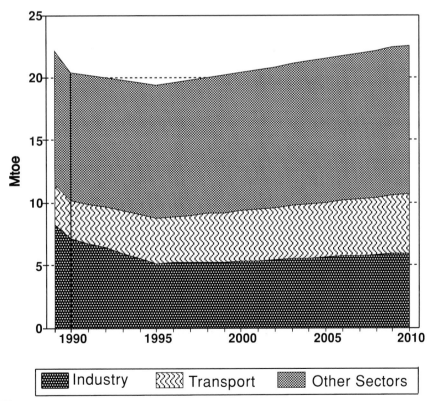

Figure 7
Forecast TFC by Sector, 1989-2010

Source: AEEF.

Government's electricity demand forecast up to 2000 seems reasonable for most end-use sectors. However, it takes insufficient account of new electricity demand in industries that will grow as the economy is restructured. This industrial growth must occur if the assumed increase in GDP is to be realised. But since economic cost-based pricing and the impact of a large part of industrial restructuring on growth in electricity demand will presumably have had their full effect by 2000, a projected average growth rate of 1.8% per year in total electricity demand between 2000 and 2010 may be too low in view of the average annual projected GDP growth rate of 4.3%.

There are uncertainties about future household electricity demand. Households accounted for 27% of total electricity demand in 1990. Demand grew 6% per year during the 1980s with no deceleration in 1990 despite a shrinking economy and the fact that virtually all dwellings have already been connected to grid supply. Since per capita household demand is only 60% of the level in OECD Europe it is probably far from saturation. However, residential electricity price increases have been very large since 1989, and further very large increases are needed to reach economic cost levels. These will restrain demand over the next few years, though by how much is unclear. The Government's forecast that household demand will grow from 0.74 Mtoe in 1989 to 0.89 Mtoe in 1995 and 0.98 Mtoe in 2000 seems reasonable. Less reasonable, perhaps, is the assumption of only 1.6% annual growth from 2000 to 2010.

The increase in electricity generation between 1989 and 2000 is seen as coming largely from new gas turbines, some in combined cycle. Some of the new units would generate both heat and electricity. The thermal efficiency associated with the incremental electricity generation over this period is 49%, compared with an average of 32% in 1989. Net electricity imports are projected to be 6.3 TWh per year throughout the forecast period. Own use and losses at power stations plus losses in transmission and distribution are forecast to fall from 22.3% of total demand in 1989 to 19.6% in 2010.

Total final consumption of heat is projected to fall from 1.67 Mtoe in 1989 to 1.38 Mtoe in 2010. This forecast reflects the likelihood that district heating will be uncompetitive with other energy carriers, especially natural gas, in new buildings and industrial establishments. Unexpectedly, own use and losses in the supply of district heating are shown rising from 0.51 Mtoe in 1989 to 0.63 Mtoe in 2010. It should, however, be feasible and economic to reduce these losses.

Coal demand is forecast to fall from 7.37 Mtoe in 1989 to 4.28 Mtoe (nuclear scenario) or 7.33 Mtoe (lignite scenario) in 2010. Demand for coal in electricity generation and combined heat and power (CHP) generation falls from 2.44 Mtoe to 1.12 Mtoe. Consumption at single-purpose district heating stations is shown falling from 0.78 Mtoe to 0.6 Mtoe. Demand by industry falls from 1.27 Mtoe to 0.51 Mtoe, largely because of contraction in the iron and steel and non-ferrous metals industries. Residential demand falls from 2.45 Mtoe to 1.97 Mtoe — a projected reduction that may be unduly small. According to the forecast, coal would account for 25% of total household energy demand in 2010, compared with 37% in 1989 and 7% in OECD Europe in 1988.

Total demand for natural gas is forecast to increase modestly from 9.36 Mtoe in 1989 to 10.62 Mtoe (nuclear scenario) or 11.62 Mtoe (lignite scenario) in 2010. Increased use is shown in CHP generation, households and the commercial sector. Household demand increases from 1.52 Mtoe in 1989 to 2.90 Mtoe in 2010, partly because of conversion from coal but mostly from new demand. Gas demand in industry is projected to fall from 3.44 Mtoe in 1989 to 2.47 Mtoe in 2010, though demand for gas as a petrochemical feedstock falls less, from 0.74 Mtoe to 0.63 Mtoe. Total gas demand could grow at a greater rate than forecast if gas is substituted for oil and coal in power generation — up to 0.75 Mtoe more if gas is used fully in dual fired oil/gas power generating capacity, and by even more if gas is used to the maximum in dual fired coal/gas power stations. Such a situation would require additional gas storage facilities, or other measures, to ensure that all peak demand is met. The extent of substitution of gas in dual fired generating capacity will depend, however, on the price differentials between gas, heavy fuel oil and coal. Heavy fuel oil may well prove more competitive. Further increases in gas demand could arise for power generation if electricity demand grows more quickly than currently forecast by the Government.

Oil consumption is projected to fall from 8.79 Mtoe in 1989 to 8.65 Mtoe in 1995, then rise to 9.49 Mtoe in 2000 and 9.82-9.94 Mtoe in 2010, with the transport sector accounting for nearly all of the increase as well as offsetting reductions in demand by other sectors. Given its versatility, oil will probably be used to make up for any possible shortfalls in supplies of other energy carriers or to meet unexpected increases in demand. Thus the actual increase in oil consumption may be greater than projected if Hungary has difficulties in obtaining increased gas imports or if oil demand for transportation rises more quickly than forecast.

Indigenous energy production registers a net decline from 1989 to 2010. In the nuclear scenario the Government projects that reductions in coal, oil and natural gas production will more than offset increases in nuclear power generation. In the lignite scenario projected reductions in oil and gas production more than offset increases in domestic lignite production, with nuclear power remaining constant. The production of oil, and to a lesser extent gas, will decrease, even if expected new finds are taken into account. The development of coal production is rather uncertain. Much depends on the pace of rationalisation in the coal mining industry as well as on decisions on a new baseload power station.

Rising energy demand coupled with declining indigenous production implies growing energy imports. Import dependence is expected to rise from 46% of total primary energy demand in 1989 to 57% in 2000 and 60% (nuclear scenario) or 63% (lignite scenario) in 2010. The increase in projected natural gas imports is particularly large, from 4.84 Mtoe in 1989 to 6.96 Mtoe in 2000 and 8.24-9.24 Mtoe in 2010. Hungary now has only two firm contracts for the import of natural gas, both with the former USSR. The first is for 2 billion cubic meters per year until 2008, and the second for 2.8 bcm per year to 1999. These two contracts amount to only 3.9 Mtoe per year. It is important for Hungary to negotiate additional firm gas import contracts as soon as possible to assure supplies. Without this assurance significant risk is introduced into currently planned investments in combustion turbine power generating units, which are designed to run on gas and for which oil product fuels would be very expensive. Several studies are being prepared to determine how best to secure reliable additional gas supplies.

The energy forecasts provided to the IEA were prepared using a combination of two approaches. First, a top down approach produced estimates of total primary energy demand and electricity demand, based on economic growth projections and assumptions about the pace of industrial restructuring and energy efficiency, using as guidelines experiences in western Europe. Second, a bottom up approach was used, under which detailed sectoral estimates were made for supply and demand based on discussions with energy producers and consumers. Explicit price and income relations were not accounted for in the forecasts, which is understandable as relative price variations were limited until recently.

The two-fold approach using western European experience as a guide is satisfactory. However, the following comments should be considered in summary:

- Given the assumptions for GDP growth, energy demand could be higher than projected in the transportation sector.

- The projected average growth rates of 1% per year in total energy demand and 1.8% per year in electricity demand over the same period may be too low to support a projected GDP growth rate of 4.3% per year between 2000 and 2010.

- Given the uncertainties of forecasting energy demand during Hungary's economic transition, the range of parameters examined in the Government's energy demand scenarios is unduly small.

- Existing gas import contracts cover only part of expected gas imports. It would therefore appear important for Hungary to negotiate additional contracts as soon as possible.

- The increase in oil consumption may be greater than the Government projects if Hungary has difficulties in obtaining increased gas imports or if oil demand for transportation rises more quickly than forecast.

Energy and the Environment

Institutional Organisation

Protection of the environment in the energy sector is the joint responsibility of the Ministry of Environmental and Regional Development and MOIT. Within the former, the Department of Air, Water and Soil Protection and the Department of Environmental Policy and Analysis are particularly concerned with energy policy while the National Agency for Environmental Protection, which includes 12 regional Environmental Inspectorates, is responsible for enforcement of regulations. The Ministry of Welfare is responsible for setting ambient air quality standards and monitors air quality through its regional offices. Some municipal authorities also monitor air quality. The Ministry of Transport, Telecommunications and Water Management not only has responsibility for the management of water resources (excluding pollution control), but in addition transport policy has a significant impact on emissions of air pollutants.

The environmental protection unit of MOIT is charged with the integration of environmental considerations into energy and industrial policy and liaisons with other parts of government on matters of environmental protection in industry. The establishment of such a unit, charged specifically with integrating protection of the environment into energy and industrial policy, is welcome. It is of great potential value, and efforts should continue to be directed at the difficult task of integrating energy and environmental policy. Consultation between government and industry on development of appropriate regulations appears good. However, procedures for obtaining agreement between ministries on energy/environment policy statements need clarification and streamlining.

The role of municipal and regional government in licensing the construction and operation of industrial plants and enforcing regulations is unclear and will remain so until the approval of legislation under development by the Ministry of the Interior to reorganise local government. This situation has contributed to problems in administering the system of fines for non-compliance with emissions regulations, compounded by difficulties in establishing liability while issues of ownership remain unresolved. These problems apply more to small industrial combustion plants than to the electricity supply industry, where liability is more clearly identifiable.

Priorities and Government Policy

Air pollution, waste management and working conditions present serious environmental and health hazards locally in industrialised areas of Hungary, though the overall magnitude of environmental problems in the energy sector fortunately is not as great as in Poland or the CSFR. The priority areas for action on protection of the environment in the energy sector are identified by the Ministry of Environmental Protection and Regional Development as:

1. vehicle emissions;

2. emissions of SO_2, NO_X, hydrochloric acid and toxic substances in highly industrialised regions where local air quality is seriously impaired;

3. emissions of SO_2 and NO_X from coal fired power stations.

Problems in the energy sector concerning the protection of water resources are of secondary importance compared with the control of air emissions. The Ministry confirms the view of the Hungarian electricity industry that there is negligible environmental impact from the normal operation of Paks nuclear power station.

Difficulties in dealing with environmental protection issues appear generally to be institutional and policy related rather than technical in nature. Issues common to restructuring the economy as a whole — questions of liability and ownership, enforcement of regulations, the organisation, responsibilities and powers of institutions, management incentives, resource pricing and investment planning — are all fundamental to environmental protection and need satisfactory resolution in order to achieve adequate protection in the energy sector.

In the field of vehicle emissions, diesel bus and truck engines are of most immediate concern, particularly in Budapest. Both design and poor maintenance contribute to very high emissions of particulate matter and unburnt hydrocarbons. Most of the existing fleet of diesel vehicles could not meet existing emissions regulations. Though the latest locally produced engines meet the requirements, regulations are not enforced. A proposal to introduce buses fuelled by gas (LPG and perhaps compressed natural gas) in Budapest is under examination. This initiative merits support and should be pursued as a matter of priority. Measures for controlling emissions from heavy goods vehicles also need to be evaluated.

Private car ownership and use in Hungary are expected to show marked growth in the medium term. As a result, NO_X, CO and hydrocarbon emissions are expected to increase substantially. Lead emissions, on the other hand, are expected to decrease with the progressive reduction of the average lead content in gasoline marketed in Hungary. Recent measures to reduce emissions from passenger cars include prohibition of imports of cars with two stroke engines; reduction of the import duty on imported cars equipped with catalytic converters by five percentage points; abolition of the excise duty on catalytic converters; and abolition of the import duty on four stroke engines imported to replace two stroke engines. Legislation being developed to control emissions characteristics of imported cars may necessitate the use of catalytic converters. However, the large market for imported used cars unsuited to catalytic converters requires special attention. Emissions from the existing car fleet are greater than might be expected because maintenance facilities and spare parts are scarce. Enforcement of existing regulations for car exhaust emissions, which is the responsibility of the police, is ineffective. The system clearly needs review, for diesel as well as gasoline vehicles.

Plans to reduce the gasoline lead content and the sulphur content of diesel oil are commendable. The current programme of planned investments at the DKV refinery in Százhalombatta will enable the maximum lead content of premium gasoline to be reduced from 0.4 grammes per litre to 0.15 g/l by 1992 and the output of unleaded gasoline to be increased. At the same time the sulphur content of diesel oil is to be reduced from 0.5% to 0.2% by April 1992. In addition, investment to improve the environmental impact of the refining operation itself appears to be necessary, particularly with respect to the treatment and processing of heavy vacuum residues. Crude oil from the former USSR processed in Hungary contains a moderate amount of sulphur (1.3%) and heavy metals. Limitation of the sulphur content of heavy fuel oils marketed in Hungary may become necessary.

Air pollution from stationary sources gives rise primarily to a problem of local air quality in industrialised parts of the country. Air quality is significantly below World Health Organisation standards in approximately 12% of the country — regions regarded by the Ministry of Environmental Protection and Regional Development as suffering from serious air pollution. These areas are mainly in a belt running southwest to northeast from Lake Balaton through Budapest to Miskolc. Emissions of SO_2 from combustion represent a health problem where associated with emissions of particulate matter. Measures to control emissions of particulates from the energy supply industries have been implemented. Between 1980 and 1990 emissions of particulates from power stations were reduced 85% through installation of electrostatic precipitators. These are reported to operate at generally high efficiency. Completion of the programme to install precipitators at all coal fired stations by the end of 1991 should bring such emissions down to a very low level.

The electricity supply industry accounts for 40% of Hungary's SO_2 emissions. The low quality indigenous coal, which the power stations are designed to burn, has a relatively high sulphur content. Most of this sulphur is in organic forms, and thus cannot be removed by any economic coal cleaning techniques. No power stations are equipped with flue gas desulphurisation (FGD). To retrofit power stations, the electricity trust, MVMT, would require external financial assistance. MVMT does, however, plan to improve control of NO_X emissions through modification of boiler designs when power station

boilers are reconstructed. The current refitting programme for coal fired power stations will end in 1992.

Hungary has made international commitments to reduce emissions of sulphur and nitrogen oxides under the United Nations Long Range Transboundary Air Pollution (LRTAP) convention. National targets for SO_2 emissions agreed under the Helsinki protocol of the LRTAP convention — emissions to be reduced 30% by 1993 from 1980 levels — are expected to be met. Most of the projected reduction will be accounted for by structural change in the economy and depressed demand for energy due to economic stagnation during the early 1990s. Overall growth in CO_2 emissions in the medium term is similarly expected to be limited through structural change and the effects of the recession. An examination of energy forecasts, emissions factors and plans for reconstruction at a detailed subsectoral level would be necessary to quantify the reductions in emissions that can be expected. Achievement of the NO_X emissions reduction targets agreed under the Sofia protocol of the LRTAP convention — limiting emissions to no more than 1987 levels from 1994 onwards — is likely to prove more problematic, mainly because of the expected growth in oil consumption in the transport sector. The same may be true for targets under the protocol on emissions of volatile organic compounds agreed in November 1991.

As already indicated, control of emissions to the atmosphere takes precedence over protection of water resources in the Hungarian energy sector. However, excessive rates of water extraction have led the Ministry of Transport, Telecommunications and Water Management to reduce the quantities of water permitted to be extracted from groundwater reservoirs, which limits mining operations in some areas. The levels of salts and heavy metals in waste water from Hungarian coal mines are low and disposal is not a major issue. The potential impact of uranium mining near Pécs on groundwater quality is under examination. Sites for the disposal of deep coal mine wastes and fly ash from power stations are limited in some areas, and the disposal of slurry from FGD plants would present an additional problem.

Regulation and Control of Air Pollution

Air emissions from existing stationary combustion sources are regulated by national emissions limits (expressed in grammes per hour) under the Clean Air Protection decree of 1968, amended in 1986. Limit values are determined according to a fairly complex formula that includes parameters related to stack height and plant locality (the country is divided into three categories for this purpose). Where the Ministry of Environmental Protection and Regional Development judges it necessary to improve air quality, emissions limits for an existing source can be revised, with a grace period for reconstruction work. Fines are payable where emissions limits are exceeded. Revenues so raised (approximately Ft 1 billion per year) are paid into a central fund and used to subsidise investments aimed at reducing emissions to levels below the statutory limits.

New installations require licences from the National Agency for Environmental Protection for each separate emissions source. These licences set emissions limits, under a formula that takes local air quality into account, and require the installation of specific facilities so as to rule out the possibility of paying fines as an alternative to investing in pollution control equipment. Environmental impact assessments are also required under the licensing system. No new emissions sources are permitted where local air quality does not meet statutory regional limits. Current emissions regulations require all new coal fired power stations to be equipped with FGD in addition to filters to control emissions of particulates. They also require NO_x emissions to be limited through the control of combustion characteristics.

Monitoring of plant emissions is undertaken by the plant management and sometimes by local government authorities, and verified when judged necessary by the regional office of the National Agency for Environmental Protection. Local air quality is monitored by the local public health organisations of the National Public Health and Medical Service. The National Institute for Hygiene collects and evaluates air quality data. Measurements recorded by these various bodies has frequently been contradictory, undermining the reliability of local air quality data. A more coherent framework for the organisation of monitoring is required. Legislation to this effect should separate the roles of industry and of central and local government and assign specific responsibilities for monitoring. Background ambient air quality and transboundary air pollution flows are monitored by the National Meteorological Service and the Institute for Atmospheric Physics.

Proposals to introduce new regulations for the control of emissions from all large combustion sources are under development, as local air quality in industrialised regions continues to be unacceptable. If adopted, these will limit SO_2 emissions from a typical power station to

$400\mu g/m^3$, which would necessitate the retrofit of 90% efficient FGD equipment on all existing coal fired power stations. Dissatisfaction with the regulatory system has also led to proposals to replace it with uniform national standards for all air emissions, similar to the German (TA Luft) regulations; these similarly would limit SO_2 emissions to around $400\mu g/m^3$ in coal fired power stations.

Conclusions

The need to replace the existing system of air pollution control should be carefully assessed. The system appears to have certain advantages in adapting regulations to local air quality requirements. Possibilities for improving rather than replacing this system might usefully be explored. It could be adapted for compatibility with EC emissions targets, which appears to be the implicit goal of Hungary's environmental policy. If the existing framework of regulation is retained, however, rationalising the system of monitoring local air quality would appear necessary. The role of local authorities in setting, monitoring and enforcing environmental standards needs clarification at the earliest opportunity. Rationalisation of responsibilities for monitoring, co-ordination of data collection and quality control in monitoring should be objectives of government environmental policy. Strengthening environmental monitoring and management systems in the power sector and other energy intensive industries would also be useful.

Proposals for change in many areas of the regulatory and institutional arrangements for environmental protection in Hungary are under development. In addition to changes in air emissions regulations, an additional revenue-raising tax on gasoline and perhaps other fuels has been considered on a number of occasions. Should any revenue-raising systems — such as environmental levies on gasoline or pollution charges — be established in addition to current fines for non-compliance with air emission limits, clear responsibilities and targets for spending the revenue would have to be defined. The current system of non-compliance fines is ineffective and needs review both in regard to enforcement and the level of fines. There appears to be no policy framework to direct and co-ordinate the development and operation of these various regulatory and economic instruments.

The Government lacks a coherent statement of environmental policy in the energy sector; a statement should be developed for agreement by the institutions concerned, addressing the development of a legislative framework for regulations and other instruments aimed at environmental protection. Provision for air quality management plans, to address the paramount problem of local air quality in industrialised areas, would be welcome. A review of the priorities for environmental protection in the energy sector and the ranking of any corresponding investment requirements would also be welcome.

Average concentrations of SO_2 in the air appear to be relatively low in Hungary. SO_2 emissions are of most concern in some industrial areas, particularly where concentrations of particulate matter in the air are also high. The ranking of priorities for pollution control in the energy sector by the Ministry of Environmental Protection and Regional Development — first, improved control of vehicle emissions, and second, reduction in emissions of SO_2 and other pollutants to improve local air quality in highly industrialised areas — seems appropriate. However, in regard to SO_2 emissions, current policy on the reform of air pollution regulations would appear to overemphasise transboundary pollution control to the potential detriment of local air pollution control.

ENERGY SUPPLY INDUSTRIES

Oil and Gas

Organisational Structure

The Hungarian National Oil and Gas Trust (OKGT) was established in 1957 as the sole entity responsible for all activities in the oil and gas sector, excluding imports. The organisation, now being restructured, has extensive experience in exploration and production, gas storage, pipelines, refining, distribution and retailing. Significant amounts of natural gas were discovered during the 1960s, leading to its increasing importance as a primary energy supply source for the country and the decision to have OKGT take over responsibility for town gas manufacturing, distribution and supply from the local municipal administrations from 1965 to 1967. The exception was Budapest, where Budapest Gas Works, owned by the municipal authority, continues independent distribution of gas.

Until 30th June 1991 OKGT was the umbrella organization for 22 affiliated companies and one subsidiary, listed in Table 5. In June 1991 OKGT had about 40 000 employees and total assets of about Ft 185 billion (US $2.5 billion) depreciated book value. OKGT reported primarily to MOIT. Although nominally governed by a Council of Directors — the managers of the 22 affiliated companies and the president of the trust, who was also chairman of the council — OKGT was, for all intents and purposes, supervised by MOIT. This relationship was reinforced in November 1990 when the council was relieved of all decision making powers.

Two additional organisational aspects of the oil and gas industry (and OKGT's role therein) are most important. First, OKGT, through its oil and gas pipeline affiliate, Gáz-és Olajszállító Vállalat (GOV), is responsible for transit of oil and gas through Hungary from, and between, neighbouring countries. Second, until 1st January 1991, all imports and exports of crude oil, refined products, natural gas and gas liquids were contracted for by Mineralimpex, a foreign trade company supervised by the Ministry of International Economic Relations. As of 1st January 1991, the Hungarian Government liberalised the regulations governing this activity, thereby permitting new entrants, though Mineralimpex continues to play a dominant role.

OKGT is being substantially restructured. Effective 1st July 1991, 12 of the 22 affiliated companies, together with the drilling activities of the KFV affiliate, were separated from OKGT and established as independent joint stock companies, initially 100% state owned. These 13 entities, which accounted for 44% of OKGT's workforce, 23% of its assets and 8% of profits, will be privatised once plans are approved by MOIT and the SPA.

The remaining nine core companies of OKGT, along with its supply subsidiary, were legally established as a joint stock company on 1st October 1991 and renamed the Hungarian Oil and Gas Company (MOL). International management consultants assisted in the organisational development of the new company. The full reorganisation is likely to take at least one year to complete. MOL is to be a vertically integrated oil and gas company with two divisions, upstream and downstream, as shown in Table 6. The two divisions are to operate as financially separate profit centres to improve financial and managerial accountability. The general management of MOL has responsibilities for strategic and long term commercial planning, approval of major investments and contracts, advice to government on privatisation issues and

Table 5
OKGT Affiliated Companies, to 30th June 1991

Name	Initials	Location
Exploration, Exploitation and Transportation		
Geophysical Exploration Company*	GKV	Budapest
Lowlands Petroleum Exploration Company	KV	Szolnok
Lowlands Hydrocarbon Production Company*	NKFV	Szolnok
Trans-Danubian Petroleum Company*	KFV	Nagykanizsa
Gas and Oil Transporting Company*	GOV	Siófok
Refining and Marketing		
Danube Petroleum Refinery*	DKV	Százhalombatta
Komárom Petroleum Refinery*	KKV	Komárom
Zala Petroleum Refinery*	ZKV	Zalaegerszeg
Tisza Petroleum Refinery*	TIFO	Tiszaújváros
Petroleum Products Trading Company*	ÁFOR	Budapest
Gas Supply and Distribution		
Southern Lowlands Gas Company	DÉGÁZ	Szeged
Trans-Tisza Gas Company	TIGÁZ	Hajduszoboszlo
South Trans-Danubian Gas Company	DDGÁZ	Pécs
North Trans-Danubian Gas Company	ÉGÁZ	Györ
Middle Trans-Danubian Gas Company	KÖGÁZ	Nagykanizsa
Carbon Dioxide Production Company	SZTV	Répcelak
Machine Manufacturing, Construction and Installation		
Petroleum Machine Works, Budapest	BKG	Budapest
Trans-Danubian Petroleum Machine Works	DKG	Nagykanizsa
Lowlands Petroleum Machine Works	AKG	Orosháza
Pipeline Construction Company	KVV	Siófok
Technical Development and Miscellaneous		
Hungarian Hydrocarbon Institute	SZKFI	Százhalombatta
General Contracting and Designing Company for the Oil Industry	OLAJTERV	Budapest
Supply Subsidiary of the Hungarian National Oil and Gas Trust*	AGEL	Budapest

* Retained in the integrated oil and gas company.

preparation of company accounts. The management reports to a nine member board of directors appointed by the Minister of Industry and Trade.

In the past, OKGT affiliates reported profits and financial performance independently, and from these reports OKGT compiled a consolidated balance for tax purposes. Under the new arrangements, the nine former affiliates lose their independent status; MOL will prepare integrated financial balances using internal transfer prices

calculated on the basis of import prices (CIF basis). In the upstream sector, the system of royalties from oil and gas production is to be altered in anticipation of new concession type exploration and production ventures. A new concession law for mineral exploration and production is being prepared. It is proposed that its implementation would be overseen by a new independent regulatory body.

A number of changes are of particular interest. All of the gas supply and distribution affiliates are

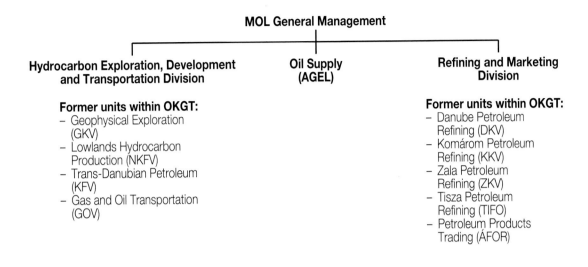

Table 6
MOL Organisation, Effective 1st October 1991

MOL General Management

Hydrocarbon Exploration, Development and Transportation Division

Former units within OKGT:
– Geophysical Exploration (GKV)
– Lowlands Hydrocarbon Production (NKFV)
– Trans-Danubian Petroleum (KFV)
– Gas and Oil Transportation (GOV)

Oil Supply (AGEL)

Refining and Marketing Division

Former units within OKGT:
– Danube Petroleum Refining (DKV)
– Komárom Petroleum Refining (KKV)
– Zala Petroleum Refining (ZKV)
– Tisza Petroleum Refining (TIFO)
– Petroleum Products Trading (ÁFOR)

being set up as discrete enterprises under direct public supervision. While it is expected that these affiliates will all eventually be individually privatised, the process appears to be quite advanced in the case of the carbon dioxide production company, SZTV. It is to be hoped that the SPA will capture full value for this affiliate, which seems to be a very successful carbon dioxide producer and exporter. With respect to the five natural gas distribution and supply affiliates, it is interesting to recall that OKGT took over the town gas manufacturing and distribution companies from the local municipal administrations in the mid-1960s. In recent years these affiliates have had to establish their own design, construction and services departments. One of the five hydrocarbon exploration, production and transportation affiliates, Kőolajkutató Vállalat (KV), has been removed from the MOL organisation and its operations absorbed by the NKFV affiliate. AGEL will continue to be part of MOL initially, operating as an oil trading unit. The Hungarian Hydrocarbon Institute, SZKFI, has been dissolved by incorporation into the DKV and NKFV affiliates.

All of the "background" or service affiliates are being separated from the OKGT organisation, presumably to encourage them to provide competitively priced products and services to MOL and new industry participants. This includes

the machine works and pipeline construction affiliates. Perhaps somewhat overlooked are plans to separate and privatise the propane and butane distribution and supply operations. On the surface, this would seem potentially a very successful business activity, one to which the SPA should give due consideration.

The decision of the Hungarian Government to restructure OKGT is laudable. In addition, re-establishing the five regional natural gas distribution and supply affiliates as separate entities responsible for their own operations is most commendable. The decision to separate the non-core business service affiliates from the former OKGT organisation is also positive, assuming that they will become competitive service companies to a revitalised oil and gas industry.

Central to the Government's restructuring plan is the creation of MOL as a vertically integrated oil and gas company having the following business activities:

Upstream Operations:

– Crude oil and natural gas exploration and production;

– Crude oil and natural gas transportation (including in-transit movements);

- Natural gas imports (in competition with Mineralimpex and others);
- Natural gas storage;
- Natural gas sales to industrial markets.

Downstream Operations:
- Oil refining/processing;
- Refined products production;
- Petrochemicals production;
- Refined and unfinished products transportation;
- Refined products marketing/retailing;
- Petrochemicals marketing;
- Crude oil and refined products imports and exports (in competition with Mineralimpex and others).

Other Operations:
- Telecommunications (GOV).

A number of advantages can be attributed to such an organisation. MOL would retain sufficient power to negotiate equitable and balanced supply, transportation and sales arrangements in its upstream and downstream operations with all foreign countries, industry participants and investors. The organisation would be cost-effective, able to capitalise on the benefits provided by common, integrated operations and use of resources. For example, the production of crude oil and natural gas and the construction and operation of the natural gas storage facilities currently represent an integrated technological system operated by a common staff. Individual divisions and cost/profit centres can readily be established within such an organisation, at minimal cost. Legal regulations can be enacted to address the question of competition and access to facilities owned by MOL or any other organisation in a monopolistic position.

The organisational efficiency associated with larger organisations may not, however, be as significant as sometimes believed and an oil and gas infrastructure concentrated in one large integrated company could inhibit the development of an economically efficient industry, comprising both domestic and foreign participants and investors. The smaller companies likely to favour investment in the Hungarian market could perceive lessened chances of success in competing with MOL as presently structured. Integration also may interfere with potential interfuel competition between natural gas and oil products.

The Hungarian Government should review its rationale for restructuring OKGT and determine if there is merit in further restructuring. Such a review should clarify the objectives of restructuring and the priority accorded to each. It should also seek to balance the objective of positioning the oil and natural gas industry in Hungary as an efficient and viable competitor in the regional economic environment, as such an environment is expected to develop in the next five to ten years, with the interests of maximising economic efficiency.

The initiatives of the Hungarian Government with respect to privatisation are to be commended. Issues of competition, access and ensuring effective independent management of the industry, however, may be of greater importance to the public interest than privatisation and the level of foreign ownership, particularly at this time. The Hungarian Government should clearly separate the objectives and processes of restructuring and of privatisation in the oil and gas industry, and the objectives should be clearly identified and explained to industry participants and to the general public.

Investment and Financing

Until the mid-1980s, OKGT's investment programmes were financed primarily by central government funds. More recently, direct government contributions have all but disappeared as a possible source of project financing in the oil and gas sector. Other major sources of financing for OKGT projects have included commercial banks, the World Bank, the CMEA Development Bank, some municipal sources and OKGT's own cash flow. Table 7 presents actual and projected investment and investment financing in the oil and gas sector for 1988-1992 based upon MOL's most recent five-year plan. By October 1991 it was clear that plans for 1991 would not be realised and that the planned expenditure for 1992 is unlikely to be fully realised. It would therefore appear essential for MOL to reassess its project development plans and prepare a revised capital budget forecast as quickly as possible.

Oil

Exploration, Development and Production

Hungary is a mature oil and gas producing region that has been well explored and no new large

Table 7
OKGT Financing Sources and Oil and Gas Investments, 1988-1992
(billions of 1988 forints)

	1988[1]	1989[1]	1990[1]	1991[2]	1992[2]
Financing Sources					
Commercial Banks	1.06	.41	.88	2.74	5.00
World Bank	1.54	.68	.17	2.34	2.30
Own Resources[3]	9.89	11.43	10.55	14.12	28.90
State Loans	1.02	-	-	-	-
Municipal Sources	0.18	0.26	0.47	0.32	-
CMEA Development Bank[4]	-	0.34	1.32	3.22	1.50
Total	**13.69**	**13.13**	**13.38**	**22.74**	**37.70**
Approved Oil and Gas Investments					
Exploration and Drilling Equipment	1.93	1.78	0.78	2.60	0.60
Development	4.98	4.06	3.11	3.66	4.50
Pipeline Construction	2.26	2.59	2.80	4.92	9.90
Petroleum Refining	2.18	1.74	3.66	9.04	15.10
Underground Gas Storage	1.12	1.91	1.48	0.60	0.30
Storage and Transportation	0.42	0.43	0.61	0.83	4.10
Carbon Dioxide Production	0.13	0.15	0.21	0.33	-
Lubricant Production	0.13	0.13	0.49	0.56	1.50
Other	0.54	0.33	0.24	0.20	1.70
Total	**13.69**	**13.12**	**13.38**	**22.74**	**37.70**

Notes:
1. Actual expenditure.
2. Planned expenditure.
3. Profits, depreciation and miscellaneous development funds.
4. Financing of development of gas transit to Yugoslavia is expected to continue from the CMEA Development Bank or a successor organisation.

Source: MOL.

fields are expected to be found. Oil production is expected to decline substantially in the 1990s because proven reserves are likely to be depleted more rapidly than new reserves are discovered. Hungarian oil production depends heavily on the use of secondary recovery methods, with tertiary enhanced recovery methods now being introduced, including displacement by carbon dioxide, in-situ combustion and chemical treatment; 20% of production is through secondary recovery methods and 5% through tertiary recovery techniques. Production costs therefore are likely to continue rising. Domestic oil production, however, remains highly valuable for economic reasons as well as security of supply.

Domestic oil production in 1990 was 1.99 million metric tons (40 000 barrels per day), accounting for about 25% of Hungary's domestic oil consumption. In addition, there is annual production of about 0.7 Mt of natural gas liquids. Hungarian oil production has remained stable for more than two decades, as shown in Table 8. Production began in 1937 and since then more than 70 Mt has been produced. As of 1st January 1991 estimated remaining proven reserves were approximately 26 Mt, yielding a reserves to production ratio of 13 at present rates of extraction. The quality of Hungarian crude oil is excellent. Most of the crude output is light (higher than 40 degrees API) with a very low sulphur content (less than 0.5%). This crude produces a high yield of light, low sulphur products and is useful in making high quality lubricants. A small amount of heavy crude is also produced, used primarily for manufacturing asphalt.

Table 8
Hungarian Domestic Crude Oil Production

1970	1.81 Mt
1975	1.75 Mt
1980	2.03 Mt
1985	2.01 Mt
1990	2.00 Mt

Note: Excludes natural gas liquids.

Source: MOL.

Hungary's submission to the IEA Secretariat projects a steady decline in domestic crude oil production to 1.1 Mt in 2000 (plus 0.7 Mtoe of natural gas liquids) and to about 0.5 Mt in 2010 (plus 0.5 Mtoe of natural gas liquids). MOL gives slightly different projections for crude oil production: 1.52 Mtoe in 2000 and 0.8 Mtoe in 2010. This pace of decline is not inevitable. There is still potential for oil discoveries and for improved recovery. To stem the decline, increased investments will be necessary for exploration, making use of the latest technological improvements for geological and geophysical data collection and analysis, and for enhanced exploitation. MOL's exploration and production arm should be enabled to make adequate investments in the search for and development of additional domestic reserves where economic.

The Government's decision to encourage foreign investment in the upstream sector is welcome. Geological data packages have been made available to potential participants since 1st May 1991 and there has been a good response from foreign oil companies. Parliament has yet to pass the necessary legislation to enable foreign upstream participation, but action was expected by the end of 1991. In any event it will take time for the geological and geophysical data to be evaluated. Exploration activity by foreign companies is unlikely to begin before 1993. The involvement of foreign companies would be a useful supplement to Hungary's own efforts through MOL.

Imports

Continued uncertainty regarding Soviet crude oil availability represents a problem for the Hungarian refining sector. Until 1990 foreign crude oil supplies to Hungarian refineries were provided entirely from the former USSR via the Friendship pipeline system. In 1989 Soviet crude accounted for about 80% of supplies and domestic production the remaining 20%. As a result of supply problems in 1989 and 1990, Hungary purchased about 0.8 Mt of crude oil from other sources in 1990. In 1991 Hungarian crude oil purchases from non-USSR sources are expected to increase to more than 2 Mt. For 1992 Hungary has not received a firm commitment on crude availability from the former USSR.

Imports of oil products over the last five years have been mainly diesel oil and gasoline, primarily high octane grades. Imports are expected to

Table 9
Crude Oil Imports
(thousand metric tons)

Delivery	Trade terms	1989	1990	1991 Jan-June
Friendship pipeline	Rouble	6 321	5 027	0
	US $	0	350	1 451
	Barter	0	250	0
Adria pipeline	US $	0	1 390*	1 146

* Of the total crude oil delivered to Hungary via the Adria pipeline in 1990, 1180 kt was delivered between 1st July and the end of the year.

Source: MOL.

Table 10
Oil Product Imports
(thousand metric tons)

Product	1985	1988	1989	1990
Gasoline	345	332	470	266
Diesel	763	741	804	825
Fuel oil	790	201	66	187
Others	77	73	64	56
Total	**1975**	**1347**	**1404**	**1334**

Source: MOL.

decrease substantially in 1991 as demand falls in response to price rises and economic stagnation, and as a result of increased domestic production of high octane gasoline.

Refining

Hungary has three petroleum refineries and one lubricant blending plant. On 1st January 1991 primary distillation capacity was about 11 Mt per year (220 000 barrels per day). Capacity has declined from 14.7 Mt in 1980 through the elimination of redundant and excess capacity. The Hungarian refining industry produces about 95% of the refined products consumed domestically. Primary distillation capacity is expected to remain stable in the 1990s, but more complex conversion capacity will be required to meet future product requirements and specifications. The three Hungarian refineries operated by MOL are managed by the following three affiliates: the Danube Petroleum Refining Company, Dunai Kőolajipari Vállalat (DKV); the Tisza Petroleum Refining Company, Tiszai Kőolajipari Vállalat (TIFO); and the Zala Petroleum Refining Company, Zala Kőolajipari Vállalat (ZKV).

The major DKV refinery complex is about 30 km south of Budapest at Százhalombatta on the Danube. DKV is Hungary's largest refinery with a primary distillation capacity of 7.5 Mt per year (150 000 barrels per day). A highly complex refinery, it began production in 1965 and has been continuously upgraded; it now contains more than 30 processing units. In 1990 DKV processed 7 Mt of crude oil and provided about 90% of the refined products manufactured in Hungary. The utilisation rate of the DKV refinery has averaged around 94% over recent years. The refinery produces fuel products, lubricating oils and petrochemicals (both intermediate and finished products). Most of the refinery capacity is geared toward production of primary fuel products, which account for about 85% of the total product output. The lubricant and petrochemical products are high value added products, and thus have an importance beyond that indicated by their share of refinery output. A representative breakdown of output into the various product categories is shown in Table 12.

Table 11
Crude Oil Processing Capacity, 1990
(barrels per day)

	DKV	TIFO	ZKV	Total
Crude	150 000	60 000	10 000	220 000
Vacuum Distillation	84 000	30 000	6 000	120 000
Thermal Operations	13 300	-	-	13 300
Catalytic Cracking	20 000	-	-	20 000
Catalytic Reforming	23 000	-	-	23 000
Catalytic Hydro-Treating	76 000	-	-	76 600
Alkylation	3 300	-	-	3 300
Isomerisation	9 800	-	-	9 800
Lubricants	4 000	-	-	4 000
Asphalt	6 300		4 500	10 800

Source: MOL.

Table 12
DKV Production, 1990

Product	Percentage of Output
Gasoline	27%
Gas Oil	36%
Jet Fuel	4%
Aromatics	4%
Lubricating Oil	3%
Fuel Oil	18%
Bitumen	5%
Other	3%

Source: MOL.

content and meeting higher octane requirements. About $200 million will be invested from 1990 to 1992 in reducing the sulphur content of diesel oil and reducing the lead content of gasoline, with production of unleaded gasoline planned at over 20% of total gasoline production in 1992, compared with 6-7% in 1990, and the maximum lead content of leaded gasoline expected to be reduced to 0.15 grammes per litre by April 1992. Environmental protection projects that MOL has planned for the DKV refinery include processing of heavy vacuum residues from 1997, biological treatment of sewage water, reduced gas flaring and vaporisation recovery systems. Hungary's downstream sector has incurred substantial debt during its modernisation programme. External financing will continue to be needed in the foreseeable future and it is likely that the restructured MOL will seek joint venture partners as part of its plan to meet investment requirements.

Pipelines

Hungary has three crude oil pipelines, of sufficient capacity to handle required imports for the foreseeable future. The crude oil pipeline network, managed by GOV, includes transportation of domestic crude oil to the Hungarian refineries. The three major pipelines are the Friendship I pipeline from the former USSR through the CSFR, entering Hungary from the north and proceeding directly to DKV; the Friendship II pipeline, direct to TIFO from the border of the former USSR in the northeast, then on to DKV; and the Adria pipeline from the Adriatic Sea, through Yugoslavia and southwestern Hungary to DKV. The Adria pipeline has capacity of 10 Mt per year. GOV agreed with the Yugoslavian enterprise JANAF (formerly Naftovod) on imports to Hungary in 1991 of 3.0 Mt of crude oil through the Adria pipeline. However, deliveries were suspended in September as the result of the disturbances in Croatia. For 1991 GOV contracted with the Czechoslovakian company Chemapol for the transit of 2.0 Mt of crude oil through the Adria pipeline and across Hungary to the border with the CSFR. Figure 8 illustrates the location of Hungary's existing crude oil and petroleum product pipelines.

The TIFO refinery is in northeastern Hungary at Tiszapalkonya on the river Tisza. Current capacity is 3 Mt per year. Far less sophisticated than the DKV refinery, it is designed to utilise only crude oil from the former USSR that is lower in quality than Hungary's indigenous production. The refinery is heavily under-utilised as a result of declining supplies from this source and MOL's intention to maximise use of the DKV refinery. The TIFO refinery is used primarily to provide naphtha feedstock to the Tisza Chemical Works. In 1990 the refinery operated at only about 15% of its rated capacity and in 1991 it was projected to be used at about 25% of capacity.

The small ZKV refinery, in the western part of the country at Zalaegerszeg on the river Zala, has capacity of 0.5 Mt per year and is currently used to process heavy Hungarian crude into asphalt. Finally, the Komárom Petroleum Refining Co. (KKV), at Szőny on the Danube northwest of Budapest, operates a lubricant blending plant utilising feedstock from the DKV refinery. The two plants are about 75 km apart. A review of Hungarian refining capacity, with a view to rationalisation, would appear appropriate.

Investment requirements in the refinery sector during the 1990s will be directed to continued modernisation of the DKV refinery to meet product requirements and environmental protection efforts. They include a new naphtha reformer with continuous catalytic regeneration and a new hydro cracking unit with hydro-desulphurisation. The modernisation programme will focus on improving the quality of gasoline, diesel and home heating oil by reducing sulphur

The majority of petroleum products from Hungary's two largest refineries, DKV and TIFO, are dispatched via pipelines, with the remainder being transported by rail, barge and tank truck. Both refineries have extensive rail transport loading facilities and switchyards. The largest of the product pipelines are described in Table 13.

Figure 8
MAJOR CRUDE OIL AND PRODUCT PIPELINES AND REFINERIES IN HUNGARY

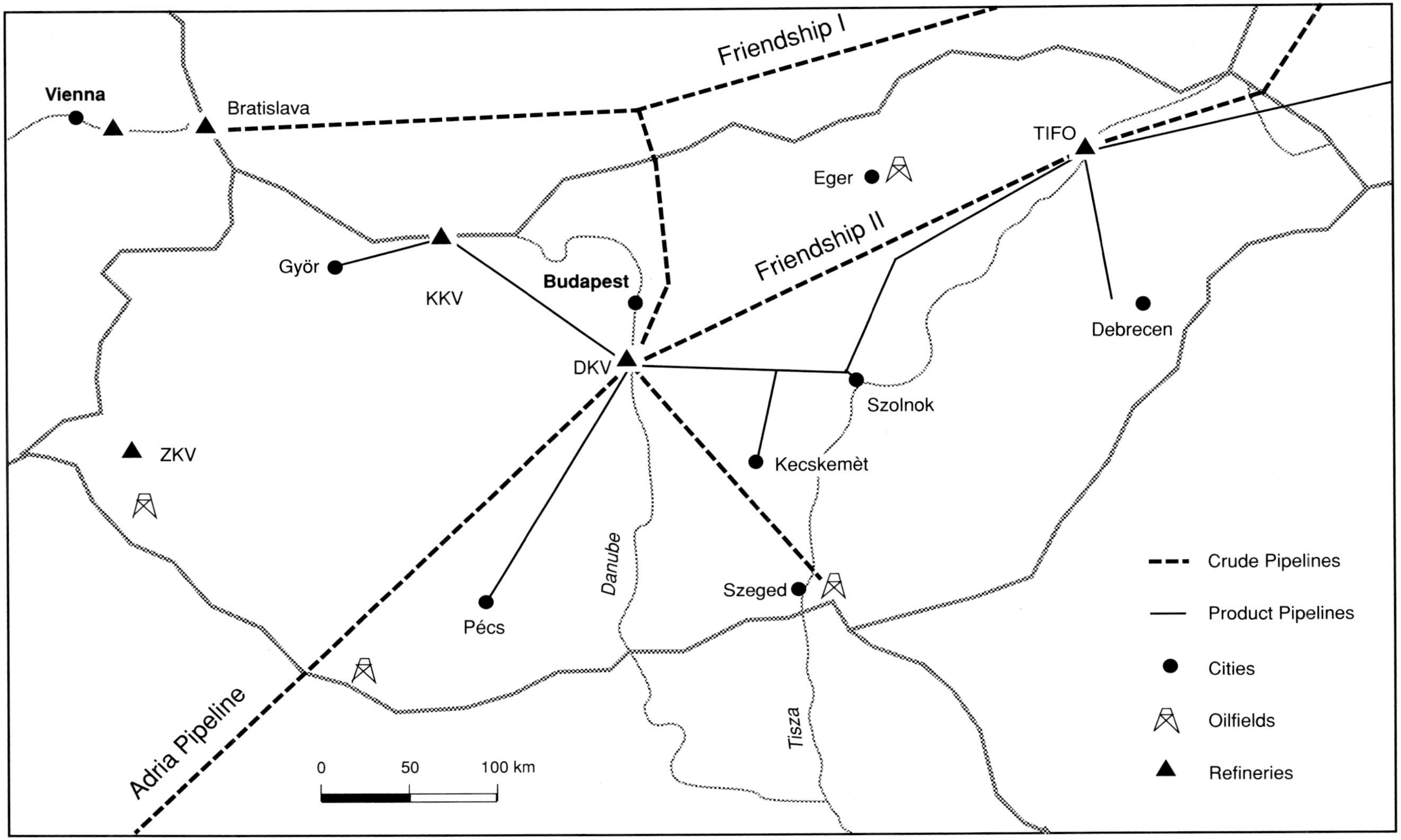

Table 13
Major Hungarian Product Pipelines

Route	Diameter (mm)	Length (km)	Capacity (10^3 t/yr)
DKV-Szajol	150	113	450
Szajol-TIFO	200	126	650
DKV-TIFO	300	237	1 950
DKV-Pécs	200/300	198	1 000
DKV-KKV	150/200	88	460
DKV-KKV	300/400	88	2 100
KKV-Györ	150	47	450
TIFO-Ebes	200	63	850
DKV-airport	150	39	750

Source: MOL.

Stocks

Hungary does not have a compulsory government controlled strategic stock program. The only current requirement is the obligation for oil importers to stock 5% of total imports and 8% of refined product imports. In 1991 total oil stocks were estimated to range between 20 and 30 days of domestic consumption — far below average commercial stock levels in western Europe. It would be advisable for Hungary to increase its stocks from the current level of about 25 days to closer to 90 days of net imports, the oil stock requirement in IEA Member countries.

Increasing Hungarian oil stocks to meet IEA requirements would involve substantial costs, including the purchase price and carrying cost of the oil as well as the need to increase storage capacity. The Hungarian Government recognises the necessity of increasing stocks, though mechanisms for financing such increases equitably are yet to be investigated. Appropriate legislation and regulations will be required to establish a programme and its financing mechanism. Hungary might investigate the stockpiling programs of some IEA Member country governments to assist in the determination of a system appropriate for Hungary.

Distribution and Marketing

Petroleum product marketing in Hungary is being substantially restructured. ÁFOR, the Petroleum Products Trading Company, a MOL affiliate, was formerly responsible for all wholesale refined product sales within Hungary and had a dominant market share in retail sales of gasoline, diesel and home heating oil. As of 1st January 1991 oil companies are allowed to buy products directly from the refineries and oil product import restrictions have been removed.

Hungary's retail network for gasoline is likely to expand substantially in the 1990s, aided by new laws encouraging foreign investment. ÁFOR had about a 60% market share for gasoline retail sales at the end of 1990, with about 400 filling stations out of a total of 700. Under new laws preparing for privatisation in the sector, ÁFOR will have to transfer ownership of all but 240 service stations either to private Hungarian individuals or to joint ventures established with foreign investors, thereby reducing its market share.

Shell Interag, a joint venture between Shell and the Hungarian company Interag, has the second largest retail network, with about 50 filling stations (about 30% of market share) at the end of 1990, and it is likely to continue expanding. Agip and BP have been active in Hungary since 1969 and 1972, respectively, but only through franchise agreements that left ownership of the ten Agip and ten BP brand name filling stations with ÁFOR. BP is to buy its brand name stations from ÁFOR in the near future. The Agip brand name stations have now been apportioned to the joint venture company Agip Hungaria. A number of additional foreign oil companies are entering Hungary or expanding their presence there, including Total, Esso, Mobil, ÖMV, Q8 and Aral. The number of filling stations in Hungary is likely to expand rapidly during the 1990s, particularly along motorways. A potential obstacle to this expansion is the lack of resolution of property ownership issues, making it difficult for companies to acquire land for new filling stations. Procedures to enable competition for building new retail gasoline stations, including those on motorways, should be implemented as soon as possible.

Demand Outlook

Hungarian oil consumption declined steadily during the 1980s, from 10.6 Mtoe in 1980 to 7.4 Mtoe in 1989, as a result of reduced economic activity as well as substitution of other energy carriers, such as natural gas and nuclear generated electricity. Figures submitted to the IEA Secretariat by the Hungarian authorities (Table 14) show domestic oil consumption declining further in the 1990s before picking up again towards the end of the decade. The level of refined product exports will depend heavily on Hungary's ability to obtain financing for refinery modernisation.

Pricing

Crude oil and refined product prices moved towards world oil price levels in 1991. Crude oil imported from the former USSR is now priced at world market prices on a convertible currency basis. Product prices have been liberalised but gasoline prices are still subject to government influence — a pricing committee within MOL recommends the refinery gate price for petroleum products, subject to informal approval by the Ministry of Finance. The retail price, excluding taxes, for gasoline in Hungary is somewhat lower than the average price in western Europe. As a result, imported refined products, particularly gasoline, are uncompetitive within Hungary. In addition, importers of refined products are obliged to keep stocks equivalent to 5% of total oil imports and 8% of product imports.

Pre-tax oil prices in both the producing and consuming sectors should fully reflect world oil market prices, taking into account quality differences, transportation differentials and regional supply and demand imbalances. Government should refrain from intervening in pricing decisions by the restructured state enterprises and private companies in the oil and gas industry. Completing the process of separating the functions of management, ownership and regulation is vital in this regard. The Government should focus its efforts towards enabling effective competition as the principal means of influencing prices.

The Government has imposed large nominal taxes on gasoline and automotive diesel oil. In continuing this policy the Government may also wish to consider taxing other oil products. In any event the Government should review oil product

Table 14
Oil Supply and Demand Balances
(Mtoe)

	1989	1995	2000	2005*	2010*
Domestic Production	2.72	2.45	1.85	1.45	1.03
Imports	6.08	6.39	7.96	7.82-8.60	9.04-9.22
Estimated Transit	2.00	4.50	4.50	4.50	4.50
Exports	n.a.	0.19	0.33	0.08-0.43	0.25-0.31
Primary Supply	8.79	8.65	9.49	9.19-9.62	9.82-9.94
Est. Final Consumption	7.42	7.16	7.55	7.86	8.19

* Ranges represent nuclear and lignite scenarios.

Source: AEEF.

Table 15
Structure of Gasoline and Automotive Diesel Oil Prices, 15th April 1991
(forints per litre)

	Gasoline				Diesel
	86 Octane	92 Octane	98 Octane	95 Octane Unleaded	
Road fund	3.20	3.20	3.20	3.20	0.70
Compulsory insurance	6.20	6.20	6.20	6.20	0.00
Consumption Tax	33.20	33.20	33.20	30.00	15.90
Estimated ex-refinery price	7.00	10.70	13.50	13.50	14.90
Estimated wholesale + retail margin	3.40	2.70	2.90	4.10	1.50
Retail Price	**53.00**	**56.00**	**59.00**	**57.00**	**33.00**

Source: National Bank of Hungary.

taxes periodically with a view to adjusting the tax system to take into account the structure of taxes in other European countries — including those in the EC while membership of the Community remains a policy objective. Tax is currently Ft 33.2 per litre on leaded gasoline and Ft 30 per litre on 95 octane unleaded gasoline. Tax on automotive diesel oil is Ft 15.9 per litre. A special "road fund" tax is also charged on all gasoline and diesel (Ft 5.2 per litre for gasolines and around Ft 2.3 per litre for auto diesel at the end of 1991).

Oil refining and retailing in Hungary are insulated to some degree from international market pressures by the high transportation cost component in imported oil product prices and by Hungarian import duties. These duties are high relative to the value added by refining and allow for an upwards bias to product prices. This reduces incentives to improve the efficiency of the domestic refining industry and optimise product supply from it, and reduces effective competition in Hungary. It is therefore recommended that consideration be given to eliminating import duties on refined petroleum products. The Government is considering a proposal to introduce duty-free quotas for specific oil products and assign quotas to companies on a first come, first served basis. Such a system is not recommended, as it would impose an additional burden on administrative resources with no significant benefits, particularly with respect to improving competition and efficiency.

Table 16
**Import Duties on Oil Products,
15th February 1991**

Product Categories	Duty
Light products except aviation fuel, gasoline and naphtha:	9.8%
Aviation fuel and naphtha:	0
Gasoline, gas oil and heating oil:	4.5%
Kerosene for motors:	0
Other middle distillates:	4.5%
Heavy products:	10.5%

Source: National Bank of Hungary.

Competition and Access

The restructuring of OKGT should be accompanied by legislation clearly establishing the rules of participation and investment in the oil industry and ensuring competitive access for new participants to all aspects of the industry, including refining, transportation, storage and marketing. It is further recommended that the Government seek to enable the development of competitive participation in the oil industry. To do this the Government, in consultation with MOL, will need to determine the preferred means for participants to gain access to oil processing facilities, crude and product pipelines and other facilities.

Access can be defined in a number of ways. At an oil processing facility, for example, it could mean an entitlement to a share of the output of products at negotiated prices, or an entitlement to a share of processing capacity whereby crude oil would be supplied and the corresponding output of products taken at a negotiated processing fee. Two options that can be considered are:

- pro-rata access, where each company seeking access to a facility is allocated capacity on the basis of the capacity requested as a proportion of the total demand for capacity;

- limited access, where a specific proportion of capacity is set aside for the negotiation of commercial contracts with industry participants under terms and conditions no less favourable than those provided MOL.

OKGT drafted a legislative proposal in August 1991 to establish the rules of access to MOL's facilities. It is being considered by the Government. Such rules and their implementation almost certainly will need to be adjusted in the light of operational experience.

Natural Gas

Exploration and Production

The oil and gas upstream activity in Hungary can best be described as mature. Most of the hydrocarbon producing zones containing the bulk of the country's reserves are located between depths of 120 and 2 200 metres, although there are some producing wells at 3 400 metres. A majority of the fields contain multiple pay zones, but most wells are of single or, to a lesser extent, double and triple completion. Extreme temperature and pressure conditions exist in most fields, along with gas caps. Gas producing zones can contain lean gas, wet gas with high gas liquids content or a combination of the two with carbon dioxide. Little hope is held for the discovery of major new fields at these depths. A recent deep drilling programme discovered much less gas than expected and was scaled back.

Domestic production of natural gas is declining. Annual production peaked at 7.5 bcm[1] in 1985 and fell to 4.9 bcm in 1990. Production in 2000 is optimistically forecast at 4 bcm in the absence of

significant new investments. As of 1st January 1990, Cedigaz estimated Hungary's remaining proven gas reserves at 123 bcm. Based on actual gross production data for 1989, this yields a reserves to production ratio of 19. The World Energy Conference 1989 Survey of Energy Resources estimated additional resources of natural gas with 233 bcm identified as "in place", of which 175 bcm is recoverable with reasonable certainty. Additional resources are defined as those in addition to proven reserves and do not include resources whose existence is merely speculative. By way of comparison, the United States has had a reserves to production ratio of the order of 10 since the 1970s. While the situations are not necessarily comparable, Hungary's relatively high ratio suggests that production might be increased or its decline arrested, subject to a comprehensive geological and reservoir assessment.

As noted earlier, Hungary is seeking foreign participation and investment in upstream oil and gas activities. Given the relatively small size of the hydrocarbon resource and its exploration and development maturity, Hungary may find more interest on the part of small to medium-sized foreign companies. Major oil and gas companies tend to focus on larger upstream projects where they can secure a controlling position. The Hungarian Government may also wish to adopt the procedures followed in some OECD countries with respect to the collection and systematisation of hydrocarbon exploration and production information, such as seismic data, core samples, well logs and production history. Such information is generally available to any interested party after a period of confidentiality. In Hungary such a service would be of great assistance to both foreign and domestic companies in identifying the best oil and gas prospects. At the same time, the Government could be better assured that the resource base is optimally and effectively exploited. Such data services are generally administered by a government agency, which could also assume responsibility for the proposed oil and gas exploration licensing programme.

MOL's exploration affiliates should refocus on domestic resources, with a view towards comprehensive geological and reservoir assessments, possibly with foreign participants and investors. The objective should be to slow the decline in indigenous production of natural gas through optimal development of projects on an economic basis.

---

1. Measured under normal conditions at 15°C.

Imports

Natural gas imports have been increasing steadily since the mid-1980s to meet Hungary's domestic requirements, and there is little reason to believe this trend will not continue through the 1990s. Imports were 3.9 bcm in 1985 and 6.3 bcm in 1990. Based on projections submitted to the IEA, Hungary will have to buy about 10.4 bcm from external sources in 2000. This increasing dependence on natural gas imports (approximately 72% of Hungary's demand in 2000, up from 56% in 1990) raises security of supply concerns, which are further exacerbated by Hungary's reliance on one source of imports, the former USSR. Existing supply arrangements with this source, which delivers gas from the Yamburg field in northwestern Siberia and the Orenburg field in southern Siberia, are detailed in Table 17. The balance of imports is made up through spot purchases, generally on a barter basis.

In addition to short term options for supply diversification through links to Austria and the CSFR (described below), a number of new potential long term supply options have been proposed in the Government's energy policy papers. Major capital intensive projects under consideration, involving natural gas pipelines from the Middle East and western Europe and possible LNG shipments from northern Africa and the North Sea, include:

- imports from Algeria via an expanded Trans-Med pipeline (4 bcm per year);

- imports of LNG from Algeria, Nigeria and/or Norway from a new LNG terminal in Yugoslavia and through a new pipeline to Hungary and beyond, in co-operation with the "Hexagonale" Group of countries[1];

- imports from Iran via a new pipeline through Turkey;

- imports from Norway via a new pipeline to Denmark and Germany;

- Imports from Norway via LNG ships to Poland (Gdansk) and a new pipeline from Poland to Yugoslavia.

The Government's policy to diversify Hungary's sources of natural gas imports merits support, though long term supply contracts need to be negotiated before resources are committed to major infrastructure projects. All these potential supply projects entail significantly greater costs than current Soviet supplies or their marginal expansion, and all but the first entail greater costs than Soviet deliveries through new projects. When assessing the economics of new sources of gas supply, full account should also be taken of the effect on prices of competition from other European importers. Opportunities for regional co-operation in diversifying sources of supply should be fully explored.

As was noted earlier, Mineralimpex has played the dominant role in importing natural gas. Because of Hungary's increasing reliance on natural gas imports and the restructuring of the oil and gas industry it would appear that Mineralimpex's role will be significantly modified.

Table 17
Contracted Natural Gas Supplies

Supply Arrangement	Contract Period	Contracted Deliveries (bcm per year)
Yamburg field	1991	1.5
	1992/1997	2.0
	1998/2008 (Option)	2.0
Orenburg field	1991/1998	2.8

Source: MOL.

---

1. Austria, the CSFR, Hungary, Italy, Poland and Yugoslavia.

Transmission

In addition to its activities in the crude oil and refined products sector, GOV owns and operates the high pressure pipeline transmission system, shown in Figure 9, which transports all natural gas produced in and imported by Hungary, as well as gas transported through the country. This system has been developed gradually, taking into account the amount of gas to be delivered, the direction of the delivery, seasonal demand fluctuations and peak demand. The system consists of pump and compressor stations, gas delivery stations, branch points and the related telecommunications and computer based telemetry systems. The telecommunications system has been expanded for use throughout MOL. Cold separation is the primary means of processing natural gas for transmission. Natural gas liquids are extracted using low temperature oil absorption. Where required, the natural gas is compressed to meet pipeline pressure specifications.

The overall gas trunkline grid comprises more than 4 000 km of pipe. Natural gas is transported throughout the country (domestic production, imports, storage and in-transit volumes) at a pressure of 64 bar (6.4 megapascals) with domestic delivery made to the regional gas distribution and supply entities and to industrial customers supplied directly by MOL's upstream affiliates. GOV transports approximately 14-15 bcm per year of natural gas, of which 3.2 bcm was contracted to move in-transit to Yugoslavia from the former USSR in 1990.

Natural gas imported from the former USSR is delivered to northeastern Hungary near Beregdaróc through the Brotherhood pipeline, commissioned in 1975. The capacity of the GOV system to receive this gas has been increased several times by a combination of looping and compression. In expectation of increased imports from this source, the trunkline system is being further expanded, with sections to be constructed to the Hungarian border along with compressor plant expansions. This will add approximately 400 km to the trunkline grid.

Gas in transit to Yugoslavia enters Hungary through the Soviet Soyuz or Union pipeline. It crosses eastern Hungary through GOV's transmission network and leaves the country through a pipeline at Röszke near Szeged. The system facilities within Hungary, commissioned in 1979, have been expanded several times. The volume of gas contracted for transit to Yugoslavia was 4.1 bcm in 1991. This volume is expected to increase to 5.9 bcm per year by 1996, depending on the development of transmission and distribution capacity in Yugoslavia.

The Hungarian branch of the Brotherhood pipeline has maximum capacity of 11 bcm per year without pipeline or compressor expansions. Commitments for its use comprise 6.2 bcm of deliveries to Hungary in 1991 and 4 bcm of backup capacity for deliveries to Yugoslavia when the Soyuz pipeline is undergoing maintenance or if it fails.

Given Hungary's increasing dependence on imports of natural gas, the Government is evaluating two short term pipeline projects offering capacity for some direct and indirect diversification to Western gas supplies: 1) a connection from Györ to Baumgarten in Austria; and 2) a connection between the transmission systems of Hungary and the CSFR from Györ to Ivánka.

The Czechoslovakian transmission system moves gas in transit between the former USSR and western Europe via Baumgarten and Germany. Interconnection with this system would enable

Table 18
Proposed Natural Gas Import Diversification Projects

	Length (km)	Diameter (cm)	Capacity (bcm/yr)	Cost (MFT)	Cost (US $ M)
Györ to Baumgarten	118	80	6.0	6 000	75
Györ to Ivánka	97	60	3.9	5 840	51

Source: MOL.

Figure 9
MAJOR NATURAL GAS PIPELINES

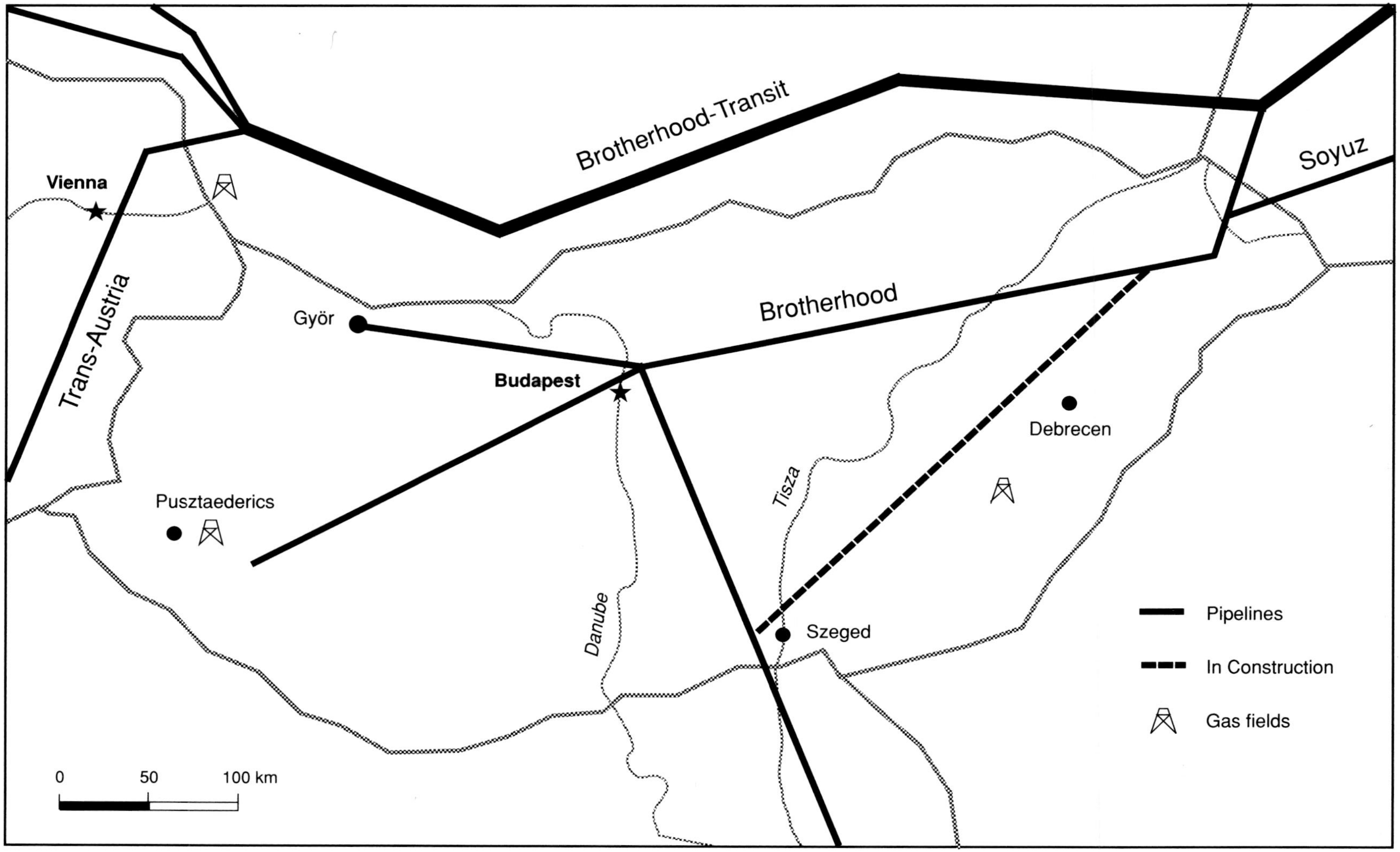

Pipelines

In Construction

Gas fields

Soyuz

Brotherhood-Transit

Brotherhood

Trans-Austria

Debrecen

Szeged

Tisza

Danube

Budapest

Györ

Pusztaederics

Vienna

0   50   100 km

Hungary to receive supplies from the West only indirectly, facilitated by a swap or exchange. Either of the alternatives in Table 18 would take about one year to construct.

It is questionable whether GOV can handle the impact of such projects and the increased seasonality of domestic demand, especially that associated with CHP generation, without major system enhancements and additional storage development. A full appraisal of the investments necessary to expand the transmission system will be required.

Hungary should actively pursue all natural gas transit opportunities. In addition to enhancing its natural gas supply diversification strategy, this would position Hungary to exploit its technological expertise, both at home and in neighbouring countries, to earn hard currency on a low risk general contracting basis.

Storage

The average daily winter demand is 2.5 times that experienced in the summer, and this difference is likely to rise, increasing the need for storage capacity. Winter peak day requirements place further demands on storage capacity. Storage provides some insulation from supply disruptions as well as the opportunity to take advantage of price fluctuations. Underground natural gas storage has been developed at three locations in Hungary, using depleted natural gas producing horizons.

There are plans to increase the storage capacities at Kardoskút to 0.210 bcm. Even further expansion would appear essential if the increase

forecast in natural gas consumption for CHP generation occurs. MOL officials are confident that additional storage can be developed. At Hajdúszoboszló, for example, only one of five zones has been used. Sites for potential increased storage capacity (initially of 0.5 bcm) are being surveyed. LPG storage capacity is 53 000 cubic metres. Upstream affiliates of MOL are responsible for developing and operating all underground storage in Hungary.

Distribution

The five regional natural gas distributors and Budapest Gas Works receive all their supply through GOV's high pressure system after the gas has been decompressed to between 6 and 10 bar. The pressure is subsequently reduced one or two times through the distribution network, as local conditions and safety factors warrant, before delivery to end-users. Over the past several years, the six distribution companies have had to exert increasing control over the development of their systems to be able to respond more quickly and with improving cost and technological efficiency to the demands placed upon them by consumers. The length of the gas distribution network was in excess of 15 000 km at the end of 1989, up from about 3 300 km at the beginning of 1981. Table 20 sets out some recent, selective data for the six gas distributors.

The five regional distributors separated from OKGT on 1st July 1991 are now financially independent. Budapest Gas Works, owned by the Budapest Municipal Assembly, was never part of OKGT. It is the sole distributor of natural gas in the Budapest area, with the exception of some direct sales by MOL to industrial consumers. Budapest Gas Works' sales are currently around 2.5 bcm per year: 1.5 bcm to industry, 0.7 bcm to households and 0.3 bcm to the commercial sector. Budapest Gas Works includes twelve affiliates engaged in activities as diverse as meter manufacturing and food retailing.

The natural gas distribution companies are continuing to expand their systems, but the rate of penetration is expected to slow significantly once 50% or so of all households in Hungary are supplied with gas. The data in Table 21 illustrate the development of natural gas supply to the household sector.

All of the gas distribution companies require new customers to contribute to the costs of connection. Residents frequently form a co-

Table 19
Gas Storage Facilities

Location	Capacity (bcm)	Withdrawal Rate (thousand cm/hour)
Hajdúszoboszló	1.400	840
Kardoskút	0.150	100
Pusztaederics	0.330	120
Total	**1.880**	**1 060**

Source: MOL.

Table 20
Regional Gas Distribution Companies

	Budapest	DÉGÁZ	TIGÁZ	DDGÁZ	ÉGÁZ	KÖGÁZ	Total
1989							
Customers	639 200	281 600	350 600	112 000	88 100	138 400	1 609 900
Sales (mcm)	2 540	1 048	1 938	428	402	757	7 113
Employees	2 947	1 632	3 933	1 479	1 090	1 633	12 714
1990							
Customers	654 900	294 500	378 300	119 900	91 900	146 500	1 686 000
Sales (mcm)	2 494	1 041	1 896	425	407	745	7 008
Employees	2 874	1 585	3 883	1 413	1 056	1 615	12 426
Ratios - 1990							
Sales per Customer (thousand cubic metres)	3.81	3.53	5.01	3.54	4.43	5.09	4.16
Customers per Employee	228	186	97	85	87	91	136

Source: MOL and Budapest Gas Works.

Table 21
Penetration of Natural Gas in the Household Sector

	1970	1980	1985	1989	1990
Households (thousands)	3 122	3 610	3 786	4 000	4 023
Households using natural gas (thousands)	525	919	1 182	1 559	1 629
Penetration	17%	26%	31%	39%	41%
Households using natural gas for heating (thousands)	n.a.	n.a.	650	989	1 084

Source: Typical Data: OKGT, 1990.

operative to pay for the excavation and construction. The cost of piping and meters is borne by the customers in some cases and by the company in others, depending on the company. The companies are responsible for safety. Meter reading and revenue collection is in some cases contracted with outside state billing companies. Problems with revenue collection and cases of interference with meters are frequent.

Privatisation of the peripheral businesses of gas distribution companies (for example, LPG distribution) is to be expected in the medium term and foreign investors have expressed interest in some of these businesses. This is unlikely to apply to the core businesses while prices continue to be controlled directly by the Government (as opposed to a transparent framework of regulation implemented by an independent agency), and uncertainty exists over the development of the role of local government authorities in the ownership of the companies and their assets. Indeed, if the low prices set for natural gas are maintained, they may result in financial difficulties for the gas distribution companies.

Supply and Demand Outlook

As noted earlier, Hungary's natural gas production peaked in 1985 and then declined through 1990. In the absence of major investments upstream, given the maturity of the industry, there is little reason to believe the production of natural gas will not continue its downward trend. Natural gas is a major component of Hungary's TPES — 29% in 1990 and 1991 — and its contribution is expected to increase, both in relative and absolute terms. Demand for natural gas, as shown in Table 22, is expected to grow by an average of 0.6-1% per year over the next 20 years. According to government forecasts, the sectors mainly responsible for this growth will be power generation and households, with a reduction in industrial demand.

Pricing

Natural gas prices in Hungary, determined by the Government, have been artificial and subsidised. In *Hungarian Energy Policy — June 1991,* the Government reconfirmed its general commitment to reforming its energy pricing system to reflect "market value relations". In the short term, however, natural gas prices are to continue to be subject to state control.

Prices in the supply sector are to be set as low as possible while covering the full cost of production. Transmission and distribution charges will include a profitability consideration in their determination. Direct and indirect subsidies to gas consumers are to be eliminated, but the Government still supports "balancing" energy bills for social purposes. The Government implemented major increases in end-use gas prices in 1991 to more adequately reflect European market prices, including the real costs of imported supplies. Further increases are expected.

Prices are set at the same level across the country. Their structure and evolution are described in Table 23. Large industrial consumers, not included in the table, pay an annual capacity charge of Ft 280 per MJ per hour in addition to a commodity charge of Ft 250 per GJ, as of 1st June 1991. LPG prices have also been set by the Government, but imports were liberalised in 1991 and domestic prices are to be deregulated.

The Hungarian Government's decision to implement a natural gas pricing policy ensuring that prices paid by final consumers reflect the full costs of gas supply is entirely commendable. This pricing policy should be fully implemented without delay.

Table 22
Natural Gas Supply and Demand Balances
(Mtoe)

	1985	1989	1995	2000	2005	2010
Domestic Requirements	8.71	9.36	9.65	10.17	9.52-10.82	10.62-11.62
Indigenous Production (Net)	5.76	4.72	4.20	3.21	2.85	2.38
Imports (Net)	3.16	4.82	5.45	6.96	6.67-7.97	8.24-9.24
Import Dependency (Based on Heating Values)	36%	51%	56%	68%	70-74%	78-80%
Gas as % of TPES	28%	31%	34%	34%	30-34%	32-35%

Note: Heat Contents of Indigenous and Imported Natural Gas
Imported gas from former USSR: 34.000 MJ/m³
Indigenous production average: 32.177 MJ/m³
Indigenous gas with high N_2 and CO_2 content (used in power stations): 16.500 MJ/m³

Source: MOL; and MOIT submission to IEA Secretariat, AEEF.

Table 23
Structure and Evolution of Gas Prices
(forints per gigajoule)

Customer category	1987	1988	1989	1990 (Nov 1)	1991 (June 6)
Residential	86.6	94.1	104.7	150.0	230
Small Commercial/Industrial[1]	144.3	148.0	151.0	358.7	350
Fertiliser Manufacturers	95.8	94.0	94.0	212.3	212
MVMT Interruptible	115.2	115.0	115.0	254.3	238
% change on previous year					
Residential	-	8.7	11.3	43.3	53.3
Small Commercial/Industrial[1]	-	2.6	2.0	137.5	-2.4
Fertiliser Manufacturers	-	-1.9	0	125.9	0
MVMT Interruptible	-	0	0	121.1	-6.4
Consumer Price Index	-	15.5	17.0	28.9	37[2]

Notes: 1. Customers consuming less than 200 m³ per hour.
2. Projected.

Source: MOL.

Furthermore, sustainable natural gas pricing structures should be established, giving due consideration to:

- differentials between summer and winter prices;

- different prices for firm and interruptible supplies;

- responsibility for connection costs and related payment policies;

- actual transmission costs to and distribution costs for the separate distribution companies.

In addition, cross-subsidisation should be eliminated without delay in all natural gas prices, both across the producing and consuming sectors, and within the sectors themselves.

Any financial assistance judged necessary to buffer cost based prices for specific groups of consumers should be provided in the form of direct support, not through any kind of price management. Interference with the operation of proper pricing signals must be avoided in all aspects of the industry. This is important to the success of energy conservation initiatives as well.

Regulation

It is recommended that the Hungarian Government establish an independent natural gas regulatory agency to safeguard the public interest where competition does not exist. Monopolies such as natural gas distribution companies, pipelines and storage would be subject to the jurisdiction of such an agency. It should be an independent body responsible for administering regulations enacted by the Government, but should not be subject to political interference from the Government. Some of its responsibilities would include:

- supervising tariffs and rates of return on investments for natural gas monopolies such as distribution companies, pipeline companies and gas storage companies;

- supervising terms of gas supply and service levels for the various categories of natural gas consumers;

- ensuring that government safety and environmental standards are met;

- monitoring data on supply and demand and on prices in all segments of the industry.

Coal

General

In 1990 coal represented 23% of the total Hungarian primary energy supply. Production of coal in 1990 was 17.6 million metric tons (4.53 Mtoe), of which 6.8 million were mined from open cast pits. Imports were 1.43 Mtoe in 1990. Production has been falling steadily in recent years. Figure 10 shows the trend since 1983. Before that, production had been stable for a decade at about 25 million metric tons per year.

The industry produces three distinct primary products, classified in Hungary as hard coal, brown coal and lignite. Each has geographically distinct sources and some differentiation of markets. Figure 11 shows the distribution of coal fields in Hungary. Hard coal of very low calorific value is produced from the Mecsek mines in the southwest. Brown coal of even lower calorific value is produced from deep mines in two basins, separated by the Danube, along the low mountains in northern Hungary. Lignite comes from an area in the northeast. Conditions for deep mining of coal are generally unfavourable. Calorific values of both deep mined and open cast coal are low. Most coal has high sulphur and ash contents. Productivity is low, with average output from deep mines of 1.54 metric tons per shift per man.

Most coal mined in Hungary is sold for power generation. A large part of the remainder is used for space heating with a small part used in industry, mainly as coke for metallurgy. The financial condition of the sector is bad as a result of the conversion of state capital subsidies into debt, bad investments, overmanning and controlled low prices for coal. Comprehensive restructuring is being undertaken.

Organisational Structure

All of Hungary's coal mining and preparation capacity belongs to eight state owned, regionally based companies: Mecsek, Veszprém, Oroszlány, Tatabánya, Dorog, Nógrád, Borsod and Mátraalja. They are independent economic entities, not subordinated to a trust as is the case with electricity and was the case for oil and gas.

Considerable central influence on the industry has been exercised through control of producer and consumer prices, allocation of capital and policy guidance on employment. State ownership and control are exercised through MOIT. Contact between the Ministry and companies is direct. The mining companies have established a joint stock company, Mininvest, to:

- exercise a delegated right to sign contracts with MVMT and industrial consumers;

- maintain data and information resources;

- protect the professional interests of the mining industry;

- develop policy papers and studies on matters of interest to the collieries;

- give expert opinions and advice to the collieries.

The creation of Mininvest was an attempt to partially redress the imbalance in negotiating positions between the monopsony purchaser of power station coal and the competing coal producers. In the present climate of falling power station purchases, Mininvest tries to arbitrate the allocation of cuts among the companies. Decisions on investment and borrowing are made by the companies independently.

The financial condition of the sector is critical. The accumulated investment debt of the companies was Ft 35 billion in 1989. All eight companies are in a more or less serious state of financial collapse. Mecsek, Borsod, Nógrád, Dorog, Veszprém and Mátraalja have filed for bankruptcy: They have ceased to trade as independent companies and their affairs, including their debts, have been taken over by the Coal Mining Restructuring Centre, SZÉSZEK, established by government resolution in September 1990. SZÉSZEK's principle task is to reorganise the companies to make them financially viable. This involves debt write-offs, managerial reform and closures of inefficient production units.

In the government resolution, provision was made to write off Ft 9.1 billion from existing state allocations and state loans to mines in liquidation. It was recognised that a further Ft 21-22 billion of allocations and loans would have to be written off in future years and that it would be necessary to pay from the state budget the costs of mine closures, including claims for damage and rehabilitation of the environment.

Technical and Economic Structure

The output of coal from each mining company in 1990 is shown in Table 24, along with the average calorific value of the coal produced. The

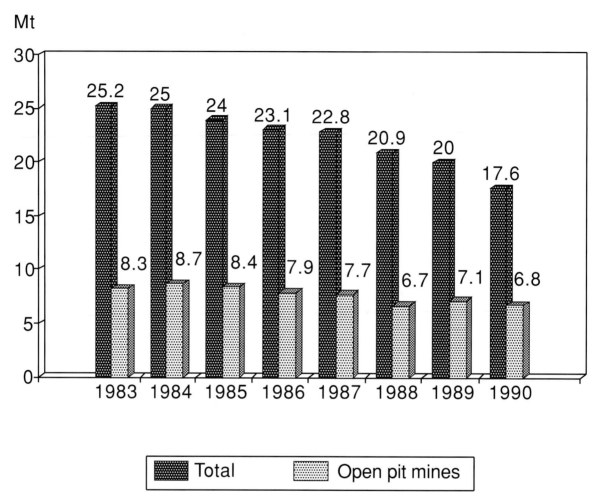

Figure 10
Trends in Coal Production, 1983-1990

Mt

Legend
Total
Open pit mines

Source: Mininvest.

marginal cost production schedule of the industry is not known with any certainty, as marginal cost analysis has not been widely and systematically applied. Mininvest calculates that of the 21 mining units in operation in 1990, ten produced coal at costs below the sale price. The most profitable units made surpluses of Ft 50-100/GJ. Losses of the least competitive units reached almost Ft 200/GJ. These figures must be treated with some caution, as in the absence of a proper accounting system the elements included in the production cost are not clear. Some cross-subsidisation probably exists and the

administered prices may not reflect the coal's true value. The figures do, however, indicate the variability of profitability within the coal industry.

Since 1990 the change from rouble to dollar accounting standards has had a radical effect on the absolute and relative costs of the industry. Mining machinery and auxiliary materials are now paid for in dollars and many prices have increased by 300%. The effect is uneven across the industry, with some mines more exposed to the changes than others. Those using machinery imported from western Europe, such as

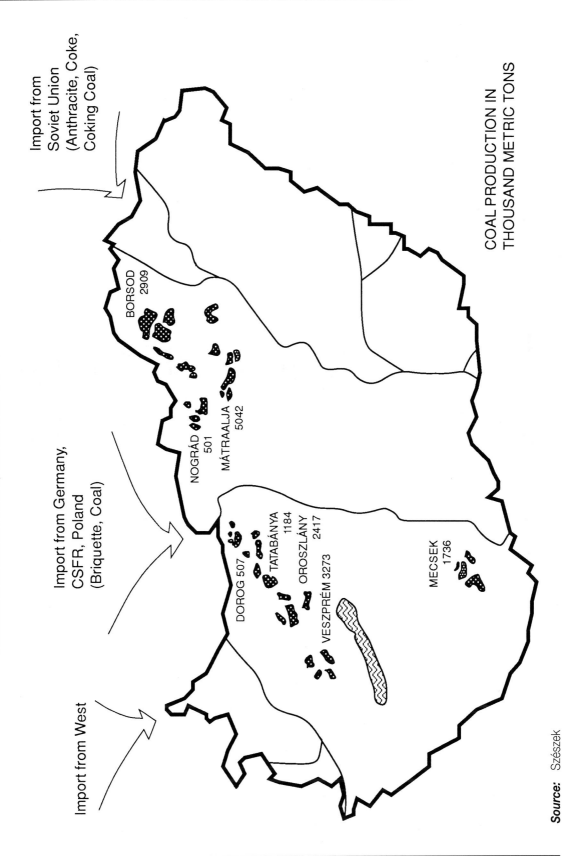

Figure 11

HUNGARIAN COAL FIELDS, COAL PRODUCTION AND IMPORTS, 1990

Import from
Soviet Union
(Anthracite, Coke,
Coking Coal)

Import from Germany,
CSFR, Poland
(Briquette, Coal)

Import from West

COAL PRODUCTION IN
THOUSAND METRIC TONS

BORSOD
2909

NÓGRÁD
501

MÁTRAALJA
5042

DOROG 507

TATABÁNYA
1184

OROSZLÁNY
2417

VESZPRÉM 3273

MECSEK
1736

Source: Szészek

Tatabánya, were less affected than those equipped with Soviet and Polish equipment, such as Oroszlány. In the first half of 1991 production costs increased by an average of 37%. Trends on the demand side were also unfavourable. Coal prices are aligned with a reference price for heavy fuel oil, fixed in 1990 and not adjusted since the decline in oil prices in 1991. At average oil prices in mid-1991 a large part of the industry is not viable. A substantial contraction appears inevitable and it is essential for that contraction to be managed in an orderly fashion.

Low calorific value hard coal is produced at Mecsek from the Szászár, Komló and Vasas deep mines and the Pécs open pit. Mecsek has the worst conditions in Hungary for deep mining and a dangerous environment. Productivity is low at 60% of the Hungarian average. Production has continued because the coal is of higher quality than other indigenous coal and is suitable for metallurgy. Hard coal for metallurgy was separated out by a physical process with the by-product burnt at the power station in Pécs nearby. The metallurgical sector now imports better coal more cheaply. The most difficult conditions are at Komló, where a town of 30 000 people depends on the mine as the primary source of almost all employment. In 1989 Mecsek Coal Mines disposed of 33.7 PJ of coal, of which 16.1 PJ was used at Pécs thermal power station. The open cast pit is profitable but small. The deep mines are unprofitable. By 1990 annual production had fallen to 26.7 PJ.

Brown coal mines form the largest part of the Hungarian industry. In 1990, 129.5 PJ was produced from 16 mining units; of that, 73.8 PJ was burnt in power stations. The mines lie in two regions, one in Trans-Danubia (Veszprém, Oroszlány, Tatabánya and Dorog) and the other in northern Hungary (Nógrád and Borsod). Because of the different characteristics of the collieries in terms of financial condition, production cost and reserves, and because of the different relationships with nearby power stations, the brown coal sector is the most complex to restructure. An incremental cost analysis of existing production facilities has been made, but it is not comprehensive or systematic and more work must be done before the long term prospects of these mines are clear.

The Veszprém mines have the best geological deep mining conditions in Hungary, producing coal mainly for the power stations at Ajka, Oroszlány and plants in northeastern Hungary. The most productive mine in this region is Ajka, with productivity at 5.5 metric tons per man shift in 1991, using a retreating long wall and modern equipment. The area generally is a low cost producer, relatively distant from the power stations it now serves and therefore burdened by transport costs. The geological reserves could support higher capacity, but owing to present marketing conditions no expansion is feasible.

Oroszlány produced 29.8 PJ of coal in 1990, mostly for the mine mouth power station of the same name. It also supplies Tisza power station

Table 24
Disposal of Coal by Company, 1990

Company	Fine Coal (PJ)	Steam Coal (PJ)	Total (PJ)	Calorific Value (kJ/kg)
Mecsek	13.7	13.0	26.7	14 906
Dorog	4.8	3.0	7.8	12 229
Tatabánya	9.4	7.3	16.7	13 174
Oroszlány	10.4	19.4	29.8	12 325
Veszprém	12.0	24.0	36.0	10 916
Borsod	18.3	14.3	32.6	11 155
Nógrád	0.8	5.8	6.6	9 172
Mátraalja	1.1	32.3	33.4	6 429
Total	**70.5**	**119.1**	**189.6**	
Total in Mtoe	*1.68*	*2.84*	*4.53*	

Source: Coal Mining Yearbook, Hungary, 1991.

in northeastern Hungary, because proven reserves and output are declining at Borsod, the original source for Tisza. The area has proven reserves for twelve years, but is burdened by high debt and works somewhat below design productivity and efficiency. The cutback in coal demand by MVMT has caused severe problems for both Veszprém and Oroszlány.

Three years ago, Tatabánya was the least profitable company in Hungary, producing 1.6 million metric tons of coal from newly opened shafts. The investments proved bad. Water intrusion was severe and high rates of pumping had to be maintained, threatening the water table as far away as Budapest. Eventually the new shafts were closed. The labour force was cut by 50% and production dropped to 1.2 million metric tons, returning the mine to apparent profitability. The company has good beneficiation and briquetting facilities, which means it can sell all production as household coal if price differentials warrant it. Consequently, in 1989 the mine supplied only 487 000 metric tons to the pit head power station at Tatabánya, remaining requirements being supplied from Veszprém and Oroszlány mines. Following a change in price differentials, Tatabánya has since switched back to supplying the local power station, exacerbating the difficulties of Veszprém and Oroszlány. The company has reserves accessible from existing shafts until 1997.

Dorog, in Trans-Danubia, produces mainly household coal and has a large briquetting plant. The company filed for bankruptcy and succeeded in establishing financial viability following the write-off of debt. It has since been bought out by private individuals and creditors from Hungary. Dorog has reserves for six to seven years.

Generally in Trans-Danubia it appears that production capacity will fall over the next four years by at least 30%. Shafts are close together and in principle labour can move between the units. It would appear sensible to unite the companies and to rationalise activities among them.

In northeastern Hungary, brown coal is mined at Borsod and Nógrád. Nógrád has begun the procedure for financial liquidation, but is making losses even in these circumstances because the production cost is greater than the price for its coal and writing off its debts is not enough to restore viability. The mine produces only steam coal and supplies the Tisza power station, which also obtains supplies from Dorog, Oroszlány and Veszprém. The coal has relatively low sulphur content.

Borsod has also begun financial liquidation prior to restructuring. The company produces about 3 million metric tons of coal and serves both power station and household markets. To maintain production capacity at this level it is necessary to open a new mine. Preparations for a new shaft at Dubicsány to produce an additional 700 000-800 000 metric tons per year are well advanced. The company is seeking new investors, one of which might be MVMT. The new shaft apparently has good prospects and the brown coal power stations of northeastern Hungary are short of supplies. If the shaft at Dubicsány is not opened, then coal must be brought from Veszprém, which entails substantial transport cost and could be problematic after 1995/96 as production declines.

The northeastern Hungarian basin also includes lignite deposits in a province about 100 km long and 10 km wide between the Mátra and Bükk hills, mined by the Mátraalja company. There are two pits, one at Visonta and one at Bükkábrány. They produced 33.4 PJ (0.77 Mtoe) of lignite in 1990, almost all used by the Gagarin power station adjacent to the Visonta pit. In Visonta 200 million metric tons of lignite were originally available, of which 130 million have been mined. More lignite reserves are located in a contiguous territory that has not yet been developed.

Bükkábrány is 50 km from the power station and coal must be transported by road or rail. The coal field is large, containing 570 million metric tons of lignite in a layer 12-15 metres deep, comprising alternating seams of lignite and clay, which are mined together. The heating value averaged over the layer is 6 200-7 000 kJ/kg. The sulphur content of the lignite is 1.5%, but as only 25% of the material is combustible the sulphur emissions per unit of heat are high. At Visonta the overburden is about 8 m^3 per metric ton, productivity is 6 metric tons per shift per man and the mining cost is Ft 220/GJ, which results in a substantial loss. At Bükkábrány the overburden is 4 m^3 per metric ton and productivity is 12 metric tons per shift per man. The mining cost of Ft 100/GJ yields a profit more than enough to compensate the Ft 30/GJ cost of delivering the lignite to Gagarin power station by rail. The lignite is brought from Bükkábrány to the power station by a main railway line, eventually joining a single track branch to Gagarin. The maximum capacity of the branch line is 3.5 million metric tons per year. The line was built for the construction of the power station and is not really suitable for its present function. Insufficient foundations limit speed to 20 km per hour. Transport costs are paid by the power station, which buys lignite from the two pits at the same price. The power station evidently prefers to buy coal from Visonta even though it has a higher production cost. There appears to be an agreement whereby the power station is supplied 50% from each pit. The loading facility at Bükkábrány is capable of handling only 1.5 to 2 million metric tons per year but is being upgraded to 3 million tons per year capacity. Meanwhile the mining company carries extra lignite from Bükkábrány to Visonta by truck at its own expense.

The generating sets at Gagarin have recently been through an extensive and successful refitting, which has improved their availability and will increase demand for lignite to 48 PJ (1.10 Mtoe), or 8.0-8.3 million metric tons per year by 1995. Bükkábrány could meet this requirement, but only with a substantial new investment in transport. The Mátraalja coal mines propose to limit production from Bükkábrány to the capacity of the existing railway line and to open a new mine at Visonta on the as yet undeveloped lignite territory. The investment required is Ft 5 billion; the mine would produce 3 million metric tons per year. Production cost is expected to be similar to that at Bükkábrány.

Markets

The structure of the market for coal in 1990 is shown in Table 25. Power stations provide the largest market, but residential sector demand is also significant. In 1990 a small quantity of coking coal was produced at Mecsek and sold to the state owned Danube Iron Works. These sales ceased because metallurgical coal of better quality can be imported more cheaply.

The coal mines are mainly located close to the power stations they were originally intended to supply. This geographical relationship still translates into a close market relationship at Pécs and the lignite mines, where coal of the quality burned in the power stations cannot be supplied from other sources in Hungary. The brown coal flow is more complex. Severe imbalances have developed and substantial flows occur among mines and power stations in Trans-Danubia. There is also a major flow from Trans-Danubia to the power stations in northeastern Hungary. These flows are detailed in Figure 12.

Overall, domestic brown coal production enjoys effective geographical protection from imports. The power stations are designed to burn low calorific value, high ash coal that is not available elsewhere and in any case would be expensive to transport. Conversely, the brown coal mining industry cannot sell its products to power stations outside Hungary.

Sales to households in 1990 amounted to 74.6 PJ or 36% of total coal sales. About half of this was in the form of briquettes and half as sized coal. Briquettes and coal for briquetting are imported from the former USSR and from producers in

Table 25
Coal Markets in 1989/90
(Mtoe)

	Power Stations & District Heating	Metallurgy	Households	Other	Total
1990					
Domestic Supply	2.975	0.220	1.816	0.207	5.218
Net Imports	-	0.752	0.363	0.281	1.396
Total	**2.975**	**0.972**	**2.179**	**1.488**	**6.614**
1989					
Domestic Supply	2.985	0.347	2.042	0.161	5.535
Net Imports	-	0.810	0.621	0.703	2.134
Total	**2.985**	**1.157**	**2.663**	**0.864**	**7.669**

Source: Ministry of Industry and Trade.

Figure 12

FLOW OF COAL BETWEEN MINES AND POWER STATIONS, 1989

(thousands of metric tons)

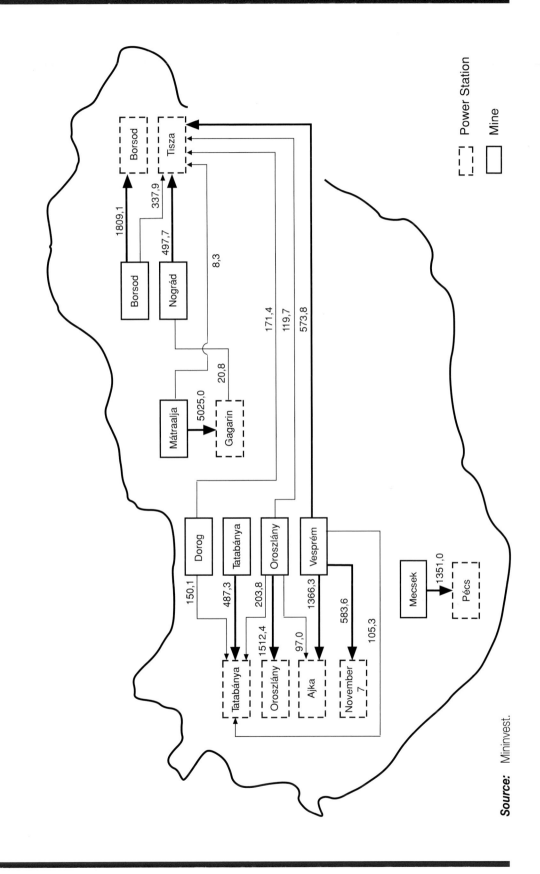

Source: Mininvest.

central and eastern Europe by both private agencies and the coal mining companies themselves. Imports, required because of the deteriorating quality of Hungarian coal, are further stimulated by the low prices of coal from the former USSR and the CSFR.

Most household fuel is distributed through TÜZÉP (Fuel and Building Material Trade Enterprise), a company undergoing privatisation, although there is no monopoly and other companies are active. Sales to the domestic sector have recently been irregular as a result of large price increases in 1989 and anticipation of another price rise in 1991. There are difficulties in meeting the seasonal fluctuations in demand because TÜZÉP does not have the money to finance adequate stocks. In the cities household coal and briquettes compete with natural gas and district heating and represent a small share of the market. In the suburbs, where gas and district heat are not available, coal is a common household fuel. Natural gas is beginning to penetrate these areas, but the cost of connection is high. The tendency is clear: Coal will be replaced by natural gas, but it will take time. In the countryside coal supplies 90% of household fuel requirements and heating oil about 10%. About 9 PJ (0.21 Mtoe) of wood was used for fuel in Hungary in 1990.

The briquetting plants are in poor financial condition. Recent winters have been mild, consumer preferences have shifted towards sized coal, disposable incomes have fallen and cheaper briquettes could be imported from eastern Germany until reunification in 1990. Imported briquettes are now too expensive to market, which has benefitted local producers. Total plant capacity is about 2.4 Mt. Utilisation in 1990 was about 1.8 Mt, falling from a peak of full utilisation in 1988.

Prices

Prices for coal in Hungary have been, and still are, determined by the state. Until recently the price of household coal was held down by large subsidies to dealers. Depending upon the quality of coal, a company might sell to a dealer for Ft 4 000 per metric ton. The householder would buy at around Ft 1 000 per metric ton and the state would pay the dealer Ft 3 200. Subsidies were eliminated as of 1st June 1991; the householder now pays the authorised producer price plus a margin for the dealer. Demand presumably will be reduced substantially at the beginning of the 1991/92 heating season.

Successive changes to the coal price regime have had major effects on the differentials between steam coal and household products. In 1989 a mining company might sell coal, depending on the quality, for Ft 100/GJ to a power station or the same coal, after beneficiation and briquetting, to households for Ft 160. The difference covered the cost of the beneficiation. In subsequent price reviews the differentials were changed and now a mine is likely to obtain a higher price from the power station than from the household, so there is no incentive for beneficiation.

Prices for coal and coal products are set by MOIT. Coal was excluded from the 1991 Bill on Prices as the state wished to maintain control of producer prices while the consumer price subsidy system still operated; the state would otherwise have been liable for open ended subsidies. Now that the subsidy system has been abolished, liberalisation of prices is feasible. There was no opposition to the idea, but it proved difficult to introduce it into an overburdened parliamentary schedule. Coal prices finally ceased to be a matter for government regulation with approval of the 1992 state budget.

There is not a fully competitive market to determine the price for coal supplied to MVMT. MVMT is a monopsony purchaser of coal — the mines cannot sell the bulk of their output to any other buyer and MVMT cannot supply its power stations from elsewhere because their stations are designed to burn very low grade coal. MVMT does, however, have the option to purchase heavy fuel oil and burn it at Dunamenti and Tisza power stations. As noted earlier, coal prices are aligned with a reference price for heavy fuel oil, fixed in 1990 and not adjusted since the decline in oil prices in 1991. In the future prices for coal are to be agreed between the coal and electricity industries and it is understood that the prices will continue to be aligned with the price of heavy fuel oil.

The contractual relationship between the mining companies and MVMT is unsatisfactory. As late as July 1991 the mining companies still had no legal contractual basis to supply the power stations in 1991. MVMT announces its requirements annually; as a result of falling demand for electricity it has stipulated that it will reduce its coal requirement from 125 PJ in 1990 to 115 PJ in 1991 and 100-105 PJ in 1992. The mining companies cannot agree how to allocate these cuts. Normally a mining industry would attempt to stabilise its operations by long term contracts to cover a large part of its output.

Restructuring

Within the context of the programme of economic liberalisation the coal industry is to be restructured. Under the terms of a loan from the World Bank the Government has undertaken to make the industry profitable without subsidy, to abandon centralised decision making on production levels and to generate investment funds internally by borrowing at market rates, with a goal for investment projects of a 12% rate of economic return.

A government resolution of 30th August 1990 regarding the restructuring of the coal mines agreed to the following measures:

- establishment of the Coal Mining Restructuring Centre;
- a producer price system aligned on the price of import substitutes;
- a write-off worth Ft 9.1 billion from the existing state debt;
- recognition of the need to write off a further Ft 21-22 billion;
- state budgetary provision for the cost of mine closures, including claims for damages and rehabilitation of the environment.

The restructuring centre, SZÉSZEK, is charged with making cost based analyses of production units and defining rationalisation and investment programmes; managing closures and investment programmes; preparing and implementing financial and organisational restructuring; and organising future operations in the national interest.

Restructuring at a company level is under way, but the eventual structure of the industry is still uncertain. There is scope for rationalisation by combining companies, which would reduce overhead, ease labour mobility, help in closing uneconomic units and concentrate resources in the best new investment projects. The main points at issue are the optimal size of the new company or companies and the relationship to the electricity supply industry.

A number of arrangements could be envisaged:

- At one extreme, the mines could be absorbed into the electricity supply industry.
- Alternatively, they could be combined into a single unit, or several basin level units, with an administered price relationship to the electricity supply industry.
- The basin level companies could be put together with the coal fired generating stations and be allowed to compete for electricity sales within a liberalised electricity supply system.

The future form of the industry cannot be determined until its approximate future size and the geographical distribution of viable activities are known. More importantly, its form cannot be determined independently of the new structure of the electricity supply industry.

The future of the briquetting industry raises a number of further issues. On one hand, it can be argued that briquetting should be separated from the mining companies, as current arrangements provide for cross-subsidisation of inefficient mining from profitable briquetting. Current arrangements may also restrict competition in the supply of briquettes, particularly as imports of high quality briquettes from eastern Germany are no longer economic. On the other hand, briquetting provides mines with some market flexibility in an otherwise extremely constrained situation. It permits them to switch production, within limits, between household and power station supply according to prevailing prices. It can also be argued that adequate competition will be provided by new private briquetting companies. It would appear pragmatic for briquetting plants to remain part of the mining companies, though in the preparation of accounts briquetting should be separated from other mine operations.

Conclusions

Deep mining conditions in Hungary are difficult. All indigenous coal has low calorific value and high sulphur contents, damaging to the environment. Production is expensive, and supply and quality are deteriorating. On the other hand, coal is a significant national energy resource. The situation of the industry has been distorted by poor technical decisions and low fixed prices. The current financial condition of the industry is no guide to future decisions.

Clearly a substantial contraction is inevitable. It is essential for this contraction to be managed in an orderly and economically optimal fashion, preserving such parts of the industry as are economic and taking into account the social costs. A comprehensive analysis of the industry's prospects should be undertaken, based on a marginal cost analysis complemented by shadow pricing to account, among other things, for the social costs of contraction. Some government intervention to manage the transition appears inevitable. One possibility would be to determine medium term contracts between MVMT and the coal industry, with contracted volumes declining until the industry reaches a viable size.

Resources should be concentrated into the most economic areas. The present structure does not permit the best rationalisation and allocation of investment resources, management skills and labour. Reorganisation into three or four companies might be beneficial; detailed examination of this option is recommended. The industry might be separated into companies producing 1) lignite, 2) brown coal in each of the Trans-Danubian and northern Hungarian basins and 3) low calorific value hard coal at Mecsek if analysis shows this area to be viable. Investment in new production facilities for brown coal is economically marginal and could be undertaken only with a long-term plan for the simultaneous development of new mines and coal fired generating plants.

Decisions about the future of the industry should not be prejudiced by monopoly distortions. Coal companies are faced with a monopsonistic purchaser of power station coal and market forces will not lead to an optimal solution. Three possible solutions are: a) that the mines would be transferred into the electricity supply industry, in which case decisions about them are theoretically optimal but in practice are made by an industry with a primary focus elsewhere; b) that the purchasing monopoly would be managed by price and quantity agreements; or c) that control of coal fired power stations would be transferred to the regional coal mining companies so that competition could be exercised in the supply of electricity to the high voltage grid. Choosing among these options is the responsibility of the Hungarian Government, but whatever institutional restructuring may be agreed upon, this problem should be explicitly addressed and its solution clearly specified.

Restructuring the industry and achieving a satisfactory financial position, by re-evaluating company assets and liabilities and writing them off where appropriate, are more urgent than ownership changes.

Electricity

Organisational Structure

All aspects of electricity supply and distribution come under the control of the Hungarian Electricity Board, Magyar Villamos Múvek Tröszt (MVMT). MVMT also supplies heat from some of its power stations to district heating systems and for industrial process steam.

Table 26
Main Characteristics of Hungarian Power System, 1990

Installed Capacity	7 184	MW
Peak Load	6 534	MW
Electricity Demand	39 224	GWh
Net Imports	11 147	GWh
MVMT Generation	27 463	GWh
Heat Supplied by MVMT	55.6	PJ

Source: MVMT.

MVMT has 22 subsidiary companies falling into three groups: power and heat generation; network transmission and distribution; and investment, construction and installation. The first group includes eleven power station companies and a repair enterprise; the second includes a company (OVIT) to control the high voltage lines and six regional distribution companies, including one for Budapest; the third comprises various companies providing subsidiary services.

Until the end of September 1991, MVMT preserved the characteristics of state control and functions around a central decision making structure established during the period of central planning. The volume of investment is decided by the state, funds are made available by the state budget and surplus income is taken back by the Treasury. Pricing, investment and funding are the subject of an annual negotiation between MVMT and the Ministries of Finance and of Industry and Trade.

The relations between MVMT and the subsidiaries display similar characteristics: Targets are set, funds are made available and surplus revenue flows back to MVMT. The companies produce separate balance sheets, but MVMT settles the financial accounts of the industry with the state. An inner price system regulates revenue flows between the subsidiaries and MVMT. The power stations sell to the trust at fairly uniform tariffs and the trust sells on to the distributors. There are differences between the operating conditions of the power stations and in the varying circumstances of the distributers, which would normally lead to financial differentiation among the units. These differences are taken into account in the preparation of an annual business plan and internal transfers are agreed to compensate distribution companies for differences in revenue resulting from differences in customer mix. If a company reduces its operating costs below those foreseen in the business plan, it keeps the extra profit. From this surplus the company can raise salaries, make social investments (such as recreational facilities) and sometimes make productive investment. The improved performance is taken into account in setting the next year's business plan. The outcome of each annual negotiation determines what remains with the company and what passes to MVMT and the state.

Electricity Supply

The structure of fuel inputs to the MVMT system since 1955 is summarised in Table 27. The main trends are clearly visible. Brown coal and lignite predominated in the 1950s and '60s. An important penetration of fuel oil and natural gas occurred in the '70s. Nuclear energy entered the system in the early '80s and to some extent has displaced all fuels, but especially fuel oil.

The generating plants of MVMT reflect this pattern of fuel use in their age (and therefore size) and geographical location. Plants burning brown coal, generally rather small and old, are located near the coal mines. They were mostly commissioned in the 1950s and early '60s but some date back to the '40s.

Table 27
Structure of Fuel Inputs to the MVMT System, 1955-1990 (PJ)

	Lignite	Brown Coal	Hard Coal By-products	Fuel Oil	Natural Gas	Nuclear	Total	Net Cons. (GWh)
1955	19.3	47.8	4.1	1.6	0.0	0.0	**72.8**	4 691
1965	22.0	92.2	13.6	19.6	8.7	0.0	**156.1**	10 410
1975	41.8	91.0	19.3	63.9	52.5	0.0	**268.5**	20 807
1985	46.5	75.4	14.8	59.8	85.0	72.7	**354.2**	31 771
1986	44.5	77.6	18.7	59.8	92.1	80.2	**372.9**	32 400
1987	45.8	79.2	18.3	48.4	77.8	119.5	**389.0**	33 836
1988	36.9	79.3	17.5	26.3	74.8	147.3	**382.1**	33 735
1989	35.8	75.3	16.7	20.4	82.0	151.0	**381.2**	33 942
1990	35.5	72.8	16.1	18.6	73.8	148.4	**365.2**	32 991

As a proportion of the total (%)

	Lignite	Brown Coal	Hard Coal By-products	Fuel Oil	Natural Gas	Nuclear	Total	Net Cons. (GWh)
1955	26.5	65.7	5.6	2.2	0.0	0.0		
1965	14.1	59.1	8.7	12.6	5.6	0.0		
1975	15.6	33.9	7.2	23.8	19.6	0.0		
1985	13.1	21.3	4.2	16.9	24.0	20.5		
1986	11.9	20.8	5.0	16.0	24.7	21.5		
1987	11.8	20.4	4.7	12.4	20.0	30.7		
1988	9.7	20.8	4.6	6.9	19.6	38.6		
1989	9.4	19.8	4.4	5.4	21.5	39.6		
1990	9.7	19.9	4.4	5.1	20.2	40.6		

Source: MVMT.

In the mid-1960s the big lignite deposits in the northeast were developed and construction began on the large Gagarin power station. The first 100 MW block of the station was completed in 1969. Another 100 MW block and three 200 MW blocks were connected in the following three years.

Around the same period large oil fired stations were built on the Danube and Tisza rivers to supply electricity and process steam to adjacent oil refineries, from which they also received a supply of heavy fuel oil. Dunamenti has capacity of 1 870 MW in two power stations spread over 13 units. Tisza 2 has capacity of 860 MW in four units. (A coal fired station, Tisza 1, is not included in this total.) Dunamenti and Tisza 2 were constructed for dual oil/natural gas firing. Both operate at a rather low load factor because natural gas and oil are largely used for load following.

No further new plant was constructed until the nuclear power station was built on the Danube at Paks. It comprises four 440 MW pressurised water reactors of the Soviet VVER type, commissioned between 1983 and 1987. Two more units of 1 000 MW each were planned for the early 1990s but the decision was rescinded in 1990.

Gas turbines for peaking duty have been installed at Inota and Kelenföld and the first of a group of 145 MW sets is under construction at Dunamenti, to be commissioned before the end of 1991. Table 28 shows the principle power stations of Hungary with some technical data, and Figure 13 shows their locations.

The total installed capacity of hydroelectric plants in Hungary is 47.8 MW. There are two large plants on the Tisza river, 28 MW and 11.4 MW respectively, with 27 mini-hydro systems totalling about 8 MW

Table 28
Principal Power Stations

Name	Fuel	Power Capacity (MW$_e$)	Contracted Heat Capacity (MW$_t$)	Combined Heat+Power Capacity (MW$_e$)
Paks	N	1 760	5	13
Dunamenti 2	HO+NG	1 290	-	29
Tisza 2	HO+NG	860	-	-
Gagarin	L	800	28	6
Dunamenti 1	HO+NG	580	394	65
Inota	C, DO	270	63	-
Tisza 1	C+NG	250	237	35
Pécs	C	245	370	45
Oroszlány	C	235	39	4
Borsod	C+NG	171	331	47
Ajka	C	113	266	23
Bánhida	C	100	8	2
Kelenföld	FO+NG	98	672	66
Tatabánya	C+FO	32	196	32
Dorog	C	13	147	13
TOTAL GENERATING CAPACITY (not all included above)		**6 925**	**5 025**	**485**

Notes: DO - diesel oil L - lignite
HO - heavy fuel oil, residual fuel oil N - nuclear
NG - natural gas C - coal
FO - fuel oil

Source: *Technical Data 1990*: MVMT, 1991.

Figure 13
MAJOR POWER STATIONS IN HUNGARY

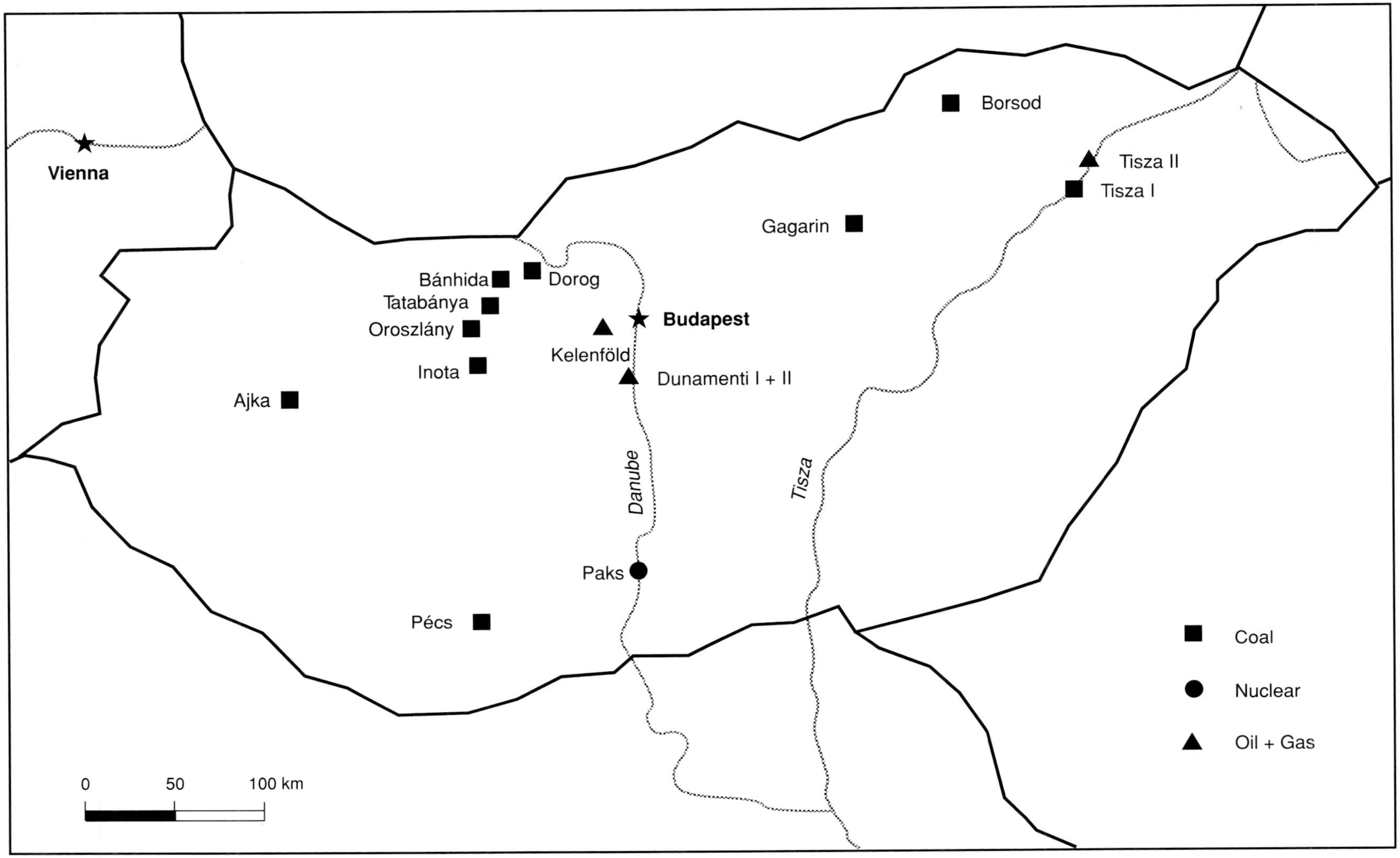

Legend:
- Coal ■
- Nuclear ●
- Oil + Gas ◄

Locations: Vienna, Ajka, Pécs, Dorog, Bánhida, Tatabánya, Oroszlány, Inota, Kelenföld, Budapest, Dunamenti I + II, Paks, Gagarin, Borsod, Tisza I, Tisza II

Rivers: Danube, Tisza

Scale: 0 — 50 — 100 km

capacity. Hungary has withdrawn from a larger project, agreed with the CSFR, which would have involved co-ordinated management of two large plants on the Danube. The upstream plant close to Gabcikovo (Bös) in the CSFR would have been operated by a diversion from the Danube where it forms the border between the two countries, with the water being returned downstream. Regulation of the water level in the Danube would have been achieved by co-ordinated operation of a second plant at Nagymaros, 150 km downstream from Gabcikovo, where the Danube flows through Hungary. Co-ordinated operation of the two dams would have allowed generation of peakload electricity. The capacity for power supply from Gabcikovo would have been around 720 MW and from Nagymaros 174 MW. Hungary withdrew because it believes the environmental costs and interference with associated water tables would be excessive. The matter is a serious issue of contention with authorities in the CSFR, which have virtually completed construction of the power station and associated installations at Gabcikovo. Attempts to renegotiate the agreement have not been successful.

In 1980 MVMT initiated a comprehensive programme of refitting for its coal fired stations, which is now coming to an end. The dates of refitting are given in Table 29. The programme has been generally successful and some highlights are worth mention. The Gagarin lignite power station was the first such station built in Hungary and many components in the boiler, turbine and cooling systems were prototypes. Not all functioned well and availability of the plants was only some 5 000 hours per year. Refitting is expected to increase availability to 7 500 hours per year (trials achieved 8 000 hours). Boiler efficiency has increased from 77% to 85% and control has improved. Only the station's three 200 MW units have so far been refitted. Plans to refit the two 100 MW units are in abeyance because of the falling demand for electricity and uncertainties about supplies from the lignite mine.

Another interesting refit was the installation of a fluidised bed burner (FBB) on a boiler with capacity of 100 metric tons per hour at Ajka power station. The base of the old boiler was cut off and replaced with the fluidised bed. A characteristic feature of the high sulphur Ajka brown coal is its high limestone content. The FBB is of a recirculating design and the retention time is sufficient to take out much of the sulphur. Sulphur retention varies from 60% to 70% depending on the load. NO_x emissions are also reduced, the slagging conditions are improved and control is easier. The project was funded from a number of sources: retained profits of the Ajka power station, the EC's PHARE programme, state credits and the refund of environmental fines. The success of the FBB conversion has led to the conversion of a second boiler in the power station and reconstruction is planned for the three remaining boilers of similar capacity.

Table 29
Dates of Refitting of Coal Fired Power Stations

Station	Number of Units	Commissioning Dates	Refitting Dates
Ajka	5	1960-62	1980-86
Borsod	10	1955-57	1976-88
Gagarin	5	1969-72	1986-91
Inota	5	1952-55	1976-91
Oroszlány	4	1962-63	1985-89
Pécs	10	1960-62	1986-92
Dorog	3	1943	1983-86
Bánhida	1	1968	-
Tatabánya	8	1940-42, & 1951	1987-91
Tisza	8	1957-59	1981-87

Source: MVMT.

A serious problem with the brown coal stations is the deteriorating quality of coal. In many mining areas known reserves are becoming exhausted and funds are not available to develop new deposits, the economic viability of which is in any case marginal. New mining development is not feasible in the absence of a common plan for mines and power stations.

Trade, Transmission and Distribution

Hungary is a member of the former CMEA countries' Interconnected Power System (IPS) and is synchronised to that system. A 750 kV line connects the substation at Albertirsa in central Hungary to the former USSR's 750 kV network linking Chernobyl and other major power stations in Ukraine to Poland, Hungary and Bulgaria. Hungary participated financially in the construction of the line and of some of the power stations to which it connects. A 400 kV line and a 220 kV line enter Hungary from the USSR along a parallel corridor, terminating at Sajószöged in northeastern Hungary. The combined capacity of all these lines is 4 000 MW. Very large amounts of electricity (30% of gross consumption) have been imported from the former USSR under a contract that expires in 2004.

The maximum permitted imports from the former USSR were 1 800 MW and 10.5 TWh per year, reduced in 1990 to 1 100 MW and 6.5 TWh per year following the change from rouble to dollar based accounting, which had the effect of greatly raising the price. Electricity imported from the former USSR is now expensive. The import prices contain a capacity element that makes comparisons difficult, but the standard price appears to be 50% higher than almost any domestically produced electricity, with peak prices more than double the cost of domestic peak generation. The import contract is negotiated annually, and MVMT hopes to reduce volumes further in the future. The present downturn in demand, the commissioning of new capacity at Dunamenti and future connection to western Europe strengthen the case for diminishing Soviet imports. MVMT, however, plans to preserve some access to Soviet capacity for flexibility. Spot imports of electricity from the former USSR, on a barter basis, generally cover one to two months of the year and are cheaper than domestic supplies.

Exchanges are made with the CSFR, and Hungary transmits electricity from the former USSR to Yugoslavia, from the CSFR to Yugoslavia and from Austria to Romania. Exchanges with Austria are made in a coursed mode of operation whereby islands of the Hungarian grid are temporarily synchronised to the Austrian network. Exchanges with Yugoslavia are on a similar basis. Figure 14 summarises imports and exports for 1990. Hungary has frontiers with Austria, the CSFR, the former USSR, Romania and Yugoslavia, and is close to Germany and Italy. This strategic position should be borne in mind when considering future development of the power system.

Figure 15 shows the main features of the transmission network. The 750 kV line from the former USSR is connected to the network at only one point, Albertirsa, southeast of Budapest. A 400 kV network begun in 1967 interconnects most of the large power stations. Some power stations, including Gagarin, feed into a 220 kV network begun in 1960, which has not been added to since 1970. A substantial 120 kV network connects load centres throughout Hungary and also connects with some smaller power stations. Distribution, including control of the 120 kV network, is the responsibility of six regional distribution centres. The total rated capacity of transformers connected to the distribution system in 1990 was 26 040 MVA. This capacity has grown steadily since 1970 at a little under 5% per year. The route length of medium and low voltage lines has grown somewhat less rapidly. Low voltage line length has grown at around 2.5% a year over the past 20 years, reflecting a campaign of rural electrification begun in 1963 and now essentially complete.

Dispatch

The Hungarian system is integrated into the IPS, controlled by the Central Dispatch Station in Prague. Hungarian output is only some 2-3% of overall IPS production. The task of the Central Dispatch Station is to maintain stability in frequency and voltage, and the task of the smaller members of the system is to maintain national power balance. The hydrocarbon fuelled power stations at Dunamenti and Tisza 2 are used for real time control of the power balance and the system is reoptimised on an incremental cost basis every two or three minutes. Six regional dispatch centres control the 120 kV lines and the lower voltage networks are controlled by 39 local centres.

The computer control system is 13 years old and now functioning at the limits of its capabilities. Only three of the six regional centres and 15 of the 39 local centres are supported by computer control. A feasibility study has been prepared to specify a new system for 2000 and beyond. It is envisaged that this system would be capable of

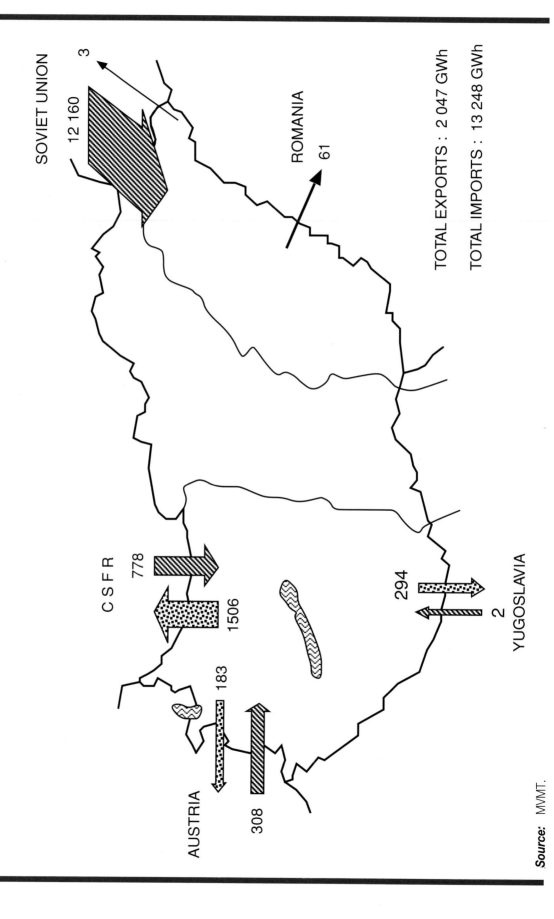

Figure 14

IMPORT AND EXPORT OF ELECTRICITY, 1990 (GWh)

SOVIET UNION

12 160

3

ROMANIA

61

CSFR

778

1506

AUSTRIA

183

308

YUGOSLAVIA

294

2

TOTAL EXPORTS : 2 047 GWh

TOTAL IMPORTS : 13 248 GWh

Source: MVMT.

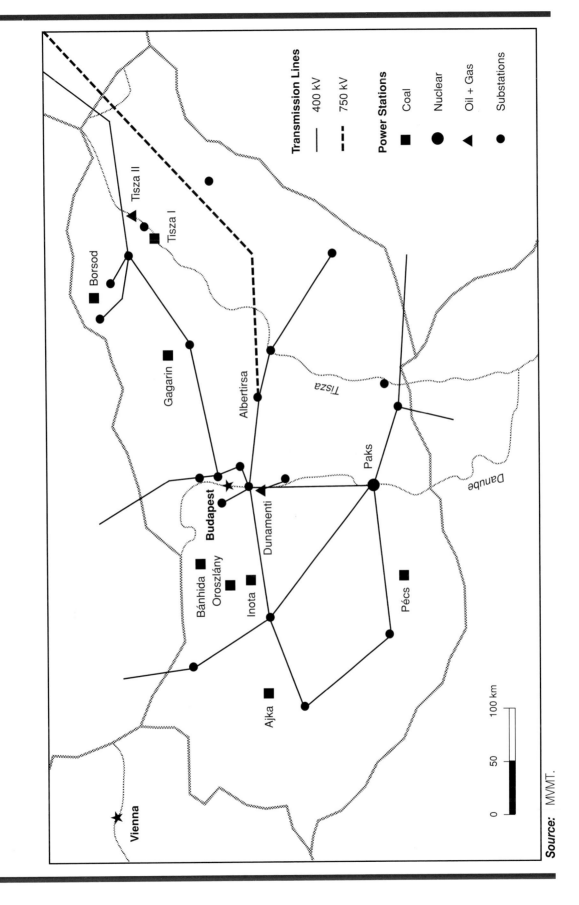

Figure 15

HUNGARIAN POWER NETWORK AND MAJOR POWER STATIONS

Transmission Lines

— 400 kV

--- 750 kV

Power Stations

■ Coal

● Nuclear

▲ Oil + Gas

• Substations

Tisza II

Tisza I

Borsod

Gagarin

Albertirsa

Tisza

Paks

Danube

Budapest

Dunamenti

Bánhida

Oroszlány

Inota

Pécs

Ajka

Vienna

100 km

50

0

Source: MVMT.

69

finer control of voltage, frequency and reactive power and would allow load management for smaller users.

The main characteristics of the dispatch of plant are indicated in Figure 16. Nuclear power is dispatched first and maintains a constant output on baseload. Indigenous coal is also used largely in baseload mode. Load following is achieved mainly by the hydrocarbon plants and with imports. Imports are made at three price levels, corresponding to off peak, normal and peak times. The contract has a take or pay form specifying a maximum offtake in MW and a minimum consumption in MWh, which must be paid for whether it is taken or not. Gas turbines at Inota and Kelenföld are used for fast response and peak shaving.

Since the change from rouble to dollar based accounting, the price of domestic coal has risen steeply. At the same time, the market price of oil has fallen. MVMT is obliged by government decree to produce a certain amount of electricity from coal. In 1991 this amount was 8 TWh, accounting for virtually all the coal consumed by MVMT. The obligation now imposes significant costs on MVMT. In mid-1991 it was cheaper to produce electricity from heavy fuel oil at Dunamenti power station than to generate electricity in most coal fired stations, and the installed generating capacity at Dunamenti is large. A substantial increase in the combustion of heavy fuel oil at this plant and at Tisza power station is likely.

Development of International Connections

There is considerable interest in Hungary in connecting the electricity transmission system with the UCPTE system to help reduce dependence on imports from the former USSR over the long term. Interconnection with UCPTE would also facilitate proposals to build power plants in Hungary with foreign capital and pay it back with exports of electricity.

The Hungarian network is synchronised to the IPS. The first interconnection concept was to maintain synchronisation with CMEA and connect to UCPTE by an AC/DC coupling near Vienna, now under construction. Although opinion is still divided on the subject, there has been a shift towards the view that the AC/DC coupling should be moved to the Albertirsa substation at the end of the 750 kV line from the former USSR, and that the Hungarian system should be synchronised to the UCPTE system. There would be several advantages. Under this plan there would be no obstacles to any other connections to the UCPTE

system elsewhere, for example to Yugoslavia and on to Italy. The Hungarian system would also benefit from UCPTE's high standard of frequency and voltage control.

UCPTE regulations require member countries to be able to meet their electricity demand in normal operation from their own plant or contracted imports. There is some doubt whether the import contract with the former USSR would be acceptable in this respect, but the Hungarian authorities appear to believe it would be. UCPTE also establishes requirements for primary, secondary and tertiary control that are fundamentally different from the philosophy prevailing in the IPS system. The Hungarian system can meet the primary and secondary requirements, since it has adequate spinning reserve as long as the imports from the former USSR are available, though some retrofitting of control equipment will be necessary. Tertiary control will require installation of more gas turbine capacity. These problems are not insurmountable.

There could be several ways of making the transition, depending on whether the CSFR synchronises to the UCPTE system at the same time. A likely outcome will be to move the AC/DC coupling to Albertirsa and synchronise most of the Hungarian system to UCPTE except for an island in the northeast that would remain synchronised to the CSFR and the former USSR, importing directly from the latter on the 400 and 220 kV lines and exchanging with the CSFR across the existing interconnections. If the CSFR and Poland were to link up with UCPTE simultaneously with Hungary, this would offer more connections to UCPTE and a more solid system independent of the relatively weak Austrian network. However, investment costs might prove prohibitive for simultaneous interconnection. Overall, the intention to connect the Hungarian grid to the UCPTE system is sensible, the specific proposals are good and interconnection should be pursued.

Electricity Demand

The historical development of electricity consumption is described in Figure 17. Consumption fell from 1989 to 1990 by 2.7%. The rate of growth of peakload has been declining erratically since the 1950s, as shown in Table 30. MVMT's forecasts for the next 20 years are compared in Figure 18 with the projections prepared for MOIT by AEEF for its submission to the IEA. The Ministry's projections are higher than those under MVMT's "realistic scenario" throughout the period to 2010.

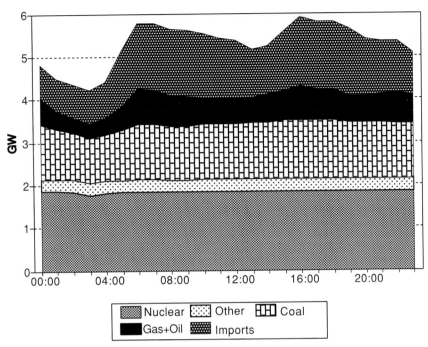

Figure 16
Typical Load Curve for the Hungarian Power System, December 1990

Legend: Nuclear, Other, Coal, Gas+Oil, Imports

Source: MVMT.

Figure 17
Development of electricity generation in Hungary, 1930-1990

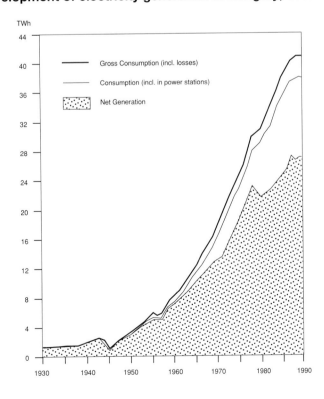

Legend: Gross Consumption (incl. losses), Consumption (incl. in power stations), Net Generation

Source: MVMT.

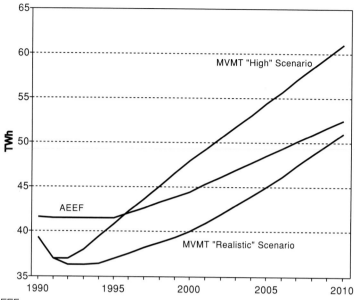

Figure 18
Electric Energy Demand Projections

Source: MVMT and AEEF.

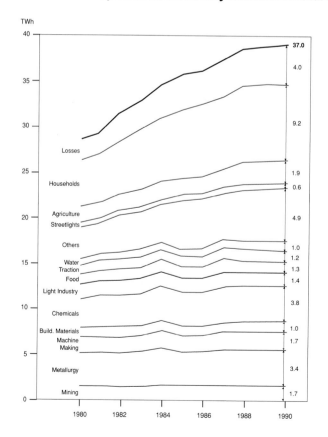

Figure 19
Historical development of electricity market structure

Source: MVMT.

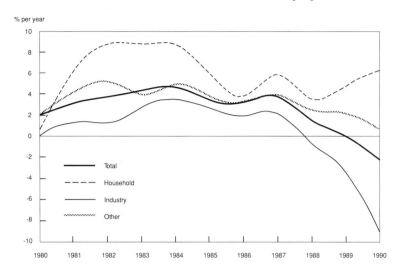

Figure 20
Rate of increase of demand for electricity by sector

% per year

Total
Household
Industry
Other

Source: MVMT.

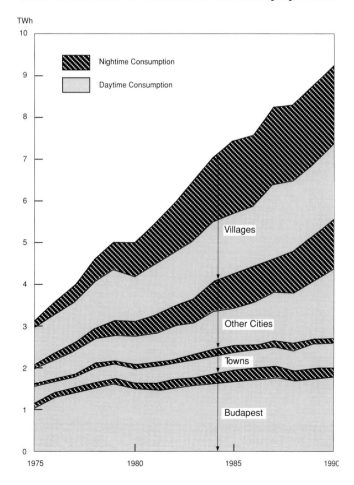

Figure 21
Rate of increase of demand for electricity by sector

TWh

Nightime Consumption
Daytime Consumption

Villages

Other Cities

Towns

Budapest

Source: MVMT.

Table 30
Growth Rate of Peakload

Period	Growth Rate (%/yr)
1950-55	12.7
1955-60	7.9
1960-65	9.0
1965-70	8.4
1970-75	6.6
1975-80	4.7
1980-85	3.3
1985-90	2.2

Source: MVMT.

The development of consumption over the past ten years, including losses of transmission, is shown in Figure 19. Stagnation of demand from the industrial sector is evident. The large proportions of the metallurgical and chemical sectors are also clear. The latter feature is important because these sectors generate little added value for the economy and a substantial retrenchment is probable, which would have the dual effect on electricity demand of reducing growth and worsening the load factor.

The disparate growth rates among sectors are even more clearly visible in Figure 20. Growth in the household sector was strong throughout the 1980s, especially towards the beginning of the decade. This strong demand has several causes. One is that during this period distinct differentiation of living standards emerged and wealthier groups made substantial purchases of appliances. A second cause is the connection of new subscribers in villages and suburbs. The statistics are, however, distorted by the inclusion of some small private enterprises within the household tariff group. A third cause is the high degree of cross-subsidisation of the household sector. The contribution of the rural electrification programme to demand is visible from Figure 21, which indicates that demand in Budapest has doubled in the last 15 years while household demand nationally has tripled. The fastest growing area has been night-time demand in villages, indicating the advantages of off peak water and space heating in outlying areas.

Load management through the tariff structure and more recently by ripple control is well advanced. The daily load factor has increased steadily since 1975 (Table 31), despite the growth in household demand, which would normally have an unfavourable effect. Ripple control, mainly on hot water heating, can reduce the system peak by 100 MW. A programme to extend ripple control is under way with the aim of controlling 30% of suitable appliances.

Medium Term Expansion

There is great uncertainty regarding demand forecasts. Increases in household tariffs and contraction of heavy industry are likely to contain demand growth in the medium term. It is possible that there will be no growth to the end of the century and MVMT is planning on this basis. Extra demand side management (DSM) measures are expected to contribute up to an equivalent of 400-600 MW capacity by 2001 and MVMT plans to install gas turbines at heat supply stations to displace some imports and make up for retired generating plant. Details of the plans are given in Table 32.

Gas turbines with heat recovery are to replace gas fired boilers in some district heating systems. The advantages of gas turbines for power supply are that such plant can be constructed in small increments of capacity, specific investment costs are low, lead times are short and thermodynamic efficiency is high. The disadvantage for Hungary is that natural gas must be paid for in foreign

Table 31
Load Factor on the Days of Maximum Load

Year	Peak Demand (MW)	Load Factor (%)
1955	885	85.8
1960	1 293	85.8
1965	1 993	86.7
1970	2 983	84.2
1975	4 185	82.3
1980	5 184	85.8
1985	6 226	87.1
1988	6 523	88.3
1989	6 550	89.2
1990	6 534	92.1

Source: MVMT.

Table 32
Projected Investments in Gas Turbine Generating Plants

Date	Location	Capacity
1992	Dunamenti	145 MW
1994	Kelenföld	145 MW
1995	Dunamenti	220 MW
1991-1995	**Subtotal**	**510 MW**
1996-2000	Ujpest	210 MW
1996-2000	Debrecen	125 MW
1996-2000	Kispest	125 MW
1996-2000	Tisza	300 MW
1996-2000	**Subtotal**	**760 MW**

Source: MVMT.

exchange, as must the gas turbines. In addition, the price and availability of gas in the next century are uncertain. In an uncertain demand situation, however, the advantages appear to prevail and it is likely that MVMT will follow this route. Figure 22 shows the likely medium term growth in capacity and its structure.

Long Term Expansion

There is a limit to the volume of gas turbine capacity that can be installed in association with heat supply. In the longer term a new baseload power station may be needed. Domestic brown coal has the disadvantages of high cost and poor environmental characteristics. A major power system expansion based on brown coal would require a new mine, entailing significant economic risk — the low calorific value of the coal implies a high specific investment cost, and foreign investors are unlikely to be interested. Hence expansion of generating capacity fired by deep mined brown coal is not under consideration. Three possibilities for baseload expansion, all very provisional, have recently received considerable attention:

- extension of nuclear generating capacity at Paks;

- a new lignite fired power station at the Bükkábrány mine;

- a power station at Komárom on the Danube in northern Hungary burning imported hard coal.

Some advantages of the nuclear option are that facilities for a large extension have already been prepared at Paks (under the earlier plan to extend the number of Soviet reactors). The prospects for international co-operation in a nuclear project are good, although the project would likely be based on reactors of around 900 MW, which is a large unit size in comparison with the Hungarian system; smaller units would appear preferable. Specific capital costs are high, as is the foreign exchange component, and the acceptability of the technology in Hungary and neighbouring countries is not assured. Of several foreign offers to collaborate in a nuclear project, some would help alleviate the foreign exchange burden.

The advantages of a lignite power station are that lignite is an indigenous resource, already successfully exploited, and new generating capacity could be commissioned in relatively small blocks, providing for greater flexibility in responding to developments in demand. The environmental impact would need to be assessed but is probably containable, though at considerable cost. FGD would be required and related investment costs could not be met without external financing. There is interest from Germany in a joint venture.

A coal fired power station using imported hard coal is a recent suggestion. Coal could be imported through the Rhein-Main Canal on completion of the Danube link, scheduled for 1992. FGD would probably be required and external financing necessary.

Tariffs and Return on Assets

The average revenue from electricity sold to households in 1990 was Ft 1.63/kWh. The average unit revenue from total sales was Ft 3.18/kWh in 1990 and Ft 4.11/kWh in mid-1991. From these figures the cross-subsidisation of the household sector is evident. It is also clear that, as the industrial sector retracts, MVMT will lose its more profitable sales, unless the tariffs are revised. Cross-subsidisation of the household sector became acute in the early 1980s, coincident with the boom in household sales. Cross-subsidisation was the result of government policy to compensate lower paid groups by making basic needs available at a low price. Table 33 summarises present tariff structures.

Figure 22
Medium-Tern Expansion of Electric Power Generating Capacity

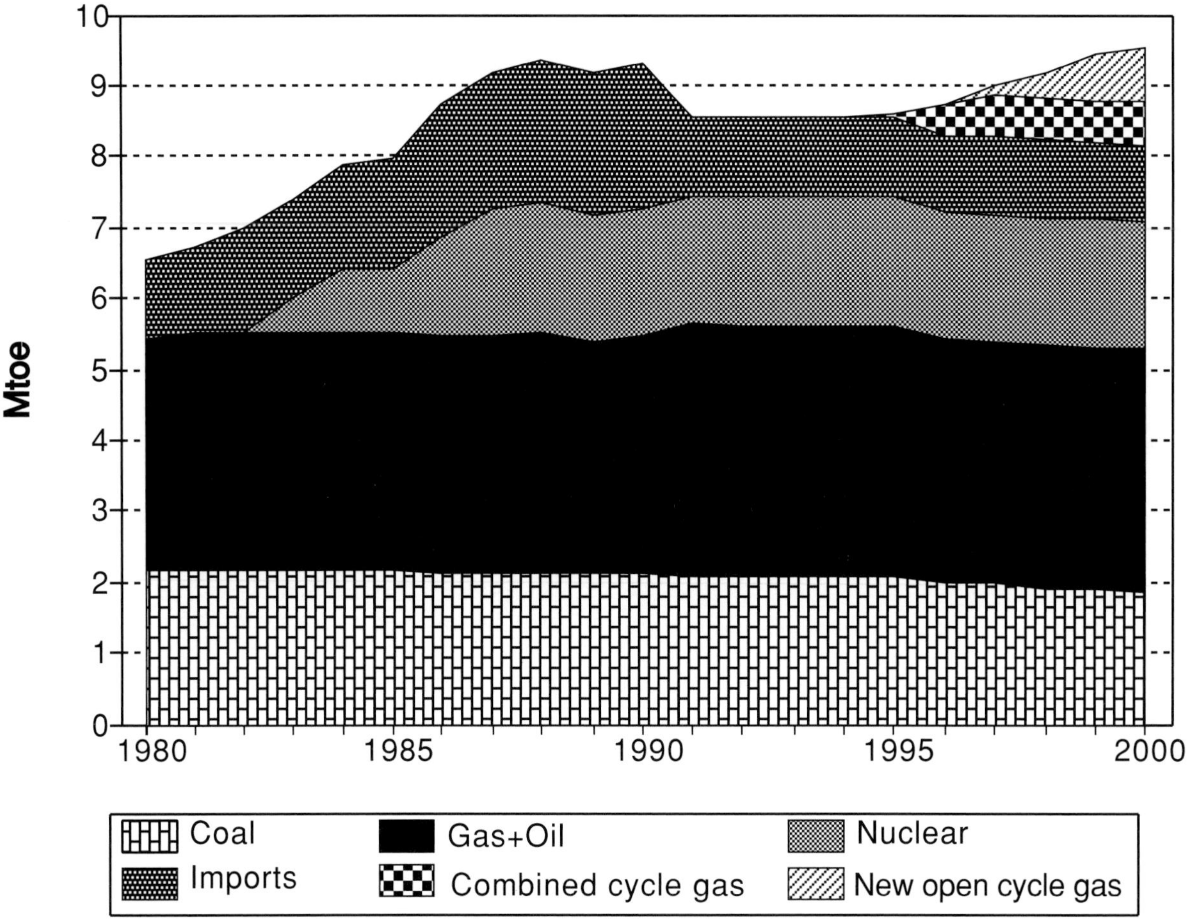

Legend:
- Coal
- Imports
- Gas+Oil
- Combined cycle gas
- Nuclear
- New open cycle gas

Source: MVMT.

The general level of prices is established on an accountancy basis, depreciating assets at historic cost. This procedure normally gives results below long run marginal costs, and in Hungary, where inflation has been strong, this is surely the case.

MVMT does not publish detailed accounts. The depreciated net value of its fixed assets in 1990 was Ft 168 billion. The distribution of assets within MVMT was estimated in 1990 to be as shown in Table 34, though it is subject to re-evaluation during the restructuring process.

MVMT's income was Ft 21.3 billion in 1990, which represents a rate of return on assets of 12.6%. To confirm this figure would require a more detailed explanation of financial accounts than has hitherto been possible.

Restructuring and Regulation

In April 1991, the Ministry of Trade and Industry submitted to the Government a proposal for the

Table 33
Some Features of MVMT's Electricity Tariffs

Category	Demand Charge Ft/kW/yr	Energy Charge Ft/kWh		
		Peak	Day	Night
TRACTION				
Railway	-	3.15	3.15	3.15
Trams	-	3.80	3.80	3.80
GENERAL TARIFFS				
Demands to 2.5 kVA	1 440	6.20	6.20	3.00
Demands to 3.5 kVA	2 280	6.20	6.20	3.00
Demands to 5.0 kVA	3 540	6.20	6.20	3.00
Demands > 5.0 kVA	720	6.20	6.20	3.00
PUBLIC LIGHTING				
Directed Lights	9 600	4.20	4.20	4.20
Intensive Lights	14 400	4.20	4.20	4.20
HOUSEHOLDS	-	3.70	3.70	1.90
(PURCHASES FROM INDEPENDENT POWER PRODUCERS	-	4.50	2.70	2.00)

Source: MVMT.

modernisation of MVMT's ownership, management and organisational structure. The restructuring is intended to:

- take advantage of the benefits of the corporate form;
- separate the functions of ownership and operation;
- render transparent the economic situation of MVMT's individual corporate parts;
- attract capital, especially foreign capital, for development projects;
- "loosen" the monopolistic structure of generation and distribution.

The Ministry proposed a two tier organisation in which a central concern is responsible for technical and economic management and co-ordination and owns part or all of the corporations. Elements of natural monopoly would be regulated by a new legal entity. In addition to this economic regulation the document proposes public control at the level of the parliament and through regional and local governments. The proposal was accepted by the Government in April and MVMT was charged with elaborating proposals for implementation.

From 1st January 1992 the industry is to be reconstituted as an assembly of corporations owned by the state. The generating companies will be grouped on a fuel or regional basis. An earlier suggestion that these companies would also take on the related coal mines appears to be defunct, although there is still some possibility of such merging at Gagarin and the hard coal mine

Table 34
Estimated Distribution of MVMT Assets, 1990

Nuclear power station	28%
Coal fired stations	15%
Hydrocarbon fired stations	12%
Transmission lines	9%
Power distribution companies	36%

Source: MVMT.

near Pécs. The power distribution companies will be reconstructed into corporations retaining present territorial boundaries.

Generating companies may accept foreign capital, should the opportunity arise. The distribution companies will be partially owned by local governments. How and when this will happen will remain unclear, however, until legislation on the conversion of assets to local government ownership is completed. The production and distribution companies will operate as affiliates of the central concern, so the "Concern" will have ownership rights, although it is not yet clear which state organisation will exercise property rights over the Concern.

An outstanding issue is the ownership of the high voltage transmission system. Several options have been considered. A common element is that the dispatch centre will belong to the Concern and operational control of dispatch will be exercised by the Concern to ensure secure, economic operation. The Concern will buy from generators and sell to the distribution companies. It seems likely that the grid will belong to the Concern, though some believe that it should be a separate state owned company. In either case an internal price system that reflects economic costs and avoids cross-subsidy is needed to regulate financial flows among the companies, and a regulatory body should be established to oversee the operation of the industry.

Under the new internal pricing system, subsidiaries within MVMT are to be given financial and technical targets. They are allowed to retain the profits they make and amounts set aside for depreciation, and to reinvest these funds in their businesses. Cash management will be handled separately, with any surplus cash in affiliates being transferred to the Concern to fund any shortfalls in other subsidiaries. The distribution companies present particular problems. Because of the cross-subsidisation between industrial and household tariffs, the income of distribution companies depends crucially on their ratio of industrial to household customers. A compensation scheme is to be established to balance the financial performances of the distribution companies.

The government obligation on MVMT to purchase fixed quantities of coal from the domestic coal industry, amounting to 8 TWh in 1991, is costly for MVMT, since it is now cheaper to produce electricity from heavy fuel oil at the Dunamenti power station, where there is significant spare capacity. However, as noted in the conclusions to the section on coal, some government intervention to manage transition in the coal industry appears inevitable. One possibility would be to determine medium term contracts between MVMT and the coal industry, with contracted volumes declining until the coal industry reaches a viable size.

Work has started on the design and role of a regulatory institution. It is recognised that the regulator should supervise consumer prices and that if independent producers appear, price supervision must be extended to cover the prices paid to them. An Electricity Act, in preparation, will remove MVMT's monopoly right of generation and permit private generators to market electricity. The wider role of a regulator to encourage economic operation of the general system through appropriate price signals seems not to be fully appreciated.

Conclusions

The Hungarian power system is relatively small and exhibits several special characteristics — the rather depressed electricity price generally, major cross-subsidisation, the close relationship with a declining domestic coal industry, the very high dependence on generation from one site at Paks nuclear power station and the high dependence on imports from the former USSR. These aspects constrain the restructuring process but the solution proposed seems generally sound.

Government should work as rapidly as possible towards eliminating cross-subsidies in consumer prices. The internal price system to be established within the electricity supply industry should be based on principles of economic efficiency. Any plan to compensate disadvantaged distributors should operate outside the internal pricing schedule. Consideration should also be given to cost based differential pricing for the retail prices of distribution companies instead of a compensation scheme.

State ownership of the electricity supply industry, in whole or in part, should be separated from administrative control of the industry. An independent regulatory agency should be established to assess system costs and regulate consumer prices and tariff structures on sound economic principles. The IEA review team agrees with what appears to be the general view, that full privatisation is a secondary objective and can be delayed until restructuring is complete.

The need for a long term strategy for power system expansion is not seen as pressing. The team has not seen fully developed analyses of future options for long term expansion. Such studies should be pursued, or, if they are already available, presented for public debate and scrutiny. It may be desirable to oblige generators to periodically submit to government a medium and long term rolling investment plan demonstrating orderly investment in the medium term and options for long term development.

Nuclear Power

Technical and Organisational Structure

Most of the country's nuclear power facilities are concentrated at MVMT's nuclear power station at Paks, 115 km south of Budapest on the west bank of the Danube. The power station is composed of four units of water cooled, and water moderated, 440 MW reactors. These are the latest model of the Soviet designed VVER reactor, which incorporates a hermetic area (containment) and "bubbling towers". MVMT has made significant improvements to the original design and the control systems.

The lifetime load factors of the four units vary between 81.2% and 85.3%. The number of reactor trips average about 1 per year per unit. Table 35 shows the performance of all four units since construction — results comparable to some of the best in the OECD. To achieve this level of performance, maintenance has to be very reliable, and in fact the maintenance programme at Paks is extensive and very well planned. About 1 100 of the site's 3 800 employees are maintenance staff. Though this number seems high, the power station management found it necessary in order to develop an independent capability to replace unreliable components provided by external suppliers. MVMT-Paks is able to fabricate many spare parts and is largely self sufficient in technical and material needs. About 100 people are contracted from outside during plant outages, mostly for civil engineering work. Otherwise work is contracted out only when special expertise is required. An example is the development of computer software for a more sophisticated maintenance database. Such work is usually carried out by institutes or joint stock companies controlled by institutes with which Paks has had a long-standing relationship.

The safety of Paks was reviewed by an OSART team from the International Atomic Energy Agency (IAEA) in 1988, with a follow-up visit in

1991. The IAEA concluded that the Paks power station is operated safely and managed effectively. In addition, the Ministry of Environmental Protection and Regional Development confirmed MVMT's view that the environmental impact of the Paks power station is negligible during normal operation.

Various international bodies have observed a history of good quality control practice dating back to the construction of the plant in the late 1970s. The quality assurance department reports directly to the nuclear safety manager. The latter reports directly to the plant manager and interfaces with the staff of the National Atomic Energy Commission.

Training is excellent, with several simulators, including a full scope simulator, available on site. There are also other excellent facilities for training staff. The Technical University of Budapest can train 25 to 30 engineers a year in the nuclear field. This is in addition to the Energy Training Institute's secondary school for engineering and a high school for power engineering at Paks.

Since MVMT-Paks has taken a lead role in addressing safety issues it is important for care to be taken to ensure that any reorganisation or other changes in the industry do not diminish this emphasis on safety. MVMT-Paks relies on the resources of various institutes for improvements in its operations. Care should also be taken, in the reorganisation of public sector R&D, so that access to these institutes and the quality of their work are not adversely affected.

Hungarian energy policy in the nuclear sector rests on two main points: Present facilities should continue to be operated safely and efficiently, and an environment for expansion should be fostered if such is determined to be desirable. MVMT-Paks has proved competent in managing nuclear technology safely, and compares well with similar organisations in OECD Member countries. It is not clear, however, that provision has been made for the costs of eventual decommissioning. This is a major issue and requires resolution.

Potential Expansion of Nuclear Power Production

Proposals to expand nuclear power production in Hungary are being developed. The Paks site was designed for a potential capacity of 4 000 MW. Present fabrication and training facilities could support additional plants with few additions to staff and without impairing performance. The

Table 35
Performance Indicators for Paks Nuclear Power Plant

	1983	1984	1985	1986	1987	1988	1989	1990	Lifetime
Production (GWh)									
unit 1	2 473	2 784	3 193	3 324	3 078	3 299	3 408	3 442	25 001
unit 2		982	3 286	3 339	3 387	3 237	3 507	3 548	21 286
unit 3				762	3 412	3 513	3 340	3 486	14 513
unit 4					1 108	3 396	3 636	3 255	11 395
Load Factor (%)									
unit 1	65.6	72.0	82.8	86.2	79.9	85.4	88.4	89.3	81.2
unit 2		77.7	83.4	84.7	85.9	81.9	89.0	90.0	85.4
unit 3				76.0	88.5	87.6	82.9	86.5	85.7
unit 4					76.0	87.9	90.6	80.8	85.3
Duration of Refuelling Outage (Days)									
unit 1		73.5	45.8	46.0	68.7	33.1	35.9	32.7	-
unit 2			47.1	42.6	34.5	59.2	33.3	30.9	-
unit 3					35.0	34.8	53.7	42.7	-
unit 4						37.1	30.3	63.0	-
Collective Dose of Refuelling Works (mSv)									
unit 1		520	546	465	948	569	610	1139	-
unit 2			404	441	387	605	571	729	-
unit 3					58	111	152	247	-
unit 4						84	87	340	-
Number of Reactor Trips									
unit 1	5	2	4	2	1	1	4	1	20
unit 2		1	4	2	1	1	0	1	10
unit 3				0	2	2	2	0	6
unit 4					0	0	0	1	1

Source: MVMT.

overall performance level to date has resulted in a generally favourable public attitude towards the nuclear facility locally, and it appears that nuclear power production is not a major issue of contention so far in public opinion nationally. Nuclear power plants are one attractive option for baseload applications. Expansion at Paks would offer a measure of independence to the Hungarian electricity supply industry. There are many sources of reactor fuel, assuring security of supply. None of the proposals under consideration, all of which include substantial participation by foreign capital, would appear likely to cause undue burdens from a technical, infrastructural or financial point of view, assuming the issue of waste disposal is addressed. With regard to maintaining grid stability, small units would appear preferable to large units.

Fuel Cycle

Paks is supplied with fuel from the former USSR, processed from uranium mined in Hungary. The cost of uranium production from the mine, near Pécs, is higher than world prices. The mine may therefore be closed, though the consequences for local employment would be severe.

Spent fuel is returned to the former USSR, which so far has retained high level wastes after reprocessing. This situation is likely to change, as the former USSR now demands hard currency and a higher price if spent fuel or high level wastes are kept for permanent disposal. Governments of the republics and regional authorities in the former USSR may also attempt to curtail trade in wastes. Several other suppliers of fuel and reprocessing services are available in OECD countries, but it is expected that they would not accept high level wastes for disposal. Whether reprocessing remains the preferred option or a once through fuel cycle is adopted, a permanent spent fuel disposal site will be required. Additional interim storage will probably also be required until a permanent site is available. The spent fuel pool at Paks can only accommodate only 2.5 more years of fuel. Possible dry storage projects are being examined.

As in many countries, there is as yet no permanent solution to waste disposal. Low and medium level wastes are stored at Paks. A geological formation adjacent to the uranium mine has characteristics that could make it a good site for disposal of all radioactive wastes, and its potential is under investigation. Developing the site for waste disposal might provide some employment if mining ceases. The issue of spent fuel repositories should be examined as soon as possible to resolve technical, social and political concerns.

Regulatory Authorities

The Atomic Energy Commission was reorganised by the Government in 1990, when it became an independent regulatory body. Until then MOIT was responsible for safety in the nuclear industry. The Commission's responsibilities include:

- licensing of nuclear facilities;
- public information;
- policy making in regard to nuclear power;
- safety;
- R&D related to nuclear safety;
- exports related to nuclear power;
- accountancy for radioactive materials;
- nuclear liability;
- emergency assistance and notification;
- international relations with the IAEA and other international organisations together with bilateral and multilateral agreements.

There are twelve commissioners, nominated by the Commission head in consultation with MOIT and other ministries. The head of the Commission currently is also president of OMFB and a Minister without Portfolio, and as such is a member of the Government. The commissioners meet twice a year, and are supported by a staff of 65 called the "Office". They can also consult outside experts via a Scientific Technical Advisory Committee. About 15 commission staff members at Paks supervise operation of the plant. The Commission has a purely regulatory function and is responsible for all facilities where there is more than 1 kg of fissionable material. It is not responsible for controlling and monitoring ionising radiation. Its role is oriented towards nuclear safety and the control of fissionable materials.

The Commission has enough funds for its immediate needs but relies on OMFB for funds for long term R&D projects that support its work. The Government should ensure that the Commission will continue to have adequate access to funds for its R&D programme. The Commission should not have to compete with private industry for the required funds, as would be the case if OMFB controls the funds. The IEA review team would suggest that the Commission investigate arrangements for the financing of regulatory bodies in OECD Member countries.

The Commission's most important role, apart from the control of fissionable materials, is the licensing of new facilities. Licensing from a radiation protection point of view is undertaken by the Ministry of Welfare. Licences are issued by the Ministry of Environmental Protection and Regional Development in respect of environmental protection, by the Ministry of the Interior in respect of provisions against accidental damage or physical threat from external sources, and by the Ministry of Defense in respect of emergency preparedness. The Commission has to resolve disputes between licensing bodies and disparities between licences. It has no responsibility for low and medium level wastes, but does have responsibility for high level wastes, though not their transport. It would be preferable for the Commission to be responsible for all ionising radiation, which would mean adding radiation protection and the control of all radioactive wastes to the Commission's responsibilities.

The steps in licensing the construction, commissioning and operation of new plants have not yet been fully determined; nor have mechanisms for public involvement in hearings. Reactors licensed in other countries are not automatically licensed in Hungary. It must be proved that they satisfy the intent of Hungarian regulations, which are being updated. Licences are given for 30 years and are not usually withdrawn. In theory, the Commission could force changes at or shut down a plant. In practice, Paks's staff has taken the lead in safety issues and are ahead of the Commission in examining questions of safety.

Licensing procedures should be rationalised. The mandate of the National Atomic Energy Commission and the division of responsibility between the Commission and other licensing bodies should be reviewed. Possibilities for streamlining the licensing process for reactors licensed in other countries should be investigated. The structure, mandate and licensing procedures of regulatory bodies in OECD Member countries might usefully be examined (in particular the Nuclear Installations Inspectorate of the United Kingdom and the Atomic Energy Control Board of Canada). Even if no new reactors are built, improvements to the Commission are suggested in view of the possible changing role and structure of MVMT. Any new responsibilities assigned to the Commission should of course be met with adequate resources.

On questions of liability relating to the production of nuclear power, the Vienna convention on third party liability is followed. Under Hungarian law there is no limitation to liability, but means of obtaining nuclear liability insurance have not been established. The need for and access to such insurance should be investigated.

While the National Atomic Energy Commission is effective, the division of responsibility among the various government bodies does not permit optimal use of resources. Nuclear power is operated safely but the lead role is taken by the operator/owner due to a concentration of all facilities in one location and the dispersal of responsibility for control.

New and Renewable Energy Sources

Wood is estimated to have contributed 0.32 Mtoe to TPES in 1989, most of it consumed in the residential sector. Though precise data does not exist, other new and renewable energy sources are estimated to contribute 0.14 mtoe (6 PJ) per year to energy supply in Hungary, or less than 1% of TPES. Of this amount, 52% is low enthalpy geothermal heat, which meets 80 000 to 90 000 toe per year of fuel requirements in the residential sector; 47% is accounted for by biomass, including forestry wastes, straw and other agricultural wastes; and solar and wind power make up the remaining 1%.

The potential resource base of new and renewable energy sources has been estimated at 1.3 Mtoe (56 PJ) per year, though how much of this will prove economic has yet to be adequately assessed. Low enthalpy geothermal reservoirs account for 90% of renewable resources. Hungary has favourable geology, with water at 110-130°C at a depth of 2 000 metres in sandstone, clay and marl structures that cover much of the country. These resources are relatively well documented through the logging of wells drilled for the exploration and production of hydrocarbons. However, high back pressure, preventing water reinjection, has proved a major problem in pilot projects, making them uneconomic. Various forms of biomass account for almost all of the remaining 10% of the renewables resource base. Solar energy technology accounts for less than 1% of the resource base, with wind energy resources negligible.

ENERGY END-USE AND EFFICIENCY

End-Use Sectors

District Heating

In 1990 about 2 Mtoe of energy was required in the production of district heat. Total final consumption of heat was about 1.5 Mtoe, of which about half was used in the residential sector. District heating supplies a considerable share of residential space and water heating as well as process heat in industry. There are 59 district heating companies in 104 communities supplying 635 000 apartments out of a total of 3.9 million.

Before 1991 subsidies were paid to district heating companies amounting to Ft 8.2 billion for residential consumption in 1989, for instance. These subsidies have been drastically reduced and end-use prices for district heating substantially increased. Prices increased 242% over the year to 1 June 1991 to reach an average of Ft 104.4/m³/year. At this level prices still do not fully cover costs and in some cases district heating companies have significant debts because of unpaid bills and fuel price increases. In Budapest, for example, unpaid bills amount to Ft 300 million. District heating companies either purchase heat from MVMT's CHP plants or generate heat at their own heating plants.

Price control and responsibilities for district heating systems are to be turned over to the municipalities after the end of the 1991/92 heating season. Municipal authorities' funds are limited, as are the possibilities for raising funds, since central government collects most direct and indirect taxes. Hence local communities will probably seek to reduce operating costs for district heating systems. This approach should be supported through measures to improve efficiency where economically viable, particularly where equipment needs replacing.

The efficiency of district heating systems could be improved to some extent on the demand side by market mechanisms and by regulation. There is considerable scope for improvements in production and transmission. An assessment for industrial consumers found that network losses could range between 30% and 40%. Some district heating companies, such as the one in Budapest, are replacing the piping of the main distribution systems. Joint ventures have been set up to manufacture pre-insulated piping and it is expected that the new piping will substantially reduce losses. Recently, district heating plants and networks have been considerably under-used as industrial closures during the recession have reduced industrial heat demand. There is also scope for increased efficiency in heat production. Upgrading thermal plants and building CHP plants, including gas turbines in combined cycle, are being considered in some cases and could be considered in others. Such measures could also make a substantial contribution to increasing electric generation capacity.

MVMT has initiated work to upgrade several thermal power plants by installing gas turbine CHP units. This will noticeably increase heat output and in the medium term could provide additional electricity generating capacity of about 700 MW, as shown in Table 36. This initiative is welcome, and the Government may wish to consider measures to support it.

Major investments are necessary in district heating networks and heat plants but the companies do not have sufficient capital. The central Government has announced that financial support to will cease by April 1992 and residential consumers may not be able to afford further price

Table 36
Major Co-generation Opportunities in MVMT

	Capacity of Extension (MW)	Electricity Output (GWh/yr)
Dunamenti	150	1 200
Kelenföld	150	614
Ujpest	210	873
Debrecen	146	597
Kispest	56	229
Total	**712**	**3 513**

Source: MVMT.

increases. It is therefore doubtful whether district heating utilities can collect sufficient earnings even to remain solvent. The Government should work with utilities and municipalities on a plan to improve the efficiency of district heating systems. The tariff structure for district heating needs to be modified and prices related to actual consumption — energy consumption and capacity charges should replace flat charges. Appropriate prices are also urgently needed to improve the financial situation of district heating companies. Should the Government determine that, for certain district heating consumers, cost based prices need to be buffered, this should be done only through specific social programmes.

Residential and Commercial

Energy demand in the residential and commercial sectors in Hungary is significantly different from that of western industrialised countries. The sectors are characterised by a high share of coal and district heating, but the share of electricity is low compared to that typical in western Europe. Low ownership of residential appliances and the relatively small size of the electricity intensive commercial/public sector explain these differences. Figure 23 illustrates fuel shares in Hungary and in OECD Europe for the residential

Figure 23
Residentiel and Commercial Final Energy Consumption by Fuel, 1989

Hungary

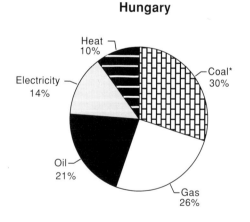

OECD Europe

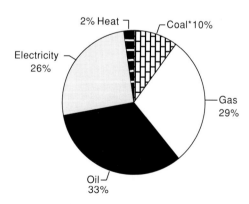

* Coal and other solid fuels. The category "other solid fuels" in the energy balances includes fuel wood, and consumption of wood is thought to be under-reported.

Sources: *Energy Balances of OECD Countries* 1980-1989, Paris: OECD, 1991; and AEEF.

sector and commercial/public service sector (together labelled "other sectors" in the energy balances, where the category includes agricultural use). In OECD Europe, the share of electricity is approximately 12 percentage points higher and coal consumption is about 20 percentage points lower than in Hungary.

Energy requirements for residential space and water heating are characterised by a relatively high share of solid fuels and district heating. Gas is also important in urban areas. For example, in Budapest the shares are about 50% for gas, 28% for district heating, 11% for oil and 10% for coal. There are about 5.1 million dwellings in Hungary, of which 3.6 million are first homes, and 2.9 million of these are in urban areas. About 60% of housing is privately owned single family houses, about 11% privately owned flats, and approximately 6% owned by co-operatives. The state owns about 22% of the housing stock. Some 635 000 multiple family dwellings are connected to district heating networks and 170 000 have central heating. For other multiple family dwellings in urban areas the overall fuel supply mix is shifting from solid fuels and oil to individual gas heating. The average size of flats in apartment buildings is 135 m^3 with a floor area of 53 m^2.

There is significant potential for improved efficiency, primarily in district heating and gas heating systems, through replacement of outdated equipment and distribution systems. Better insulation and behaviourial changes could also make a significant contribution. Current building codes should, in theory, limit energy demand for space heating to 20-25 W/m^3. However, actual demand in apartments is about 30-35 W/m^3. This inefficiency is also reflected in energy intensity figures, expressed in consumption per square meter. Table 37 shows energy and electricity intensity in Hungary and selected OECD countries. Potential for efficiency improvement also exists with regard to domestic electric appliances, as the specific energy consumption of appliances in use in Hungary is usually higher than that in western Europe. Replacing current stocks with modern equipment will gradually increase the efficiency of electricity use in the household sector. The Government should consider introducing energy efficiency labelling for residential appliances.

Apartments built between 1955 and 1985 cause the largest energy efficiency problems in the residential sector. About 1.2 million apartments were constructed in this period. Their central heating systems do not have thermal controls or individual metering. District heating is supplied in many cases by single pipe systems, where

Table 37
Energy Intensity Indicators for the Residential Sector, Hungary and Selected OECD Countries
(toe per thousand m^2)

	Final Energy Consumption	Electricity Consumption
Hungary	24.2	2.5
United States	18.7	5.8
Western Germany	22.9	4.0
Italy	17.9	2.4
Sweden	21.3	8.0
United Kingdom	21.9	4.4

Sources: *Energy Efficiency and the Environment,* Paris: OECD, 1991.

radiators have no bypass piping and can not be shut off without cutting the flow of hot water to all the radiators. These require substantial modification for installation of individual temperature regulation valves. Single pipe systems were chosen primarily because of material shortages at the time the buildings were constructed. The efficient use of energy was not then a matter of concern and district heating consumption was, as it still is, paid for through a flat rate charge that bears very little relation to actual energy use. Incentives to conserve energy are therefore limited. Improved apartment insulation, for example, would incur costs but not reduce energy bills. Even where the heat demand for a building is centrally metered and the costs are split among the tenants/owners, there is little incentive for individuals to reduce consumption. To achieve optimal resource allocation, flat owners and tenants would need both proper price signals and ways to make changes. Where there is no way to control heat demand, measures should be taken to increase efficiency in the long term.

Building codes comparable to European standards do exist but have not been enforced owing to a lack of capital and material shortages. Nor is individual metering required for heating in new or refurbished apartment blocks. Nevertheless, individual meters are usually installed for electricity in both types of dwellings and, except in some housing blocks, for gas consumption where gas is used for individual space and water heating.

Energy efficiency improvements can be expected in the medium and long term. Increased energy prices will make efficient heating systems and other measures to reduce energy expenditures attractive. In the short term there are limits to the extent to which consumers can tolerate increased energy expenditures, which were negligible under the previous social system. This may particularly be the case for consumers living in apartment blocks with central heating systems. Short term financial support for low income households may be necessary to cushion the severe social implications of energy price increases. Any such support should be made by direct income subsidy rather than price intervention.

In the long term, the thermal performance of new and existing building shells needs to be increased. Although energy prices at market levels will give the proper signals for investments in energy efficiency, government initiatives are necessary to overcome market barriers inherent in the residential sector. Building codes should mandate efficiency levels for new residential buildings and major reconstruction, be well designed, and take account of economic conditions. Effective monitoring and enforcement of the codes will also be required. For new multi-family houses, individual metering and billing are necessary to bring about economically rational behaviour. Before new building regulations are put into place, the effectiveness of various approaches, such as improved thermal insulation and individual metering and billing, could be analysed through pilot projects.

Transport

The level of car ownership in Hungary is about half the average in OECD Member countries, but higher than in other central and eastern European countries. Because the average distance travelled per car per year is lower than in most OECD countries, gasoline consumption is relatively low. Average specific consumption in the existing car fleet (calculated in litres per 100 km) is lower than in some OECD Member countries because of the predominance of vehicles with small engines. This efficiency indicator, however, does not take into account the relatively low service level (performance, safety, comfort, etc.) of many cars in use in Hungary. Comparable cars in western European countries would generally be much more efficient. Though the average efficiency of passenger cars in Hungary is nominally comparable to western European standards, as illustrated in Table 38, it should be noted that standards of maintenance are considerably lower, impairing the real efficiency of cars in operation. The Hungarian

Table 38
**Structural and Energy Indicators for the Private Transport Sector,
Hungary and Selected OECD Countries**

	Year	Ownership[1] Level (cars/1000 population)	Average Distance Travelled (km/car/year)	Gasoline Consumption (litres/car/year)	Average Fleet Efficiency (l/100 km)
Hungary	1989	177	9 000	943	8.5
United States	1988	573	15 900	3 031	10.8
Western Germany	1988	475	14 600	1 229	10.7
Italy	1988	409	11 700	729	7.6
Sweden	1988	413	14 000	1 654	10.3
Austria	1988	367	n.a.	1 246	n.a.

Notes: n.a. - not available;
[1] Total number of cars include light commercial vehicles and diesel-powered cars.

Source: AEEF; and *Fuel Efficiency of Passenger Cars,* Paris: OECD, 1991.

authorities assume that average car efficiency will increase about 20% over the next decade and that the average distance travelled will grow from 9 000 to 13 500 km per year. The gasoline price increases of 1989 and 1990 had an impact on transport fuel demand. Gasoline demand decreased 25% in twelve months.

If the economic transition is successful, income levels will rise and the expected consequent increase in mobility will have a significant impact on energy demand in the sector, especially for oil. Hungary's international trade is also likely to increase as a result of economic growth and the country's position for transit to southeastern Europe. Substantial investments in infrastructure, including motorways, railways and urban public transport, will become necessary. In *Development Trends of Transport in Hungary,* a policy paper of the Ministry of Transport, Telecommunications and Water Management, such improvements in infrastructure are emphasised. But policies should also include consideration of measures that enhance the existing public transport system. Further action will also be necessary to maintain the attractiveness of the railways for freight transport.

In the short term, the environmental impact of the transport sector appears to be more important than its impact on oil demand and energy security. Environmental problems are caused by the relatively high share of polluting two-stroke engines in private transport and by emissions from urban buses. There is scope for government action that would meet both environmental and energy policy objectives.

The Government needs to fully recognise the importance of a coherent, well funded and broadly accepted transport policy for the economic and environmental well-being of Hungary. The benefits of a relatively high proportion of urban public transport in increasing the efficient use of energy, limiting air pollution and reducing congestion should be fully taken into account in long term transport policies.

Industry

Figure 24 illustrates differences in the industrial fuel consumption pattern between Hungary and western European countries. The relatively high

Figure 24
Industrial Sector Final Energy Consumption by Fuel, 1989

Hungary

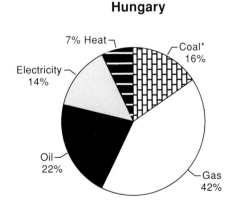

OECD Europe

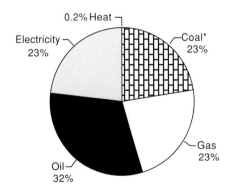

*   Coal and other solid fuels.

Sources: Energy Balances of OECD Countries, 1980-1989, Paris: OECD; and AEEF.

proportion of natural gas consumption in Hungarian industry reflects past policies to promote the use of gas and subsidisation of gas prices for some sectors of industry in the past, particularly for fertiliser production. An interesting feature is the relatively high share of heat supplied to industry from utilities in Hungary: 7% of industrial final consumption is heat from outside suppliers, whereas in OECD Europe this share is almost negligible. Another difference in the pattern of energy consumption is the use of electricity. Industrial electricity requirements in Hungary are about 9 percentage points lower than in OECD Europe, which can be explained by structural differences, as industry in Hungary generally uses less electricity intensive production technology.

The sector has a high share of energy intensive industries, and production systems are to some extent inefficient. Industrial restructuring began gradually in the early 1980s. The machinery, printing and electrical appliance manufacturing industries have grown substantially over the last ten years, whereas the fertiliser and transport equipment industries have declined. Total industrial production grew 1% in 1989 but declined by 8.5% in 1990. Heavy industry declined by 10.2% in 1990, with losses in mining (-11.8%), metallurgy (-19%) and the fertiliser industry (-20.6%). Pharmaceutical products showed the best performance with a 3.1% growth rate. Light industrial production declined by 10%, with losses in printing (-1.5%), textiles (-10.2%) and handicrafts (-25.9%), according to the *OECD Economic Survey of Hungary.*

As a result of subsidised energy prices, poor maintenance, lack of managerial incentives to use energy efficiently and unusually high shares of certain export oriented, energy intensive industries, overall industrial energy intensity is high. Economic reforms, including increased energy prices, will likely lead to substantial energy demand reductions in industry. AEEF expects two-thirds of these reductions to result from further structural change in industry and one-third from the introduction of energy efficient technology and improved management. The new priorities in industrial policy — privatisation and the creation of a market oriented business environment — as well as the price increases over the last two years and a new accounting system, are likely to help increase efficiency in industry. In early 1991, however, Hungarian industry was still almost entirely state and co-operatively owned. In the short term significant energy demand reductions will occur as a result of the recession. In 1990 industrial output was reduced 8.5% and for 1991 another 6% decline is foreseen. The

continuing decline in industrial output and the restructuring towards less energy intensive industries are likely to have a particularly important impact on electricity demand in both the medium and the long term. This impact needs to be carefully evaluated, especially in light of the decision to be made on construction of a new baseload power plant.

In the past there have been several national and international financial aid programmes designed to promote the efficient use of energy. In the absence of appropriate price signals and the presence of subsidised energy prices, these programmes generally did not achieve the results expected. Besides international loan programmes, there are currently no government initiatives for energy conservation in industry and an earlier requirement to designate energy managers in the larger industries no longer exists. Should new programmes of financial assistance for energy conservation be introduced, they should clearly not be targeted at industries that are in an essentially weak competitive position. The parliament, in any case, appears unlikely to approve any expenditure in this area in the near future. There is scope, however, for support in other areas, such as professional training and R&D projects. MVMT and regional electricity distribution companies have launched demand and load management measures, including remote load control systems.

Structural Aspects of Energy End-Use

Energy Intensity

Energy intensity is substantially higher in Hungary than in OECD countries because of inefficient production and use of energy, generally low added value in economic output and a high share of energy intensive industries. Calculating energy intensity by relating TPES to GDP poses problems because GDP data for Hungary in US dollars are still very preliminary and uncertain. Recently published data for Hungarian GDP gives $2 750 per capita in 1989 (*OECD Economic Survey of Hungary*). The average figure in OECD countries is $17 387. GDP per capita in Hungary is higher than in Turkey but below that of Portugal ($4 300). The energy intensity of Hungary as derived from these GDP assumptions is significantly higher than energy intensity in western European OECD countries, as is illustrated in Table 39. The table provides a second indicator of energy intensity, TPES per capita. On this basis, the Hungarian ratio is similar to the average in European OECD countries.

Table 39
Energy Intensity in Hungary and Selected OECD Countries, 1989
(relative to average for OECD Europe)

	TPES/Capita	TPES/GDP*
Hungary	0.86	3.91
OECD Europe	1.00	1.00
Western Germany	1.39	1.13
France	1.21	1.04
Italy	0.85	0.74
Austria	1.01	0.90
Portugal	0.49	0.86

*   Toe/thousand $, 1989 prices and purchasing power parities for OECD countries, commercial exchange rate for Hungary.

Sources: IEA Secretariat; and AEEF.

The long period of low energy prices in Hungary, together with the orientation of production towards energy intensive industries and equipment, has led to numerous investments that prejudice energy efficiency (e.g. district heating systems without radiator controls). It is possible to meter heat consumption and bill customers accordingly, but when equipment technically does not allow the consumer to save energy, efficiency improvements are limited. Increases in energy efficiency will therefore take time, and in some sectors short-term energy intensity decreases will be limited, even once energy prices rise to levels that reflect market value.

Over the next two decades the Hungarian Government expects substantial improvements in energy efficiency. According to its forecasts, energy intensity is expected to decline 1.2% per year between 1989 and 1995. From 1995 to 2010 it is assumed that energy intensity will decline 2.7% a year. It is the Government's view that strong economic growth will lead to industrial restructuring and substantial efficiency improvements. Indeed, much of the improvement cannot be accomplished without substantial economic expansion.

Institutional Structure and Policy Priorities

The main responsibility for energy conservation policy rests with MOIT. Energy efficiency is integrated into the work of the Ministry's Energy Policy Department, which develops and co-ordinates energy policy priorities. There is no separate unit or individual with explicit responsibility for energy efficiency. Other bodies exist, such as AEEF, its Energy Efficiency Office (EHI) and the Energy Management Institute (EGI). These offices were once entirely subordinate to the Ministry but are now independent bodies.

AEEF has undertaken industrial energy audits and information dissemination and has co-ordinated World Bank energy efficiency programmes, among other activities. In its new framework it is still partially funded by the Government but also carries out joint projects with energy industries. AEEF is working with MVMT on a project evaluating the impact of DSM on electricity demand. It has been found that load management and other demand side measures could reduce system peakload by 500-600 MW, primarily by load shifting via remote load control. Further studies analyse the scope for energy conservation in small and medium-sized industries and possibilities for third party financing. Third party financing is expected to replace the former financial support programmes, which were not successful in a planned economy. A comprehensive legal framework and better trained personnel are needed to assure the effectiveness of third party financing.

New tasks for AEEF and EHI include co-ordinating and managing bilateral and international projects with organisations such as the World Bank and the EC. Previously, AEEF also undertook R&D work, for example in the transport sector. These activities proved ineffective and so were suspended under the new institutional structure.

Municipalities now have a higher degree of independence from the central Government, under a new law, "Fundamental Acts on Local Self Government". Of the 3 000 or so communities, about ten are medium-sized towns. Municipalities usually exercise ownership rights over municipal utilities, such as district heating networks, though not over gas or electricity distribution companies except in Budapest, whose municipal government owns the gas distribution company and district heating systems and is responsible for public lighting. Municipalities can play an essential role in supporting energy efficiency, particularly in the housing sector but also in industry and transport. The previous institutional structure required communities to appoint managers responsible for energy, supervised by 19 regional energy management centres. These arrangements have been abolished and the influence of the regions on local communities drastically reduced. Some communities still have energy efficiency units, but their effectiveness is limited, and their activities are not co-ordinated by the central Government.

As far as initiatives by energy industries are concerned, some electric utilities have recently launched programmes to promote efficiency, though their scope so far is limited. MVMT has financed the retrofitting of public lighting, and a regional distribution company has initiated DSM programmes with emphasis on load shifting for industrial users (remote load control).

Low energy efficiency is characteristic of former command economies, and as a result the potential for energy efficiency improvements in Hungary promises to be high. The failure of prices to reflect market values, lack of private sector initiatives and managerial motivation, low maintenance levels and obsolete capital stock all resulted in substantial inefficiency. As the country embarks on transformation to a market oriented economy, efficiency improvements will be achieved in all sectors, but primarily in industry and the housing sector, which most clearly show the adverse effects of the former economic regime.

MOIT's document *Hungarian Energy Policy — June 1991* acknowledges the pivotal role that energy efficiency can play in achieving overall energy policy objectives. The document suggests economic and financial instruments to promote energy efficiency, such as tax credits for energy conservation projects, income tax credits for makers of energy efficient equipment and tax credits for residential consumers who buy such equipment. However, these proposed subsidies have not been approved by the Ministry of Finance. Taking account of the experience of OECD Member countries with such subsidies and tax deductions, as well as Hungarian conditions, there is some doubt whether such policies are an efficient way to accelerate achievements in energy efficiency. Several earlier programmes to increase efficiency, such as financial incentives for industry, have been suspended, partly because funds had been misused and partly because the programmes had not proved effective when

subsidised energy prices and lack of accountability and responsibility reduced incentives for managers to take energy use into account.

End-Use Prices

Price reform is the fundamental factor in improving energy efficiency and energy conservation in Hungary. The key principle is that where markets exist for energy carriers, prices should reflect the market price fully. In other cases, such as for district heating, electricity or gas, prices should reflect the marginal costs of supply, including environmental costs where possible. Such prices will allow energy suppliers to earn enough to renew their capital stock, providing opportunities for installing more efficient capital equipment, and will encourage consumers to invest rationally in efficient technology. The steps the Hungarian Government has taken in reforming prices for oil products and coal are encouraging. Subsidies still exist for district heating, however, and cross-subsidies were found in industry, for example for natural gas in the fertiliser industry. Further reforms are therefore necessary if the Government is to meet its target of eliminating all subsidies by the end of 1992. Appropriate prices are also urgently needed to improve the financial situation of district heating companies, among others.

End-use prices increased substantially in 1990 and 1991 in accordance with the Government's commitment to reduce and gradually eliminate price subsidies by April 1992 and establish market based pricing. For coal and oil products, end-use prices approach market levels. Gasoline prices, including duties, are approximately at the European average. For grid based energy carriers, particularly district heating and to a certain extent gas, there are still some subsidies and prices are probably below market clearing levels. Table 40 illustrates recent and current price levels for a selection of end-uses.

The Government intends to abolish price controls on energy carriers for which a market exists. For natural monopolies, such as gas, district heating and electricity transmission and distribution, price controls exercised by MOIT will remain (transferred to local municipalities in the case of district heating companies) but prices will be set to cover the economic costs of production and distribution together with provision for capital stock replacement. This principle requires an appropriate accounting framework. The necessary law has been enacted, requiring practises comparable to those in western Europe. A further concern is that inflation increased to 29% in 1990, and continuous updating of regulated prices will be required. There is no VAT on energy products.

For gas and electricity the current price structure is still not economically efficient, and cross-subsidies between certain consumer groups remain. Gas prices for residential consumers are lower than those for large industrial users (including district heating companies). End-use prices for gas are still below the full costs of supply for some consumer categories.

Residential consumers connected to district heating networks paid Ft 104/m³/year in July 1991. Prices were increased 242% in the year to June 1991. Further price increases can be expected. The structure of the district heating tariffs, which consist for residential customers of a flat charge with no direct relation to actual load or demand requirements, needs to be modified. The Government intends to turn over the regulation of prices to the municipalities during 1992. By the end of the 1991/92 heating season government subsidies are to be eliminated and it is expected that prices will rise to cover the cost of production. Costs vary but are around Ft 150/m³/year.

Conclusions

Market forces are likely to increase energy efficiency, particularly in the industrial sector. The economic restructuring and accelerated replacement of outdated production technologies that are required if companies want to compete successfully on world markets will contribute to a more efficient allocation of all production factors, including energy. Further achievements in industry are likely and could be encouraged through

Table 40
Selected Average End-Use Prices

	1987	1988	November 1990	November 1991
Households				
Natural Gas (Ft/m³)	2.9	3.2	5.1	7.8
Heating Oil (Ft/l)	8.0	8.0	11.0	21.5
Electricity-day (Ft/kWh)	1.27	1.60	2.45	3.70
Coal (Ft/t)	747	615	1 311	3 620
Coal briquettes (Ft/t)	1 137	1 089	2 004	6 460
Natural Gas (Ft/GJ)	*87*	*94*	*150*	*230*
Heating Oil (Ft/GJ)	*228*	*230*	*316*	*617*
Electricity-day (Ft/GJ)	*353*	*447*	*681*	*1 028*
Coal (Ft/GJ)	*47*	*38*	*82*	*226*
Coal briquettes (Ft/GJ)	*57*	*55*	*102*	*302*
Industry				
Gas (Ft/GJ)	144	148	359	281
Coal (Ft/t)	1 085	1 177	1 706	1 686
HFO (Ft/t)	4 340	4 280	8 950	7 606
Electricity (Ft/kWh)	2.47	2.82	3.80	5.06
Transport				
Gasoline* (Ft/l)	21.0	23.0	50.0	59.0
Diesel (Ft/l)	10.4	12.2	30.0	37.0

Notes: * 98 octane leaded gasoline.

Sources: National Bank of Hungary.

government measures that help increase industry competitiveness and can create employment. Currently, there are no such initiatives. Measures could include advisory services, professional training in business management and accounting and training of energy managers in industries. In the current transitional period, and even more so thereafter, the impact of market forces is less likely to restrain demand in the housing and transport sectors, given the expected increase in mobility. If the economic transition is successful, income levels will rise and consequently so will demand for energy, primarily oil.

In general, an improved and coherent strategy for energy conservation policy is needed on a central level, as is a better institutional structure with enhanced co-ordination among ministries and municipalities. An effective policy also requires co-operation between government and industries such as public utilities and manufacturers. In particular, it is necessary to strengthen co-ordination between the Government and municipalities to define priorities in energy efficiency policy and to identify a suitable policy mix, including appropriate regulations, economic instruments and information/training programmes. Organisations such as AEEF, which were responsible for energy efficiency under previous economic conditions, need guidelines and tasks. Again, professional training, advice to industries, consumer information, energy auditing and training of energy managers are examples.

The statistical basis for policy decisions also needs to be enhanced. An evaluation of the cost-effectiveness of technology and programmes, taking account of consumer behaviour and the impact of economic growth and increased disposable income, seems to be required. No such evaluation appears to be included in, for example, the financial incentive programmes suggested in *Hungarian Energy Policy — June 1991.* Changes in income levels can have a substantial impact on electricity use in the residential and commercial sectors and on gasoline demand for private transport. A more detailed analysis of industrial energy consumption would also provide a basis for understanding the ways in which energy demand in industry is likely to change with economic and industrial restructuring.

It is recommended that the Government specify the objectives of energy efficiency policy on a central level and set up an efficient structure of responsibilities for all parties involved, e.g. ministries and municipalities. In conjunction with this the Government will need to assess the cost-effectiveness of potential energy efficiency improvements at market price levels for energy, and use the assessment in implementing energy efficiency policies. Options for energy services, including demand as well as supply side measures (e.g. upgrading existing plants) should be evaluated systematically, particularly decisions to expand electricity generating capacity.

SUMMARY OF MAIN RECOMMENDATIONS

General Recommendations

The energy policies of the Hungarian Government are outlined in the Government's paper *Hungarian Energy Policy — June 1991,* reproduced as Annex I of this survey. The IEA team subscribes to the general thrust of the policies described in that paper, and believes that the main principles summed up in the introduction to the paper are indeed the key issues for current energy policy. These principles are:

- diversifying energy imports;

- improving energy efficiency;

- introducing market conditions in energy supply and consumption;

- improving economic efficiency in energy supply;

- improving environmental protection;

- enhancing public involvement and fostering consensus in decision making;

- addressing organisational matters (reforming regulations, restricting state intervention, curtailing monopoly powers).

To achieve these aims, the team believes that certain basic issues, outlined below, need to be addressed.

Above all else, there is an urgent need for a clear separation, within government, of the functions of ownership and administration. With restructuring of energy sector industries, management functions clearly should pass out of government hands and into the corporate sector. Ownership will rest initially with government in most of the restructured energy industries, though the rights and limitations attached to the new form of ownership have not been established. The Government must limit its interests to areas such

as setting targets for financial performance. Intervention in day to day management would be inappropriate and counterproductive to the aims of restructuring. This is particularly so with respect to pricing. The scope of the rights, privileges and duties established by the new forms of ownership must be made explicitly clear. The Government should further assess the frameworks necessary for separating ownership, regulatory and management functions, and more specifically how such frameworks will operate. The experience of OECD Member countries may prove instructive in this regard.

Where government retains an administrative role, as in the regulation of prices where the operation of the market is limited (for example in the transmission and distribution of gas, electricity and district heating), ownership and regulation should be kept separate and above all transparent. Independent regulatory authorities that can implement government legislation free from direct political control may in many cases be the most effective solution. Work on frameworks to achieve this separation has begun and its completion should be a matter of priority. In formulating frameworks for regulation appropriate for a market based economy, examination of the approaches of IEA Member countries might prove useful, though a successful framework will inevitably need to be designed to accommodate the unique features of the Hungarian economy.

Legislation is urgently required to clarify the issue of ownership of property and assets, and associated liabilities related to the implementation of restructuring policy and regulations. This is particularly so where local government is concerned. Progress has been made in defining the responsibilities of municipal and regional government authorities, but legislation to provide further clarification is required.

In keeping with the Government's goal of breaking up highly concentrated economic structures, plans exist for the restructuring of all the major energy enterprises. The key objectives of restructuring in the early stages must be to increase management effectiveness and improve accountability in terms of economic performance. Introducing competition into energy markets is an important but distinct objective of restructuring, and the priority that should be accorded it varies among the energy supply sectors. Restructuring and privatisation are two distinct processes, and the distinction should be clearly maintained if restructuring is to be fully effective and the success of privatisation maximised. For energy industries, clear statements of policy differentiating between the objectives of restructuring and those of privatisation may be required to make explicit the rationale for changes in the structure and operations of these industries.

Accounting practice is central to increasing the effectiveness and accountability of management in energy sector, and the Government's progress in reforming accounting procedures is welcome. A new accounting law modelled on practice in the EC is to be implemented on 1st January 1992. Its success should be kept under review, and further measures, such as provision for training, should be undertaken if necessary.

The process of decision making relating to restructuring energy sectors should be strengthened and clarified, not least in government itself. Co-ordination between central government and local authorities needs to be more effective. Close consultation between government and industry will also be essential. Ensuring that industry and consumer representatives work closer together in restructuring is important, as is providing the public with sufficient information to foster commitment to the necessary changes, painful as they may sometimes be.

Institutional Arrangements

Some rationalisation of government responsibilities for energy sector industries would appear desirable. In some cases, these responsibilities are the result of organisational relationships that are no longer relevant. Responsibilities in the field of energy efficiency need to be more clearly defined. The division of responsibilities for energy imports between MOIT and the Ministry of International Economic Relations may no longer be appropriate. Any such reorganisation should, however, be based on a statement of energy policy and be directed at ensuring its efficient implementation. Uncertainty over the role of municipal governments, particularly with regard to revenue raising and policy co-ordination, introduces additional uncertainty into the Government's restructuring and privatisation plans.

MOIT is understood to be reorganising arrangements for the formulation and implementation of energy policy. The reorganisation clearly should be directed at enhancing the implementation of policy set out in *Hungarian Energy Policy — June 1991* and the opportunity could be used to balance resources to reflect the requirements of market based systems. The Ministry's Energy Division has a total staff of 67, of whom 51 are professional staff; the ratio of support staff to professional staff appears too low to be efficient. A review of staffing in the Ministry would seem appropriate, to assess actual needs and examine ways in which efficiency could be improved, taking into account the development of any independent regulatory agencies. Finally, a review of the mechanisms for liaison within the Ministry and between it and other ministries is recommended. Responsibilities in this respect need clarification and mechanisms for co-ordination need strengthening, although full credit should be given for the establishment of the current procedures.

Research and Development

Priorities for the use of national funds for energy R&D must be established by the Government with reference to the priorities of national energy policy. Management of the funds should follow the customer contractor principle, with as direct a relationship as possible between the commissioning agency and the contractor. Nuclear safety research should be managed by the Atomic Energy Commission and research supporting energy policy decisions should be handled by MOIT.

The remaining funds can be disbursed by the National Committee for Technological Development (OMFB) in line with multi-year programmes defined by OMFB according to government priorities. The current competitive system might well be retained for this purpose. The present committee for scrutiny of all OMFB sponsored R&D should perhaps be replaced by advisory panels for each programme. The need to keep good scientists and effective research institutions in the country should be taken into account in OMFB's funding decisions.

Energy Forecasts

The energy forecasts provided to the IEA were prepared using a combination of two approaches. First, a top down approach produced estimates of total primary energy demand and electricity demand, based on economic growth projections and assumptions about the pace of industrial restructuring and energy conservation, using experience in western Europe as a guide. Second, a bottom up approach was used, under which detailed sectoral estimates were made for supply and demand based on discussions with energy producers and consumers.

This two-fold approach using western European experience as a guide is satisfactory. However, the following comments should be noted:

- If the assumptions for GDP growth are sound, energy demand could be higher than projected in the transport sector.

- Assuming that GDP grows an average of 4.3% per year between 2000 and 2010, the projected average growth rates of 1% per year in total energy demand and 1.8% per year in electricity demand over the same period may be too low.

- Given the uncertainties of forecasting energy demand during Hungary's economic transition, the range of parameters tested in the Government's energy demand scenarios is unduly small.

- Existing gas import contracts cover only part of the expected need for gas imports. It would therefore appear important for Hungary to negotiate additional firm contracts as soon as possible, to assure adequate supplies.

- Oil consumption may increase more than projected by the Government if Hungary has difficulties obtaining increased gas imports or if oil demand for transportation rises more quickly than forecast.

Energy and the Environment

The need to replace the existing system of air pollution control should be carefully assessed. The system would appear to have certain advantages in adapting regulations to local air quality requirements. Possibilities for improving rather than replacing the system might usefully be explored. It could be adapted for compatibility with EC emissions targets, which appears to be the implicit goal of environment policy. If the existing framework of regulation is retained, however, it would appear necessary to rationalise the system of monitoring local air quality. The role of local authorities in setting, monitoring and enforcing environmental standards needs clarification at the earliest opportunity. Rationalisation of responsibilities for monitoring, co-ordination of data collection and quality control in monitoring should be objectives of government environmental policy. It would also be useful to strengthen environmental monitoring and management systems in the Hungarian power sector and other energy intensive industries.

Proposals for change in many areas of the regulatory and institutional arrangements for environmental protection in Hungary are being developed. In addition to changes to air emissions regulations, an additional revenue raising tax on gasoline and perhaps other fuels has been considered on a number of occasions. If any revenue raising systems — such as environmental levies on gasoline prices or pollution charges — is established in addition to current non-compliance fines for air emission limits, clear responsibilities and targets for spending of this revenue will have to be defined. The system of non-compliance fines is ineffective and needs review in regard to enforcement and the level of fines. There appears to be no policy framework to direct and co-ordinate the development and operation of these various regulatory and economic instruments.

The Government lacks a coherent statement of environmental policy in the energy sector: Such a statement should be developed for agreement by the institutions concerned. It should address the development of a legislative framework for regulations and other instruments aimed at environmental protection. Provision for air quality management plans, to address the paramount problem of local air quality in industrialised areas, would be welcome, as would a review of the priorities for environmental protection in the energy sector and the ranking of any corresponding investment requirements.

Average concentrations of SO_2 in the air appear to be relatively low in Hungary. SO_2 emissions are of most concern in some localised industrial areas, particularly where concentrations of particulate matter are also high. The ranking of priorities for pollution control in the energy sector identified by the Ministry of Environmental Protection and Regional Development (that is, first to improve control of vehicle emissions, and second to reduce emissions of SO_2 and other pollutants so as to improve local air quality in highly industrialised areas) seems appropriate.

However, in regard to SO_2 emissions, current policy on the reform of air pollution regulations would appear to overemphasise transboundary pollution control to the potential detriment of local air pollution control.

The initiatives to reduce emissions from public buses in Budapest are commendable. Further measures to control emissions from diesel engines would be welcome. The system of enforcement of vehicle emissions control needs review. The IEA team supports plans to reduce the lead content in gasoline marketed in Hungary and to reduce the sulphur content of diesel and fuel oils. Investments at the DKV refinery in Százhalombatta to realise these plans should continue to be made as a matter of priority. In addition, investment to improve the environmental impact of the refining operation itself appears to be necessary, particularly for the treatment and processing of heavy vacuum residues.

Oil and Gas

Restructuring

The IEA review team supports the decision by the Hungarian Government to restructure the National Oil and Gas Trust (OKGT). Re-establishing the five regional natural gas distribution and supply affiliates as separate entities responsible for their own operations is most commendable. The decision to separate the non-core business service affiliates from the former OKGT organisation is also positive, assuming that they become competitive service companies in a revitalised oil and gas industry. OKGT's remaining nine core companies were legally established as a joint stock company on 1st October 1991 and renamed the Hungarian Oil and Gas Company (MOL).

The Hungarian Government should review its rationale for restructuring OKGT and determine if there is merit in some further restructuring. Such a review should clarify the objectives of restructuring and the priority accorded to each. It should also seek to balance the objective of positioning the oil and natural gas industry in Hungary as an efficient and viable competitor in the regional economic environment, as envisaged in the next five to ten years, against the interests of maximising economic efficiency.

While the Hungarian Government's initiatives with respect to privatisation are laudable, issues of competition, access and ensuring effective independent management are perhaps of greater importance to the public interest than the level of foreign ownership, particularly at this time. Issues of competition and access must be addressed as part of the restructuring process, which takes priority over privatisation. In the oil and gas industry, as elsewhere, the Hungarian Government should clearly separate the objectives and processes of restructuring and from those of privatisation. Furthermore the objectives should be clearly identified and explained to industry participants and the general public.

Oil Price Structure

Oil prices in both the producing and consuming sectors should fully reflect world oil market prices, taking into account quality differences, transportation differentials and regional supply and demand imbalances. The Government should refrain from intervening in pricing decisions by the restructured state enterprises and private companies in the oil and gas industry. It is vital to complete the separation of the functions of management, ownership and regulation. The Government should focus on enabling effective competition as the principal means of influencing prices.

Oil refining and retailing in Hungary is insulated to some degree from international market pressures by the high transportation cost component in imported oil product prices and by Hungarian import duties. These duties are high relative to the value added by refining and allow for an upwards bias to product prices, reducing incentives to improve the efficiency of the domestic refining industry as well as effective competition. It is therefore recommended that consideration be given to eliminating import duties on refined petroleum products. The Government is considering a proposal to introduce duty free quotas for specific oil products and assign the quotas to companies on a first come, first served basis. Such a system is not recommended, as it would impose an additional burden on administrative resources with no significant benefits, particularly with respect to improving competition and efficiency.

Enhanced Domestic Crude Oil Production

MOL's exploration and production arm should be enabled to make adequate investment in the search for and development of additional domestic reserves where economic. The Hungarian Government's decision to encourage foreign investment in the exploration for and development of domestic crude oil reserves is welcome. The Government may wish to adopt the procedures followed in some OECD countries for the collection and systematisation of hydrocarbon exploration and production information, such as seismic data, core samples, well logs and production history. Such information is generally available to any interested party after a period of confidentiality. In Hungary such a service would be of great assistance to both foreign and domestic companies in identifying the best oil and gas prospects. At the same time, the Government could be better assured that the resource base is optimally exploited. Such data services are generally administered by a government agency, which could also assume responsibility for the proposed oil and gas exploration licensing programme.

Oil Emergency Preparedness

Hungary is encouraged to increase oil stocks under government control from approximately 25 days to closer to 90 days of net imports, the requirement in most IEA Member countries. The review team suggests that Hungary investigate the stockpiling programmes of some IEA Member country governments to assist in determining a cost effective system appropriate for Hungary.

Competition and Access in the Oil Sector

The restructuring of OKGT should be accompanied by legislation clearly establishing the rules of participation and investment in the oil industry and ensuring competitive access for new participants to all aspects of the industry, including refining, transportation, storage and marketing. In addition the Government should seek to enable the development of competitive participation in the oil industry. To do this the Government, in consultation with MOL, will need to determine the best way for participants to gain access to oil processing facilities, crude and product pipelines and other facilities.

Natural Gas Pricing

The Hungarian Government's decision to implement a natural gas pricing policy ensuring that end-user prices reflect the full costs of gas supply merits full support. Such a policy should be fully implemented without delay.

Furthermore, sustainable natural gas pricing structures should be established, giving due consideration to:

- differentials between summer and winter prices;
- different prices for firm and interruptible supplies;
- responsibility for connection costs and related payment policies;
- actual distribution costs for the separate distribution companies.

In addition, cross-subsidisation should be eliminated without delay in all natural gas prices, both across the producing and consuming sectors and within the sectors themselves.

Any financial assistance judged necessary to buffer cost based prices for specific groups of consumers should be in the form of direct support, not through any kind of price management. Interference with the operation of proper pricing signals must be avoided in all aspects of the industry. This is also important to the success of energy conservation initiatives.

Gas Supply, Diversification and Pipelines

MOL's exploration affiliates should refocus on domestic resources, with a view towards making comprehensive geological and reservoir assessments, possibly in concert with foreign participants and investors. The objective should be to slow the decline in indigenous production of natural gas through development of economic projects.

The Government's policy of diversifying Hungary's sources of natural gas imports away from total dependence on the former USSR is sound. Long term supply contracts will need to be negotiated before resources are committed to major infrastructure projects. All of the potential new supply projects entail significantly greater costs than current Soviet supplies or their marginal expansion, and most entail greater costs than Soviet deliveries through new projects. When assessing the economics of potential new sources of gas supply, full account should also be taken of the effect of competition from other European importers. Opportunities for regional co-operation in diversifying sources of supply should be fully explored.

It is recommended that Hungary actively pursue all natural gas transit opportunities. In addition to enhancing its natural gas supply diversification strategy, this would position Hungary to exploit its technological expertise, both in Hungary and in neighbouring countries, in order to earn hard currency on a low risk general contracting basis.

Regulation of the Gas Industry

The Hungarian Government should establish an independent natural gas regulatory agency to safeguard the public interest where competition does not exist. Monopolies such as natural gas distribution, pipelines and storage would be subject to the agency's jurisdiction. This agency should be an independent body responsible for administering regulations enacted by the Government but not subject to political interference from the Government. Its responsibilities would include:

- supervising tariffs and rates of return in investments for natural gas monopolies such as distributors, pipelines and storage companies;

- supervising terms of gas supply and service levels for the various categories of natural gas consumers;

- ensuring that government safety and environmental standards are met;

- monitoring data on supply and demand and on prices in all segments of the industry.

Coal

Deep mining conditions in Hungary are difficult. All indigenous coal has low calorific value and high sulphur contents, damaging to the environment. Production is expensive and supply and quality are deteriorating. At the same time, coal is a significant national energy resource. The present financial condition of the industry, distorted by poor technical decisions and low fixed prices, is no guide to future decisions.

A substantial contraction of the industry is clearly inevitable. This contraction must be managed in an orderly, economically optimal fashion, preserving economic parts of the industry and taking into account the social costs. A comprehensive analysis of the industry's prospects should be made, based on a marginal cost analysis complemented by shadow pricing to account, among other things, for social costs. Some government intervention to manage the transition appears inevitable. One possibility would be to determine medium term contracts

between the electricity and coal industries, with contracted volumes declining until the coal industry reaches a viable size.

Resources should be concentrated into the most economic areas. The present organisational structure does not permit the best rationalisation and allocation of investment resources, management skills and labour. Reorganisation into three or four companies might be beneficial and should be examined in detail. The industry might be separated into companies producing 1) lignite, 2) brown coal in each of the Trans-Danubian and northern Hungarian basins and 3) low calorific value hard coal at Mecsek, if analysis shows this area to be viable. Investment in new production facilities for brown coal is economically marginal and could be undertaken only as part of a long term plan for the simultaneous development of new mines and new coal fired generating plants.

Decisions about the future of the industry should not be prejudiced by monopoly distortions. Coal companies are faced with a monopsonistic purchaser of power station coal and market forces will not lead to an optimal solution. The review team sees three possible solutions: a) the mines can be made part of the electricity supply industry, in which case decisions about them are theoretically optimal but in practice made by an industry with a primary focus elsewhere; b) the purchasing monopoly can be managed by price and quantity agreements; or c) control of coal fired power stations can be transferred to the regional coal mining companies so that competition can be exercised in the supply of electricity to the high voltage grid. The choice among these options is the responsibility of the Hungarian Government, but whatever institutional restructuring may be agreed upon, this problem should be explicitly addressed and its solution clearly specified.

Restructuring the industry and achieving a satisfactory financial position, by re-evaluating company assets and liabilities and writing them off where appropriate, is more urgent than changes of ownership. Restructuring can and should generally precede privatisation.

Electricity

The Hungarian power system is relatively small and exhibits several special characteristics — the rather depressed electricity price generally, major cross-subsidisation, the close relationship with a declining domestic coal industry, the very high dependence on generation from one site (Paks nuclear power station) and the high dependence on imports from the former USSR. These aspects constrain the restructuring process but the proposed solution seems generally sound.

All aspects of electricity supply and distribution come under the control of a trust, Magyar Villamos Múvek Tröszt (MVMT). From 1st January 1992 the industry will be reconstituted as an assembly of corporations owned by the state. A central "Concern" will be responsible for technical and economic management and co-ordination and will own part or all of the corporations on behalf of the state. The elements of natural monopoly in the structure are to be regulated by a new legal entity. The present generating companies will be grouped on a fuel or regional basis. (A suggestion for these companies to take over the related coal mines appears to be defunct, though there is still some possibility of such merging at Gagarin and at the hard coal mine near Pécs.) The power distribution companies will be reconstructed into corporations retaining present territorial boundaries.

An outstanding issue is the ownership of the high voltage transmission system. Several options have been considered. A common element is that the dispatch centre will belong to the Concern and that operational control of dispatch should be exercised by the Concern to ensure secure and economic operation. The Concern will buy from generators and sell to the distribution companies. It seems likely that the grid will belong to the Concern, though some believe it should be a separate state owned company. In either case an internal price system that reflects economic costs and avoids cross-subsidy is needed to regulate financial flows among the companies, and a regulatory body should be established to oversee the operation of the industry.

Under the new internal pricing system, subsidiaries within MVMT are to be given financial and technical targets. They are allowed to retain both their profits and amounts set aside for depreciation, and to reinvest these funds in their businesses. Cash management will be handled separately, with any surplus being transferred to the Concern to fund any shortfalls in other subsidiaries. The distribution companies present particular problems. Because of cross-subsidisation between industrial and household tariffs, the income of distribution companies depends crucially on their ratio of industrial to household customers. A compensation scheme is to be established to balance the financial performances of the distribution companies.

Government should work as rapidly as possible to eliminate cross-subsidies in consumer prices. The internal price system to be established within the electricity supply industry should be based on principles of economic efficiency. Any programme to compensate disadvantaged distributers should operate outside the internal pricing system. Consideration should also be given to cost based differential pricing between distribution companies instead of a compensation scheme.

State ownership of the electricity supply industry, in whole or in part, should be separated from administrative control. An independent regulatory agency should be established to assess system costs and regulate consumer prices and tariff structures on economic principles. The team agrees with what appears to be the general view, that privatisation is a secondary objective and can be delayed until restructuring is complete.

The intention to connect to the UCPTE system is a sound objective and the specific proposals are good. Interconnection to UCPTE should be pursued as a priority.

The need for a long term strategy for power system expansion is not seen as pressing. The review team did not see fully developed analyses of options for long term expansion. Such studies should be undertaken or, if they are already available, presented for public debate and scrutiny. It may be desirable to oblige generators periodically to submit to government a medium and long term rolling investment plan, demonstrating orderly investment in the medium term and options for long term development.

Nuclear Power

Since the management of MVMT's Paks nuclear power station has taken a lead role in addressing safety issues, it is important for care to be taken to ensure that any reorganisation or other changes in the industry do not reduce this emphasis on safety. MVMT-Paks relies on various institutes for improvements in its operations. In the reorganisation of public sector R&D, care should also be taken so that access to these institutes, and the quality of their work, are not adversely affected.

While the National Atomic Energy Commission is effective, the division of responsibility between the various government bodies does not permit an optimal use of resources. In sum, nuclear power is operated safely but the lead role is taken by the operator/owner because of the concentration of all facilities in one location and the dispersal of control among various bodies.

The Commission has enough funds for its immediate needs but relies on OMFB to fund long term R&D projects that support its work. The Government needs to ensure that the Commission continues to have adequate access to funds for its R&D programme. The Commission should not have to compete with private industry for funds, as could happen if OMFB controls the funds. Arrangements for the financing of regulatory bodies in OECD Member countries might be investigated by the Commission.

Licensing procedures should be rationalised. The mandate of the National Atomic Energy Commission and the division of responsibility between it and other licensing bodies should be reviewed. Possibilities for streamlining the licensing process for reactors licensed in other countries should be investigated. The structure, mandate and licensing procedures of regulatory bodies in OECD Member countries might usefully be examined (in particular the Nuclear Installations Inspectorate of the United Kingdom and the Atomic Energy Control Board of Canada). Even if no new reactors are built, improvements to the Commission are suggested in view of the possible changing role and structure of MVMT. Any new responsibilities assigned to the Commission should of course be met with adequate resources. By the same token, the need for and access to nuclear liability insurance should be investigated.

The issue of spent fuel repositories should be examined as soon as possible to resolve technical, social and political concerns. Whether reprocessing is retained as the preferred option or a once through fuel cycle is adopted, a permanent spent fuel disposal site will be required. Additional interim storage will probably also be required until such a site is available. The spent fuel pool at Paks can accommodate only 2.5 years of additional fuel.

Finally, it is not clear that provision has been made for the costs of eventual decommissioning — a major issue, which requires resolution.

Energy Efficiency and End-Use

In general, an improved, coherent strategy for energy efficiency and energy conservation policy is needed on a central level. The objectives of Government policy on energy efficiency need clarification. An improved institutional structure, with enhanced co-ordination among ministries and with municipalities, utilities and industry, also seems to be necessary. In particular there is a need to define priorities in energy efficiency policy and achieve a suitable mix of policy instruments, including appropriate regulations, economic instruments and information/training programmes. The Government should specify the objectives of energy efficiency policy and set up an efficient structure of responsibilities.

The statistical basis for policy decisions also needs to be enhanced. The cost-effectiveness of technologies and programmes should be evaluated in light of consumer behaviour and the impact of economic growth and increased disposable income. Changes in income levels can result in substantial increases in residential and commercial electricity use and in gasoline demand for private transport.

In conjunction with this evaluation the Government will need to assess the cost-effectiveness of potential energy efficiency investments (after the economy adjusts to market based pricing) as a basis for the design of energy efficiency policies. Various approaches to providing energy services, including demand as well as supply side measures, should be evaluated systematically, particularly with regard to decisions to expand electricity generating capacity.

Market forces are likely to lead to increased efficiency, particularly in the industrial sector. A more detailed analysis of industrial energy consumption would provide a basis for a better understanding of how energy demand in industry is likely to change with economic and industrial restructuring. Further efficiency achievements in industry could be encouraged by government measures. Currently, there are no such initiatives. Measures could include advisory services, professional training in business management and accounting and the training of energy managers. Third party financing is expected to replace the financial support programmes that were not successful in the planned economy. However, a comprehensive legal framework and better trained personnel will be required.

The Government needs to fully recognise the importance of a coherent, well funded, broadly accepted transport policy for the economic and environmental well-being of Hungary. The benefits of a relatively large amount of urban public transport in increasing energy efficiency, limiting air pollution and reducing congestion should be taken into account in long term transport policies.

Although energy prices at market levels will give the proper signals for investments in energy efficiency, government initiatives are necessary to overcome market barriers inherent in the residential sector, such as the frequent impossibility of controlling heat demand. Effective building codes, mandating efficiency levels for new residential buildings and major reconstruction, are needed. They should take account of economic conditions and require individual metering of heat as well as gas and electricity. Effective monitoring and enforcement of the codes will also be required. Before new building regulations are put into place, the effectiveness of measures such as improved insulation and individual metering and billing could be analysed through pilot projects. The Government should also consider energy efficiency labelling for residential appliances.

Major investments are necessary in district heating networks and heat plants owned by municipalities, but the companies do not have sufficient capital and the Government has announced that financial support will cease by the end of the 1991/92 heating season. Given this situation and the financial circumstances of the district heating consumers, who may not be able to afford further price increases, it is doubtful whether these utilities can even earn enough to remain solvent. The Government should work with utilities and municipalities towards improving the efficiency of district heating systems. The tariff structure for district heating should be modified and prices related to actual consumption — energy consumption and capacity charges should replace flat charges. Cost based prices are also urgently needed to improve the financial situation of district heating companies. Should the Government determine that these prices need to be buffered for certain district heating consumers, only specific social programmes should be used to accomplish this objective.

The steps that the Hungarian Government has taken in reforming prices are welcome. Subsidies still exist for district heating, however, and cross-subsidies were found in industry, particularly for electricity and for gas, where household consumption and the use of gas as a feedstock for fertiliser are favoured. Further reforms are necessary if the Government is to meet its goal of eliminating all subsidies.

Annex I

Hungarian Energy Policy — June 1991

**Reply of Hungarian Government
to IEA Questionnaire**

MINISTRY OF INDUSTRY AND TRADE

HUNGARY

PRESENTATION FOR THE GOVERNMENT

Re: Information for the Parliament on the Government's Energy Policy

Budapest, June 1991

CONTENTS

INTRODUCTION

Hungarian Energy Policy Following the Change of Political System

The new Hungarian energy policy under development is to provide for the implementation of the secure, rational and economic long term energy supply of the country. The social changes and new international relations, as well as the transformation of the economy, have called for a change of the principles and practice of previous energy policy, the essence of which had been state control through central subsidies and planning.

The major elements of the new Hungarian energy policy are:

- The elimination of one-sided energy import dependence — which results in economic dependence — and the realisation of import source diversification opportunities.

- The improvement of energy efficiency, partially through encouraging energy conservation, and partly through influencing the restructuring of production.

- The establishment of market conditions in energy supply, and the development of a liberalised pricing policy reflecting relative international values. (Which will not only assist economic clear-sightedness, but also serve as a basic factor in the motivation of rational energy conservation).

- Searching for low capital cost solutions and economic means of supply, and the creation of a flexible energy system, adaptable to demand, which promotes such solutions.

- The assertion of environmental protection priorities in the field of energy.

- Involving the public in decisions concerning the development of the system which have an impact on the whole society, and making all efforts to reach social consensus.

- Developing new organisational and control formulae corresponding to the market economy and hindering the workings of monopoly interests.

- Limiting State intervention to a justified and necessary level.

The availability of adequate supplies of energy sources for the operation of the society is the basis of economic development and improvement of living standards. However, energy supply is only a prerequisite of operation and development, and its ability to influence the economy is limited. That is why the objective of energy policy may not be more than an endeavour towards ensuring secure and economic energy supply. Economic development can be realised as a result of the energy-consuming manufacturing sectors operating efficiently, at international standards. The competence of the energy supply system in that area is only limited.

This material summarises the energy policy of the Government up to the turn of the millennium, but the principles and objectives presented here are the outcome of analyses and considerations relating to a much longer time span.

I. ECONOMIC POLICY, ENERGY POLICY AND THE ROLE OF THE GOVERNMENT IN THE ENERGY SYSTEM

In a market economy, comprehensive economic policy which defines the relationship between the state and the economy is indispensable. The energy policy is an essential part of the economic policy and both the economy and society depend on energy supplies, which are paramount from the points of view of production, living standard and social welfare. That is why energy policy should not place constraints on the operation of the economy or on the living conditions of people.

Energy policy forms the basis of a governmental level strategic programme ensuring the availability of energy indispensable to the undisturbed functioning of the society, and the economy. The most important elements of that energy policy bring to fruition the requirements of safety, environmental protection, reliability, and minimisation of costs. At the same time the possibility of social control is assured through public information, and the energy policy contains flexible solutions which enable the energy system to accept various changes and to adapt to different demand levels.

Energy policy on a regional basis must be compatible with the Government's regional policy. The development of the energy system, as a basic infrastructural system may not be independent of other regional development decisions.

Although energy policy on the basis of economic and legal norms fits into the general framework of economic policy, it needs a greater government role and greater state intervention compared to other spheres of the economy, the reason for which is that this sector has certain special elements, like natural monopolies, majority state ownership, etc. However, the regulatory measures used for central control should not limit the entrepreneurial decisions of the players in the market, but should only create a legal environment for those. Furthermore, the energy policy must guarantee the compliance with quality and environmental standards, represent the nation's interests and establish a pricing policy for transmitted energies which enables the suppliers to run a self-financing operation at a low cost.

II. THE ECONOMY AND ENERGY

Review of the Situation

After 1987 the tendency of increase in the country's energy consumption changed. The years between 1988 and 1990 can be characterised by the continuous and significant — on average 3% per annum — decrease in energy consumption. In 1990 the nation's energy consumption equalled 1235 PJ (equivalent to 29.4 M tonnes of oil). Such a low figure has not been recorded since 1977. Also the dynamic growth of electricity consumption had slowed by the end of the 80's, and in 1990 a fall (to 39.5 TWh) was observed. The slowing down, the stagnation and, in 1990, a significant decline in the development of the economy played an important role in the change in energy demand.

The absolute level of our total national energy demand is high compared to that of the Western countries. (In comparison based on purchasing parity we use twice as much energy to produce one unit of GDP as do the developed market economies.) Since 1973, the first oil-crisis, the rate of specific energy consumption (quantity of energy required to produce one unit of GDP) decrease has been rather slow (1% per year), much slower than in the developed countries (2-3% per year).

Also, the absolute level of our electricity intensity is very high, 1.5-2 times higher than that of the developed Western countries. In Hungary specific electricity demand increased at a rate of 1% per year, in the 80's even reaching 1.6% per annum. This is in accordance with international trends, as the modernisation of the developed market economies was achieved with an increase in their electricity consumption, while simultaneously decreasing their specific energy use. However, while this process was coupled with the rapid growth of the economy and improvement of living standards in those countries, in Hungary inefficient economic structures and wasteful energy use - with no positive effect on the quality of life - was preserved.

The low energy efficiency of the Hungarian economy is primarily the result of low profitability and the high material and energy-intensive, obsolete structure of production, oriented mainly toward the undemanding Soviet market and difficult to convert for other markets. The energy policy of the previous period also contributed to the economic problems. This policy - based on the belief that the Soviet Union's energy sources are inexhaustible - applied the strategy of resource development which meant the uncritical satisfaction of all demands. The bad pricing system, the government's subsidy policy, the elimination of the law of demand and supply, the monopolistic character of centralised power companies, and the partial central financing of investment, encouraged no-one to take advantage of energy conservation opportunities. Even the centrally initiated conservation programmes of the 80's could not significantly help this situation. That is how energy policy contributed to the establishment of an underdeveloped, energy and material intensive industry.

In summary, it may be stressed that beside an economy and energy policy ignoring ecology and resulting, in individual areas, in oversized energy supply systems, a society with barely any environmental and conservation awareness has also been formed. From the point of view of the future development of our energy system, it is extremely important that the citizens of our country recognise that energy conservation, and protection of our natural environment are national interests. Only such an approach can help to conserve enough energy to reduce or avoid capital-intensive developments and the need for additional environmental investments, and decrease our dependence on energy imports without risk. It must be realised that improvement of energy efficiency is mainly dependent on modernisation (partly through the renewal of production facilities using energy saving technologies, and alongside that the increase of profitability partly through supplying a satisfactory range of efficient energy consumption equipment, and finally changes in behaviour that require the introduction of a pricing system that encourages energy-saving).

Forecast for the Turn of the Millennium

It is not possible to prepare "accurate" national and regional energy demand forecasts — so characteristic of the planned economy — for long periods because demand is a function of the growth of the economy, of the changes in the requirements of society, of technical development, and also of the measures taken to improve the efficiency of energy consumption. We need to find a new path, the more so as there is no example in history for the transition of a country from a low efficiency planned economy to a market economy in which the law of the marketplace forces greater efficiency. It seems to be reasonable to split the period to the turn of the millennium into two parts. The first may be characterised by the transition, and the second by the gradual evolution of market conditions.

Taking the four year economic programme as a base, the continuation of the recession may be expected in 1991 — greatly dependent on the demand and solvency of the Soviet market. Following this nadir the economy may step on the path of growth and by 1993 GDP may reach the level of 1989. In line with that, we find it probable that electricity and total energy demand by 1993 will be somewhat lower than it was in 1990 (1200 PJ, and 38 TWh respectively). The new economic structure - the outcome of a three year process - may then serve as the basis of a progressive period in which the market forces may operate, and the positive effects of improving energy efficiency are realised.

The forecasts for the period between 1993 and the turn of the millennium may be expressed in a new flexible relationship "energy demand - energy consumption - GDP development". According to this the rate of growth of energy demand can be estimated as the sum of the specific energy demand rate and the rate of economic growth. When evaluating the potential scenarios of economic growth, it has to be mentioned in advance that the highly developed market economies reached their economic standards with dynamically increasing electricity consumption. While their specific total energy demand decreased rapidly, the total electricity intensity increased significantly. Our country may deviate from international trends only if we use all the opportunities of the transition to the market economy and restructure our economy so rapidly that the development of highly profitable but non energy-intensive fields (processing industries, services, tourism, etc.) will be possible.

It must be emphasised that in Hungary the highly energy intensive basic material industry (in contrast to the processing industry) generates only one sixth of GDP, while it uses almost 60% of the total industrial energy consumption. The specific energy consumption in the service sector is lower, only 30-50% of the consumption of the processing industries. Thus any positive change in the economic structure towards modernisation, or any efficient organisational change, will reduce specific energy consumption significantly. We based the following three scenarios on the assumption that higher economic growth makes possible a more rapid modernisation and a more significant decrease of energy intensity. Differences in energy demand growth between the alternatives are thus narrower than that for GDP.

"A" - optimistic scenario: an optimistic forecast best suited to the four year economic programme. The main characteristics of this scenario are rapid restructuring and dynamic economic growth. GDP increases at a rate of 6% per annum. Specific electricity demand increases then significantly decreases (-2.5% per annum). The decrease of total energy demand is even more significant (-3.5% per annum). Restructuring is assumed in the macro-sphere towards the tertiary sector, and in the industrial sector towards processing industries. Depending on the interdependence between economic growth and energy use, in the period 1993-2000 electricity demand may increase at a rate of 3.4% per annum, and total energy at a rate of 2.2% per annum (to reach 1400 PJ and 48 TWh in the year 2000, respectively). This scenario gives a chance for closing up the gap between Hungarian and Western levels in the long term.

"B" - moderately optimistic scenario: characterised by the elimination of obsolete production, and restructuring at a rate higher than previously but lower than that in scenario "A". GDP increases at a rate of 3% per annum. Total energy and electricity demand decreases at a more moderate rate (-2.5 and -1.0% per annum, respectively). This means that in the period between 1993 and the year 2000 total energy demand increases at an average rate of 0.5% per annum, and electricity demand increases at an average rate of 2.1% per annum (to reach 1250 PJ and 44 TWh in the year 2000, respectively). However, the implementation of this scenario would only prevent a further increase of the gap between our country and the developed nations.

"C" - pessimistic scenario: this scenario can be characterised by a relatively low, 1.5% per annum, growth of GDP. The slow elimination of obsolete production, and the protraction of the reorganisation of monopoly organisations would result in preserving the present rate of decrease in the total energy intensity and in an increase in electricity intensity (1% per annum). According to this scenario, total energy consumption would increase at an average rate of 0.5% per annum, and electricity consumption would increase at an average rate of 2.4% per annum (to reach 1250 PJ an 45 TWh in the year 2000, respectively). Hungary must avoid this pessimistic scenario. Table a. helps to review the scenarios.

In the aforementioned scenarios, the estimated total energy consumption in the year 2000 may move in a range between the 1990 level and 13% above that. Electricity consumption at the turn of the millennium may be 12-22% higher than in 1990. Based on these assumptions the probable value of total energy consumption in the year 2000 is in the range of 1250-1450 PJ (30-33 M tonnes oil equivalent), while electricity consumption may be projected at around 44-48 TWh. Several other alternatives of socio-economic development over and above the three scenarios mentioned and the effect of these upon energy consumption could be envisaged, however, it is most likely that - with regard to the transition in progress and to the main indicators of international trends - future energy needs will be within the aforementioned extreme values.

The following trends may be envisaged in the structure of energy consumption:

- the proportion of the residential-service sector increases (partly because of the rapid growth of small ventures);

- the proportion of energy sources transmitted by mains (gas and electricity) gradually expands;

- electricity - as a factor of modernisation - will play an outstanding role;

- development of mobility.

For the co-ordination of long-term energy policy matters, the Government has formed an Inter-ministerial Energy Strategy Committee

III. STRATEGIC ELEMENTS OF ENERGY POLICY

Diversification of Imports

At present 65% of our energy consumption is based on imports (10% of which is the nuclear fuel imported from the Soviet Union). The import dependence, which is the result of the moderate quantity and quality of our own domestic resources, developed historically one-sidedly towards the Soviet Union, and from the point of view of energy imports that dependence has been beneficial in the past. At the same time the undemanding Soviet market had an adverse impact on the Hungarian industry offsetting the benefits of a low energy bill by preserving the low level of development.

Because of its small volume, the decrease of coal imports from the Soviet Union does not cause supply difficulties, and it can be counterbalanced from local and other market sources. However, the problem is that the domestic combustion devices of both residential and industrial (power station) consumers, are designed for low quality coal and are not suitable for use with high quality imported coal, without its mixing with poor indigenous coals.

We are able to cover about a quarter of our 8.0 M tonnes of oil demand from domestic production, and in the previous years the balance was covered entirely from Soviet imports. However, in 1990 we were obliged to purchase about 1.5 M tonnes of oil from various sources through the "Adria" pipeline. The necessary oil supply can be provided from multiple sources if the "Adria" pipeline is better utilised and oil trade is liberalised. It is worth considering to join the oil product line connection between Schwechat in Austria and Bratislava in Czechoslovakia in order to create a regional product market as well as to implement real competition.

Nearly half of our 11 billion m^3 national natural gas demand is covered by domestic production while the balance is met by Soviet import, though domestic production is expected to show a slightly decreasing trend in the future. Import from the Soviet Union, up to a level of 5 billion m^3, is based on long term agreements but by the end of the decade the relevant contracts must be renewed. Because of the decrease in domestic production and increase in demand, as well as the need to improve the security of supply, it is a high priority task to establish the connection to the Western natural gas system. One of the short term implementation alternatives is to build a connection between Győr in Hungary and Baumgarten in Austria. Another alternative might be to reach the pipeline in Slovakia which connects the Soviet Union and Western Europe. Implementation of either alternatives would require about one year (after all the agreements have been concluded) and US $ 40 million. It is most probable that this source will be needed not later than 1994.

In the longer term — in the event of long term supply guarantees — the import of Algerian natural gas through Italy in a joint development can be envisaged, assuming that there is readiness for supply. The possibility of importing liquified Algerian gas is being studied with the neighbouring countries. Gas would be transported by sea to a Yugoslavian re-gasifying station from where the gas would be distributed by pipelines. (Of course supply guarantees would need to be assured by proper contracts.) It is also possible to import gas from the North Sea, primarily from Norway, if the necessary connection is constructed.

Our national dependence on electricity import is quite significant, too. The share of Soviet imports has exceeded 25% of domestic use in the past years and even today it is over 16%, which is high by international comparison. Such a high level of import is disadvantageous also from the point of view of reliability as sudden failure of the import may seriously disrupt our system. It is a task of strategic importance to improve the reliability of the system by diversifying the import sources and developing the generation capacities. Realistically, the primary aim of connecting our system to the Western one is not the regular import of electricity from the West in place of from the Soviet Union, but only the improvement of the reliability of our system.

Since the connection of the former COMECON system to the Western UCPTE system is only possible under certain technical conditions, at present the co-operation between the two systems is limited to island operation and to low capacities (400-500 MW). One of the conditions of connection is that the Hungarian electricity system's energy and capacity balance be stable in the longer term and another is that capacity and frequency control practices must be performed in accordance with UCPTE standards. Power transmission lines of adequate capacity have to be constructed and investment is needed on frequency-stabilisation. (Depending on the capacity required, the technical solution and the method of international co-operation, implementation time is around 3-6 years and the investment costs around US $ 300 million). There are actually several connection alternatives. Among others a unified all-European electrical trading system may be established in the longer term, in which Hungary, due to its central geographical position, could play a key role.

Short-term Energy Supply Strategy

Energy import opportunities for the forthcoming 2-3 years are determined by the present conditions. The quantity of energy offered for 1991 by the Soviet Union in foreign trade agreements with Hungary decreased compared to that of 1990, despite the fact that payment is now in dollars. The main elements of short term procurement strategy are the following:

- to explore market opportunities for multiple-source energy import,

- to prepare and initiate the technical opportunities for multiple-source procurement,

- to explore opportunities for long-term agreements.

In the course of widening the import-base, preference should be given to opportunities in which Hungarian products or services can be used as means of payment. In this way the convertible currency demand of energy imports can be directly balanced by production.

Opportunities for the regional expansion of energy imports vary greatly according to type:

a. The transportability of coal does not limit imports and efforts should be made to procure direct imports (without agents) from the former COMECON countries.

b. At present natural gas can be imported only from the Soviet Union. The conditions for covering expected short-term demand are relatively favourable (70% of our import demand is met by contracts resulting from the co-operation in Yamburg and Orenburg).

c. Potential for oil imports from the Soviet Union is low in comparison to past years, though the balance can be obtained through the "Adria" pipeline. It is reasonable though to exploit the benefits resulting from the existence of Soviet pipelines and cheap transportation, and efforts should be made to increase imports from the Soviet Union Besides the Soviet government, reasonable agreements should be reached with the individual republics, with preference given to long-term barter type agreements.

d. The volume of our electricity import is determined decisively by the readiness of the Soviet Union to supply electricity to us. Based on the indicative list, 6.2 TWh (1100 MW) is offered for 1991 and a similar volume is expected by the forthcoming 2-3 years. The import volume should be increased through barter agreements with the Soviet Union, and through utilising the opportunities of co-operation with the neighbouring countries.

Ensuring the country's energy supply requires a direct state role in energy supply, primarily in:

- negotiating and concluding bilateral and multilateral agreements,

- establishing the possibility of multiple-source energy imports through regional co-operation,

- as well as working out the conditions for accumulating the strategic energy reserves required for the operation of the economy.

The conditions and opportunities for foreign capital involvement in setting up a domestic base load power station must be explored with governmental assistance.

Energy Pricing System

The basic requirements for the modernisation of our energy pricing system are the following:

- producer and consumer prices should follow import prices at the frontier,
- they should reflect real value conditions,
- and they should ensure sector-neutrality, seasonality, and elimination of subsidies

(Major changes have occurred in this field during the past six months, and today most of our energy prices are at the world market level.) In transmitted energy (electricity, gas, heat) the state's control and regulatory power is apparent, and this is reflected in the prices.

Producers' Prices

Producer prices of energy can be classified into two categories. From 1st January 1991 the complete spectrum of crude oil and all refined oil products are in the liberalised (free) price category, with the exception of propane-butane gas which has a regulated price. In order to establish security of supply it was prescribed that a certain portion of imported crude oil and fuel should be stored in reserves. Liberalisation of coal and propane-butane gas prices is expected during 1991, so regulatory intervention affecting those products will be eliminated. That goes together with the liberalisation of the import of coal and propane-butane gas. Electricity, gas and heat (district heat) which due to their physical properties are distributed through fixed pipelines or power lines, are in the category of state cost and price control. Prices of these forms of energy must be determined in such a way to be as low as possible but cover the costs incurred by suppliers. (This means that the long-term price levels are directly set by the state, while the tariff system is worked out by the suppliers based on energy management and profitability considerations.)

Consumer Prices

Incorporating consumer prices of energy into the market economy requires a responsible approach from the Government. Under the obligations undertaken to the World Bank to eliminate consumer price subsidies by 1993 and to establish a true market-based pricing system as soon as possible, elimination of direct and indirect subsidies is required. This has already been done with oil products and the same is expected with coal in 1991. A step-by-step approach is being applied to transmitted energies (electricity, gas, heat), with attention paid to the tolerance levels of the public and the World Bank's specifications. On the basis of social considerations we support all efforts which help to balance partially or entirely the energy bills of the poorest sections of society. A coordinated effort of responsible governmental and local organisations is required to achieve this.

Conservation and Efficiency Improvement

Comprehensive domestic research and international comparison both show equally that future energy consumption and specific energy demand will be mainly determined by the change of the economic structure, by modernisation and the improvement of production efficiency and change of product structure. Thus, a production structure with a lower energy demand formed as a result of sound economic policy will result in lower energy consumption. Stagnation of consumption in the early years is expected to be followed by measured growth dependent on the dynamism of economic growth as a result of Government supported and promoted economic modernisation, energy demand reduction and new production cultures, coupled with an increase in residential energy demand.

The most important factor promoting conservation and improvement of efficiency is prices which reflect real values. In line with the practice of advanced market economies, other measures to promote efficiency of energy use are required. The reason for this is that certain benefits of energy conservation appear on a national economic level instead of a consumer level. Thus the pollution of the environment is reduced by energy conservation and certain additional investments can thus be avoided, and the nation's dependence on imports decreases. To promote energy conservation and improve energy efficiency measures in harmony with the market should be used. These are the following:

a. Tax allowances for developments resulting in energy conservation. The advantage of this is that the budget only gives up an income, or part of an income which would not in any case be generated without the existence of the tax allowance. Thus the tax allowance does not place an extra burden on the economy or on the budget. Another incentive may be a system of loans on favourable terms but because of the need for refinancing this means budget expenditure. (These two incentives should be offered to both suppliers and consumers.)

b. Giving corporate profit tax allowances for entrepreneurs who manufacture energy-efficient or renewable energy source utilising equipment or other such technologies. Of course, this means a decrease of tax income to the budget, but simultaneously the volume of imports decreases.

c. Reducing customs duty on energy efficient equipment and vehicle imports.

d. Providing VAT reductions for the residential sector when buying energy-efficient products. The same allowance should be given to cultural, educational, and health organisations too. In addition to that, renovations of existing buildings and efficient new constructions meeting the energy saving requirements should be promoted by financial incentives. Also the technical and financial facilities of metering at point of consumption must be established. Conservation in the residential sector should be encouraged not only by realistic prices, reflecting world market values, and tax allowances, but also by a conservation programme which offers technical assistance for conservation and represents the interests of both suppliers and consumers.

Environmental Protection

An organic part of Hungarian energy policy is the minimisation of environmental damage. Energy must be ensured for the operation of an up-to-date competitive economic structure, although it must be understood that each element of the energy chain pollutes the environment. This is why it is a task of key importance to create harmony in energy related development and environmental protection projects when the ecological balance is endangered and capital is scarce. Because of the "indirect" impact of energy use, energy conservation should be regarded as a basic requirement during the formation of the individual sectors' development strategies.

In the formation of decisions concerning energy the protection of the natural and constructed environment must be ensured an outstanding role. Costs related to environmental and nature protection, as well as changes to the built environment must be regarded as an organic part of the costs of development. The reimbursement of such costs must occur similarly to other investments, according to the rules of the market. Before we achieve entry to the Common Market the conditions for the application of Western European standards should be established.

When evaluating the economic efficiency, in the coal mining sector restructuring programme, increased emphasis should be laid on the protection of sub-surface waters, the establishment and maintenance of their equilibrium, as well as to the compatible landscape restoration of open cast mines. Further development, right through the whole cross section of oil refining is required to adapt to European standards in the field of motor and combustion-fuels. It should be emphasised that when the proportion of gas in the energy consumption increases there is a relative decrease of environmental pollution.

The environmental impact of power plant fly ash, slag and hazardous materials is significant and the costs related to their disposal increase continuously. The aim should be the ever greater recycling of these, with attention to their chemical and radiation properties. Pollution by solid particles (dust) has been reduced by efficient electro-precipitators as an organic part of the coal-fired power plant reconstruction programme. Partly as a result of this, power plant dust emissions have decreased to one third of the 1980 level. In heavily polluted regions, to meet environmental policy resolutions, it may become necessary to supply low-sulphur coal to consumers (first of all to residents) at a competitive price.

Nuclear power generation in normal operation is extremely environmentally friendly, though at the same time it could be a potentially hazardous technology. The probability of disrupted operation (malfunction or accident) is very low with up-to-date nuclear power stations and also the risk of that happening is lower than in other industrial activities. At the same time the storage of spent fuel elements and the storage and final disposal of low and medium level radioactive wastes is difficult. Related research activities should be accelerated. Renewable energies are characterised by environmentally friendly use. Increased exploitation of renewable energy sources is justifiable for environmental reasons, too.

We have international obligations to reduce emissions of SO_2 (Helsinki Agreement) and NO_X (Sofia Memorandum). The share of power plants in SO_2 emission sources is 40%. The production and service sector is responsible for a further 40%, while the residential sector has a share of 20%. SO_2 emission was reduced by 25% between the years 1980-1990 as a result of advantageous restructuring of energy use and power station fuel structure. Our efforts to limit SO_2 emission are focused on coal-fired power plants, with the wider use of fluid bed combustion technology, which can decrease NO_X as well as SO_2 emissions. In the 1990s flue gas desulphurisation must be implemented in some of the power stations which cause the most serious SO_2 pollution. We can fulfil the obligations of the Helsinki agreement, that is we can reduce the volume of our SO_2 emissions by 30% by the end of 1993.

In Hungary 50% of nitrogen-oxide emissions are caused by transportation, 20% by the power plants and 30% by other sources. The fulfilment of the obligations of the Sofia Memorandum (according to which by 1994 we must limit our NO_X emissions to the level of 1987) is decisively dependent on reduction of emissions in the transportation sector, though the importance of decreasing NO_X emissions in the hydrocarbon fired plants by the use of modern combustion techniques is significant. In transportation the use of unleaded petrol should be promoted as well as the use of catalytic converters which simultaneously reduce lead, sulphur and NO_X emissions.

Attention should be paid to the probable development of international regulation of CO_2 emissions accompanying the utilisation of fossil fuels, with respect to the long-term changes in the structure of energy sources. Ensuring, and the methods and means of promotion of, environmental protection in the energy system should be approached in a similar way to energy conservation. Successful, comprehensive energy and environmental policy in small countries like Hungary can only be pursued on the basis of regional co-operation. Thus it is important that the environmental aspects of our energy policy should validate international co-operation.

Capital Economy, Flexible Supply Systems and Foreign Capital Involvement

As a result of previous economic policy a considerable part of the scarce available funds was spent on energy related investments. (45% of all industrial investments at the end of the 1970s and 35% in 1990.) Developments, mainly in industry, to promote the production of energy-intensive products and the investments related to these developments deprived the efficient, value producing, non energy-intensive processing industries of capital. This was true also for the tertiary sector. In the future, this pattern of allocation cannot be maintained. With the implementation of an economically oriented energy strategy a smaller portion of domestic resources should be devoted to energy related developments and wherever it is possible foreign capital should be involved. For this purpose we will create an economic, organisational, and regulatory environment which makes the energy sector attractive to foreign capital. It must be emphasised that in the past many investment projects outside the energy system have been completed in the shadow of energy-related developments. This effect should be restrained in the future.

Besides the need to conserve capital, because of the uncertainty of demand (especially in the field of power plant development) developments must be implemented using system elements which can be flexibly adapted to demand and can be built quickly. Other conditions of meeting demand flexibly are the provision for serving seasonal fluctuations of consumption, the enlargement of the circle of alternative consumers and strategic considerations. At present we are in a position to store enough oil for 30 days, our gas storage capacity will reach 2.0 billion m^3 by 1992, and we have nuclear fuel for eighteen months. Our aim is to further develop our oil storage capacity and, according to financial opportunities, to raise the level of both fossil fuel and nuclear strategic reserves. If our country joins the EC in the second half of this decade then, as required by EC standards, we will have to increase our safety reserve from the present 5% to 25% (90 days). That would mean a single purchase of 1.4 M tonnes of oil and permanent storage. With regard to low storage costs, a 4 years' reserve is desirable for nuclear fuel.

Publicity and Public Information

Because of their effect on the environment, energy related developments can be carried out only if they are accepted by both professional and general public opinion. For this reason, in the course of decision-making on the building of new base load power stations, the Government will publish all the data and expert opinions, and energy-related decision making will occur within the framework of legislation to be made public. This is the only way we can avoid the repetition of the "Bôs-Nagymaros syndrome" — that cost the country US $ 1000 Million — in other areas of energy.

In the western democracies, the approval of large energy-related developments by the public is institutionalised. As that is not to be found here, our aim is to set up such institutions as soon as possible. Over and above that, it is necessary to perform environmental impact studies which ensure the representation of professional and public opinion too. The public is insufficiently informed on energy supply and the importance of energy conservation, which is why related information, training and education activities must be augmented.

IV. ENERGY SUPPLY AND DEVELOPMENT OF RESOURCES

Coal

In recent years the technical-economic conditions of Hungarian coal mining have continuously deteriorated. At the moment the debt of coal mining approximates to the value of its assets, losses represent about 10% of income and expired financial obligations exceed Ft 6500 million. Four coal companies (Nógrád, Dorog, Borsod and Mecsek) are undergoing liquidation (in June 1991) and if circumstances remain unchanged the same fate awaits the other companies as well. The low efficiency and poor management of the enterprises were the result of an economic policy motivating only minimum achievement, a pricing system for coal and briquettes that excluded the possibility of self-financing, subsequent financial interventions and subsidies.

The present critical condition of coal-mining points to human and employment problems beyond the energy effects of future developments. State intervention is unavoidable until, as a result of a restructuring programme pursued on the basis of Government resolution, an economical coal and coal-briquette production structure is established as part of a rational, profitable and environmentally friendly structure, together with a relevant control, organisational and ownership system. Appropriate conditions (through settlement of debts, the costs of winding up uneconomic production, etc.) must be established in the course of the restructuring programme.

In 1990 deep-mine coal production was 12.6 M tonnes and open-cast production of lignite was more than 5.0 M tonnes. Based on studies to date the restructuring programme will result in production as follows from the existing mines:

- the volume of self-financing production, at mine level, will be 7.5 M tonnes (3.0 M tonnes of which will be open-cast lignite) by the turn of the millennium;

- while at company level profitable production is likely to be 11 M tonnes (3.0 M tonnes open-cast lignite). The reason for the difference is that within one company the profit of a production unit may be regrouped to one of less favourable character if the loss is temporary and the closure of the unit would cause supply problems for a power station.

A solution to the problems of the mining sector should be sought on the basis of energy supply and human policy points of view, with respect to domestic and foreign market relations and providing conditions for long-term operation.

The Position of the Long-Term Development of Coal Mining:

- For the lifetime of the coal-fired power stations it is necessary to assure the minimum fuel requirement of the power station capacities (80-100 PJ i.e. 10-12 Mt) which is in itself more than the projected capacity of the existing mines.

- It is difficult to estimate the effect of coal and briquette prices and the elimination of subsidies on the market for domestic (household) coals. Based on the gradually decreasing trend of consumption we expect that the demand will decrease to 4 M tonnes by the turn of the millennium from the present 5 M tonnes. This demand which is at present difficult to forecast (regarding both quality and quantity) will need to be satisfied by imports and competitive domestic production.

To satisfy the demand for coal in the year 2000 (on the above basis 14-16 M tonnes), in addition to the mines which may be made self-financing at company level, the commissioning of new capacities and the expansion of import sources may become necessary. The 7 M tonne per year lignite demand of the Gagarin Power Station following its rehabilitation will be supplied from the enlarged Thorez open-cast mine (4 M tonnes per annum). Satisfaction of the 7-9 M tonnes per annum deep-mine coal demand may also require the opening of new capacities.

Preparatory to that a feasibility study for the Dubicsány mine will first be completed. With regard to the present position of the companies, it is most probable that the funds necessary to open new mines will not be generated within the sector. That is why, alongside import competition, the full-scale self-financing capability of economic coal supply (production and opening of new mines) should be established partially on the level of regional energy supply companies on one hand, and with the involvement of foreign capital on the other hand.

Hydrocarbons

Domestic hydrocarbon production peaked in 1985. Even taking into account the secondary and tertiary extraction methods with higher production rates and higher costs, a future decrease in production can be foreseen. Production of crude oil will decrease from the present 2.0 M tonnes per annum to 1.5 M tonnes annum by the year 2000, while natural gas production is expected to decrease from the current approximately 5000 m^3 annum to approximately 4000 m^3 per annum or even less, including the production of new expected gas fields.

The gap caused by the decrease in domestic production and increase in natural gas demand must be filled by extra imports. This requires, in addition to the liberalisation of oil trade introduced in the beginning of 1991, the implementation of the new comparative advantage based system in Soviet-Hungarian bilateral commercial relations, and import diversification which is the fundamental strategic element of our energy policy. We must emphasise that the uncertain Soviet imports with low guarantee value make the estimation of the structure of import sources impossible.

The major expected trends in the extent and structure of energy consumption — less capital intensive, flexible development of hydrocarbon based power stations, probably increasing mobility and the demand for improved environmental protection — require the restructuring of the oil and gas industry. Beside the primary crude oil processing requirements, developments satisfying quality requirements and increasing the depth of processing are needed. In 1990 beside the 7.8 M tonnes crude oil processed approximately 1.6 M tonnes of final products were imported. Taking into consideration the uncertainties in the future structure of crude oil and final product imports, the foreseen demand for final products of crude oil processing is estimated around 10-11 M tonnes by the turn of the millennium, while the demand for imported crude oil will be close to 10 M tonnes. The new requirements in the oil industry — diversification, product and quality improvement, unleaded petrol production — form a very wide-ranging programme which can only be implemented with the help of foreign capital and foreign ownership.

Depending on the changes in demand and possibilities of import from the USSR, an increasing percentage of Hungarian oil supply will come from other sources. By 2000 we must prepare to satisfying the bulk of oil requirements from free market purchases and through other advantageous agreements, on top of the decreasing domestic production and uncertain Soviet imports. The "Adria" pipeline provides the necessary technical facilities. However, prudence requires that possible future expansion of transport capacities should also be investigated in order to ensure the transit demand and supply security. Efforts must be made to utilise foreign concession opportunities, which could provide supplemental data sources in exchange of research and production activities.

Natural gas consumption was approximately 11 billion m^3 year in 1990 and is expected to be around 12.5-14 billion m^3 per year by the year 2000. The expected decrease in domestic natural gas production and increase of power station demand requires a considerable increase in imports. The quantity of imported natural gas was 6.2 billion m^3 in 1990, while the contracted quantity for 1991 is 5.2 billion m^3. Of the approximately 8.5-10.0 billion m^3 demand in year 2000, 4.8 billion m^3 is ensured under long-term contracts with the Soviet Union, therefore if the contracts for the late 1990s are extended, some 3.5-5 billion m3 extra natural gas import will be necessary by the turn of the millennium. This may partly come from further Soviet deliveries, partly from some other procurements, such as from some Western European or North African countries (or probably Iran) provided that proper transportation lines are built. The ratio between imported crude oil and natural gas can flexibly vary within certain limits, substituting each other as necessary, depending on the procurement opportunities and the economy.

Beside the development of the national natural gas system, the opportunity of exploiting small isolated gas lenses must be taken up in future. This task may be solved by using closed or open cycle gas turbines for electricity generation. The generated electricity can satisfy local demand, or be fed into the national grid.

Electricity

Based on per capita consumption data, Hungary's domestic electricity consumption is relatively low. However, in terms of electricity intensity per unit of production, it is too high. This contradiction may be explained partly by the bad economic structure focused on the undemanding Soviet market, and partly by the low profitability of production, the wasteful attitude of Hungarian society and finally, by the low level and backwardness of services. It is basically determined that if the aim of the Hungarian economy is to catch up with the developed world, then two major tasks must be solved in the field of electricity consumption:

a. Electricity required for efficient and profitable production, for household modernisation and for a standard of service which is acceptable by foreign capital, must be supplied. The low level of electrification of our economy (low per capita consumption), and higher requirements triggered by modernisation will contribute to the increase of electricity consumption.

b. Electricity intensity is high, so its gradual reduction is a key condition for our competitiveness. In principle, decreasing specific electricity demand (not total electricity demand) provides an opportunity to achieve significant economic growth while electricity consumption decreases, stagnates or only slightly increases. To date, this potential has not been or has hardly been utilised. In addition to savings in consumption it is very important to use market means to influence consumers' peak demand, which is a vital factor in increasing power stations capacities.

There are many means to decrease consumers' demands in terms of both quantity and capacity, and by the partial or full implementation of these means and by establishing an economic environment promoting consumer and service interests, the potential electricity savings may be realised.

There are productive capacities in industry, both in power generation and transmission, which at present do not co-operate with the grid but operate at lower cost. Through their exploitation the development of the capacity of the present system may be put off for a while. High auto-consumption compared to internationally accepted levels, as well as distribution losses must also be considered as possible sources for electricity savings. The improvement of the grid, modernisation of transformers, more efficient operation of power plants (obviously reducing costs) are all further sources for energy saving. Also electricity distribution companies must take part in micro programmes aimed at decreasing public consumption.

Until the end of 1990 the capacity of Soviet electricity import was 1850 MW, its quantity was 10.5 TWh while in 1991 the contracted capacity was only 1100 MW and the contracted quantity was 6.2 TWh. Taking into account the decreased capacity of Soviet imports and current peak demands, the Hungarian power system has only 15% capacity reserves. This value represents the lowest limit of the necessary reserves under internationally accepted standards. The technical conditions of Soviet power plants question even the maintaining of the current contracted power quantity. Considering the age and technical conditions of Hungarian conventional power stations, domestic capacity cannot cover the peak demands should Soviet imports fail. This is why Soviet imports represent the highest risk in electrical power supply. This risk can hardly be reduced by long-term and large western imports, that is why sensible development of the Hungarian power plants becomes so important.

Due to the uncertainty in long-term forecasts of demand and in order to reduce risk during the next 6-8 years a power station development programme must be implemented which satisfies only the foreseeable short-term demands and must produce enough reserves to cover possible failures. At present 2-3 year plans seem adequate as we have technical solutions that may be implemented within such a time and the required electricity production capacity may be completed by them simultaneously with the development of the economy. During this period simple cycle or combined cycle natural gas fired power stations can be built. These are suitable for peak-load operation and specific investment costs are much less than those of nuclear and coal fired power stations. Their efficiency is outstandingly high and their impact on the environment is small. However, they increase the dependence on hydrocarbon imports, and their world market (oil) price risk is also significant.

Considering that the time required for construction of a power station is 6-8 years, preparation to build a base-load power plant must be made in parallel with utilising the possibilities offered by gas turbine based power stations, so that it could be commissioned following the utilisation of the most efficient elements of the gas turbine programme and the necessary closure of old power stations. Both the construction cost and the environmental impact of a base-load power station are higher than those of a gas turbine plant. (The per unit investment cost of a gas turbine is approximately 25-45 thousand Forint per kilowatt - depending on type, while that of a coal fired power plant is 74-80 thousand Forint per kilowatt, of a nuclear power plant is 120-150 Forint per kilowatt.) Yet its fuel cost is lower, so the costs of electrical power production are more balanced and besides, it causes relatively lower import dependence, so in summary it is more advantageous for higher power production and for supply security.

It is clear from the aforementioned facts that the right approach of the power plant development programme is the subsequent application of these two solutions.

District Heating

The quantity of primary energy sources used for heat supply is 112 PJ per year which is almost 10% of the total energy consumption of the country. Most of the heat — almost equally shared between residential/communal and industrial consumers — is produced in hot water boilers, in a very inefficient way without co-generation. As the heat supply systems can form the basis for the implementation of the gas turbine programme, the energy efficiency of district heating could be improved considerably.

One objectives of our energy policy is to increase co-generation in district heating by identifying opportunities, establishing motivation and ownership systems which help implementation, and involving foreign capital. Billing based on metered heat consumption in residential-communal heat supply must be made widely used. This requires, in addition to the technical facilities, the development of legal and technical framework.

Renewable Energy Sources

The role of renewable energy sources in the domestic energy supply (biomass, geothermal energy, solar energy, etc.) is currently insignificant approximately 1-2%. These sources of energy are environmentally friendly, their utilisation reduces our import dependence and to some extent eases the load of the national energy systems. Furthermore, they improve the security of energy supply, and reduce the dependence on national supply systems in their region. That is why all local initiatives aimed at the exploitation of renewable energy sources must be given all assistance. Local authorities can have an important role in this. Even marketability of renewable energy sources may be improved with proper economic environment and business policy, and the share of these sources could reach 5% by 2000. However, the public must be warned not to overestimate the quantitative opportunities of availability and efficiency of these attractive types of energy, at least on a short or medium term basis.

Elements of Risk in Energy Supply and Areas of Uncertainty in Resource Development

In addition to uncertain economic development and restructuring, and the difficulties in forecasting energy demand, several further risks lay a burden on energy supply. The most important of these are the following:

- the uncertainties of long-term domestic coal demand and the critical situation of coal mining;

- single source, single pipeline natural gas imports from the USSR;

- the type, unit size and the time of commissioning of the new base-load power plant (nuclear, lignite or imported coal based power plant), and the risk caused by the uncertainty of the electrical power imports from the Soviet Union.

Even specialists disagree over these three issues. A consensus of expert opinions (in the case of the base-load power plant a consensus of public opinion) may be assisted by the standpoint of the Government that supports:

- the regional fusion of power plants and mining companies into corporations;

- the establishment of conditions for multiple-source natural gas imports;

- immediate decisions following the identification of the opportunities and fast implementation — especially the establishment of a power transmission line interconnection or for connection with the Czech and Slovak Federal Republic, which will start operation in 1994, requires a fast decision;

- the implementation of the new base-load power plant, financed to a large extent by western capital and built on western technology. The issues of the base load-power station must be decided by the end of 1992 the latest, following a public acceptance. This is why connection with the western electricity system must be established as soon as possible.

V. OWNERSHIP AND ORGANISATIONAL STRUCTURE

The gross value of fixed assets of the energy sector is almost 450 billion Forints. More than 130 000 people are employed in this area. These data indicate that security of energy supply is not only a strategic issue, but energy policy decisions have a serious impact on high value fixed assets and thousands of jobs. Labour efficiency is about half or one-third of what we find in developed market economies. However, the number of employees in the energy sector has a declining tendency in Hungary too. This tendency is expected to be stronger in future. Especially in coal mining, further regional tension may be caused by the effect of structural and organisational changes on staff numbers. A significant task of employment policy is to ease the problems in these areas, by re-training, further training and creation of new jobs.

There are areas in the energy sector where market conditions can only be effective to a limited extent. They are the so called "natural monopolies", the utilities which supply non-storable energies. These companies (which at present are owned by the state) own the technical facilities required for energy supply and customers have no choice as there is no alternative supply. To prevent these monopolies from abuse, it is necessary that the activities of production and distribution companies should be open and controllable for the public and its representatives. Executive power is the competence of the Government and an institutional background must be established. It is also the Government's responsibility to ensure that the self-financing activity of companies with natural monopolies serve national interests and not extra profit generation for the company. Supervisory and ownership interests are contradictory, therefore they must be separated at governmental level, as required by the interest of the nation.

A basic requirement of the electricity system development and of the coal mining restructuring programme is that the minimum quantity of domestic solid fuels needed to operate the coal fired power stations should be ensured (to avoid the construction of new power plants with high investment cost). During the transformation of the organisation and control systems of coal mining and power generation, we propose organisational, financial and financing integration. Our standpoints concerning the integration are as follows:

- the relation between the power plant and the mine must be based on the mine producing coal exclusively for the power plant (power plant related mines),

- during the course of structural changes in coal mining, all other activities, not directly connected with coal production, must stop in these power plant related mines,

- the costs of pure-profile coal mining must be included in the price of electricity, within the limits of world market prices.

The hydrocarbon industry is at present supervised by the Hungarian Oil and Gas Trust (OKGT). Considering the strategic importance of this industrial sector (harnessing the national mineral resources), the successor institution of OKGT must be transformed into a joint stock company under the Governmental decision No.: 3149/1991. Initially 100% of the shares will be owned by the state. Later, as a result of involving foreign partners and/or issuing shares, a real joint stock company will be created. This will ensure its competitiveness with international oil and gas industry. The privatisation process requires the transformation of the present organisation, separation of public supply (public gas supply) activities and the background industry, as well as preserving the original profile and basic activities, adjusting them to meet market demands. Regulations should be developed to ensure that the capacity of oil, gas and other pipelines, and storage facilities are available at market prices and with a proper tariff system for all those companies which are involved in the production and trade of oil, gas and their products.

At present the electricity industry is organised as the Hungarian Electricity Trust (MVMT). The ownership, operational, control and supervisory functions in the operation and organisation of the Trust are integrated, yet the monopoly and the lack of clear interests hold back effective development. That is why it is necessary to transform the organisation, ownership, and system of operation of production, transmission and distribution companies and to dissolve the present monopoly. Within this framework a transformation must be performed as a result of which the state keeps its majority in the basic areas of strategic importance. This will ensure the implementation of state energy policy and allow domestic and foreign private capital and local authority financial resources to be provided over a wide range, even at power plant level and especially in the field of services.

The most effective way of modernisation is regional integration of generation and fuel production. Within this framework the regional fusion of coal mines, which will be transformed into corporations and restructured through liquidation, and power plants as their consumers may be established. In addition to the general advantages the aim of transforming MVMT into a corporation (concern), and its partial privatisation is to improve market competition, to involve foreign capital and to dissolve the present monopoly. In accordance with legislation and government decisions in force, the transformation of organisations in the energy sector, which has been started, must be completed by the end of 1991.

VI. REGULATION AND ENERGY RELATED LEGISLATION

Although energy policy fits into the framework of economic policy on the basis of economic and legal normative principles, some special elements originating in the special features of this industry remain in regulations. For example the controlling role of the state which is a necessary result of the monopolistic character of energy companies. (This must ensure that no misuse of monopoly can occur, neither in supply nor in pricing.)

In certain areas of the energy sector the budget still levies some special individual income taxes, which are different from the general practice of corporate taxation. These partly arise from the fact that mineral resources are state-owned property (revenues from rents, mine commissions, etc.) and partly come from the state's role in constraining market conditions. The former ones will be introduced or be maintained while latter ones should be gradually eliminated by restricting the influence of the state except through consumer taxes.

In the framework of deregulation the obsolete energy related legislation was already revised last year (regulation concerning energy penalty, temperature norms, etc.). Regulations concerning the organisational and control system of energy organisations was reviewed and modernised this year, when the authoritative character of central control was eliminated in the energy sector.

In addition to the outdated regulations, some Acts were reviewed of which the modification had been prepared through proposals for the Parliament. Thus we propose the modification of the Electrical Power Act, the Gas Energy Act and the Mine Act. It is typical of the proposed modifications that they eliminate the monopolies under the sign of heading for a market economy. The planned liberalisation of coal prices requires the modification of the price regulations too. Parliament has approved the general Concession Law and the proposals for the related sectoral mining concession laws will be proposed soon. These latter ones are related to exploration and production of solid and liquid mineral raw materials and energy sources (including geothermal energy) and will replace the Law No. III/1960 on Mining.

Investigations concerning the modernisation of the organisation of the electricity industry, oil and gas industry and coal mining have begun. The first version of the organisational development concept have already been discussed and the rate of progress ensures that by the end of 1991 the new organisational structure complying with the requirements of a market economy will be established.

Table a
Key Energy and Economic Parameters, 1993-2000

Scenario	GDP increment	Change in energy intensity		Consumption in 2000		Pace of increase of consumption		Increase of consumption from 1990 to 2000	
		Total energy	Electricity	Total energy	Electricity	Total energy	Electricity	Total energy	Electricity
	%/year	%/year	%/year	PJ	TWh	%/year	%/year	%	%
"A"	6.0	-3.5	-2.5	1400	48.0	2.2	3.4	13.0	22.0
"B"	3.0	-2.5	-1.0	1250	44.0	0.5	2.1	0.0	14.0
"C"	1.5	-1.0	+1.0	1250	45.0	0.5	2.4	0.0	12.0

Figure a
PRIMARY ENERGY DEMAND

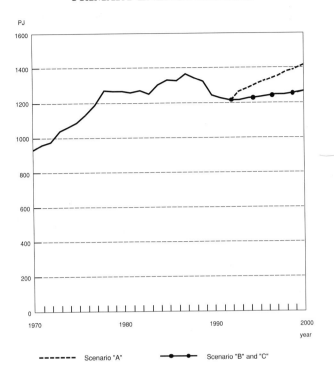

------- Scenario "A" ———•——— Scenario "B" and "C"

Figure b
ELECTRIC ENERGY DEMAND

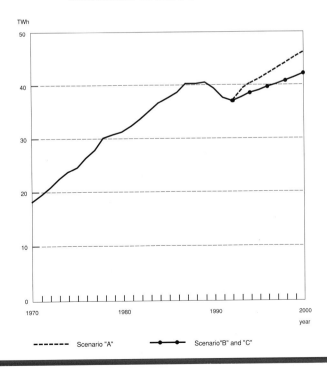

------- Scenario "A" ———•——— Scenario"B" and "C"

SPECIFIC ENERGY CONSUMPTION FIGURES IN SOME EUROPEAN COUNTRIES

Figure c

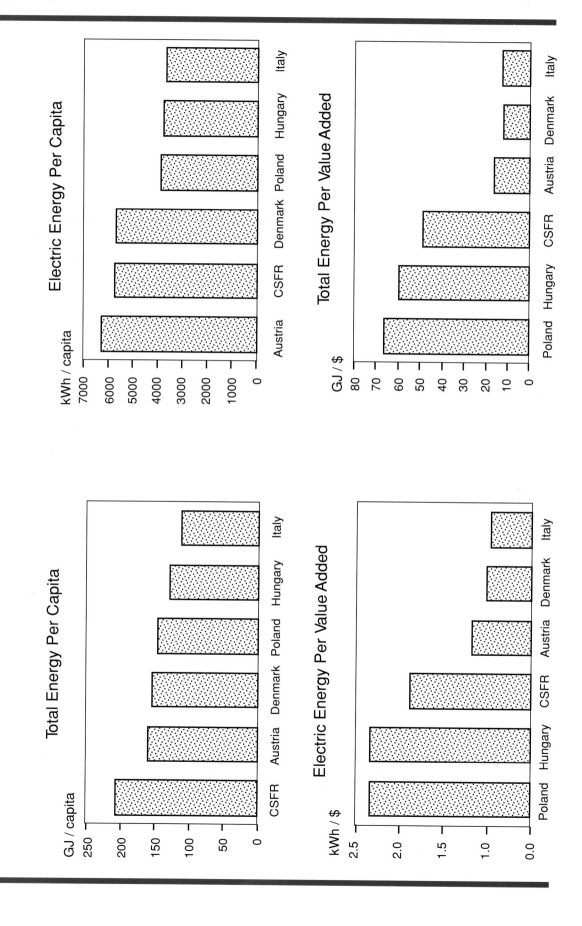

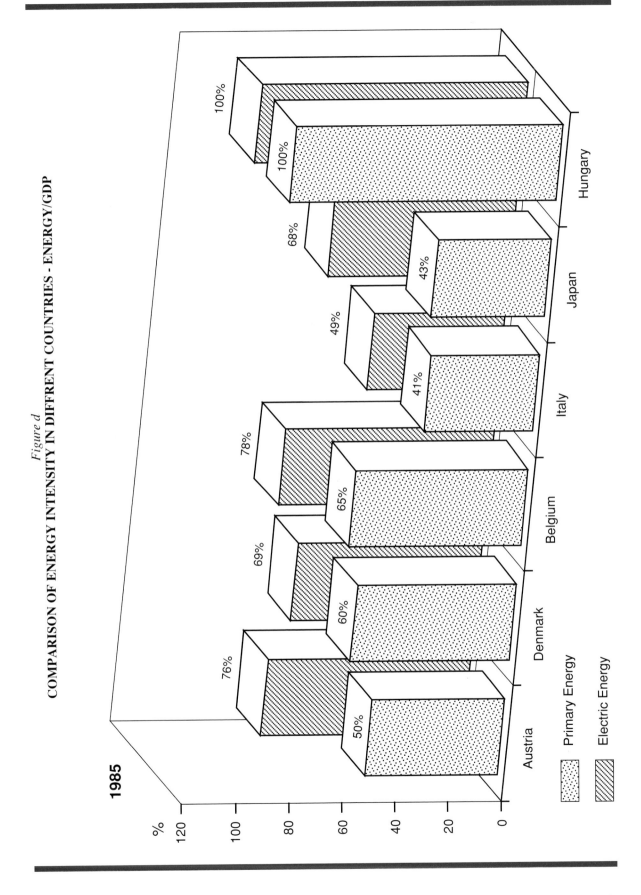

Figure d
COMPARISON OF ENERGY INTENSITY IN DIFFRENT COUNTRIES - ENERGY/GDP

Figure e
ENERGY SUPPLY STRUCTURE
1990

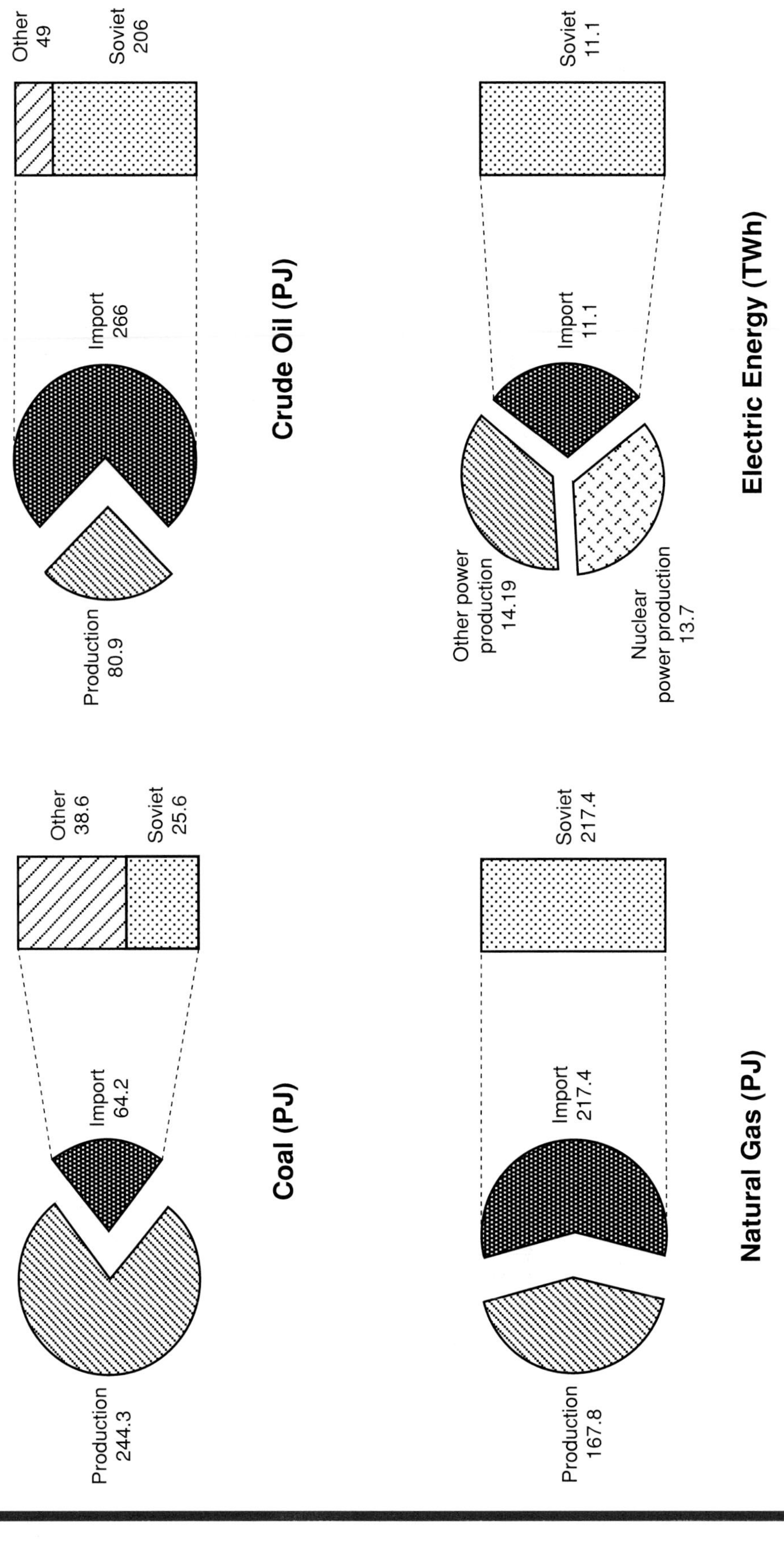

Coal (PJ)

Other
38.6

Soviet
25.6

Import
64.2

Production
244.3

Crude Oil (PJ)

Other
49

Soviet
206

Import
266

Production
80.9

Natural Gas (PJ)

Soviet
217.4

Import
217.4

Production
167.8

Electric Energy (TWh)

Soviet
11.1

Import
11.1

Other power
production
14.19

Nuclear
power production
13.7

Figure f
SHARE OF IMPORTS IN HUNGARIAN ENERGY SUPPLY (SCENARIO "A")

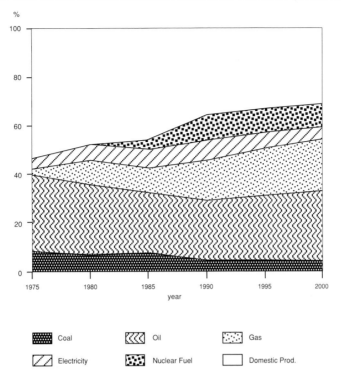

Figure g
STRUCTURE ENERGY SUPPLY (SCENARIO "A")

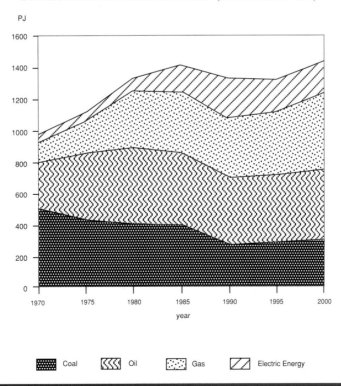

Figure h
ENERGY SUPPLY STRUCTURE
2000

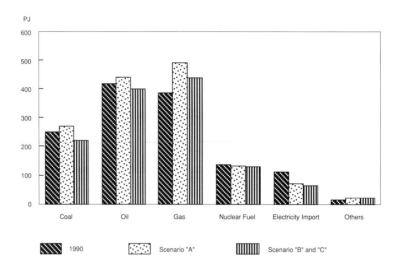

Figure i
STRUCTURE OF ENERGY CONSUMPTION
(SCENARIO "A")

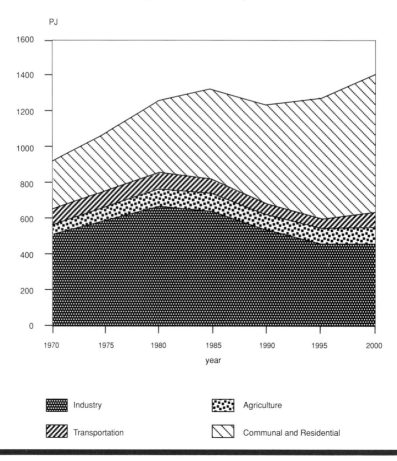

Figure j
SHARE OF INDUSTRIAL ENERGY DEMAND AND VALUE ADDED BY BRANCH, 1990

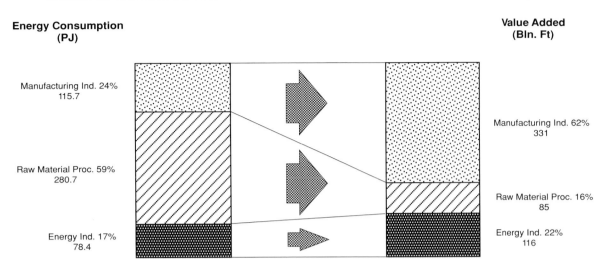

Energy Consumption (PJ)

Manufacturing Ind. 24% 115.7

Raw Material Proc. 59% 280.7

Energy Ind. 17% 78.4

Value Added (Bln. Ft)

Manufacturing Ind. 62% 331

Raw Material Proc. 16% 85

Energy Ind. 22% 116

Figure k
CO$_2$ EMISSIONS BY SECTOR 1988

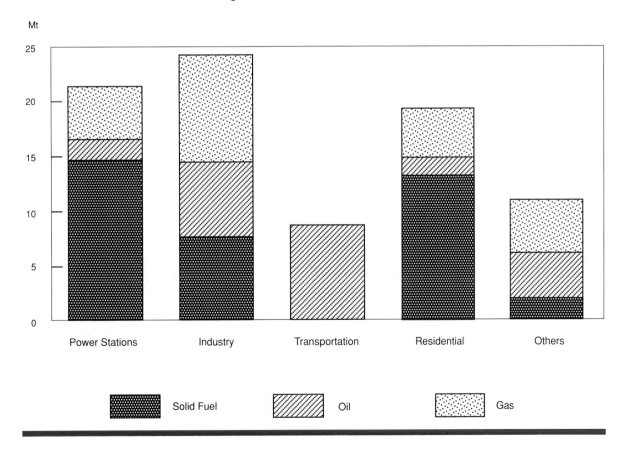

Figure l
CO$_2$ EMISSION TRENDS BY SOURCE

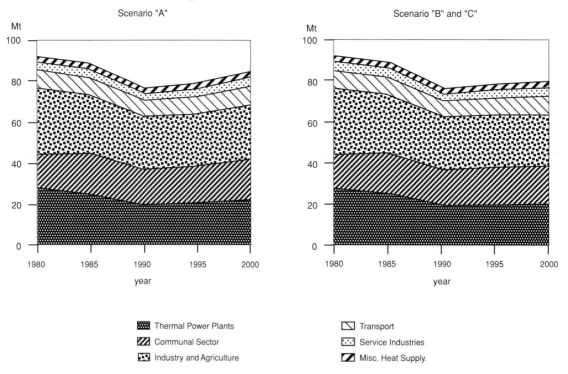

Thermal Power Plants   Transport
Communal Sector   Service Industries
Industry and Agriculture   Misc. Heat Supply.

Figure m
NO$_X$ EMISSIONS BY SECTOR, 1988

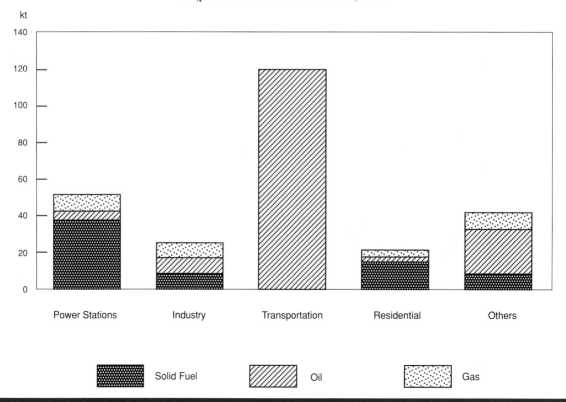

Solid Fuel   Oil   Gas

Figure n
NO$_X$ EMISSION TRENDS BY SOURCE

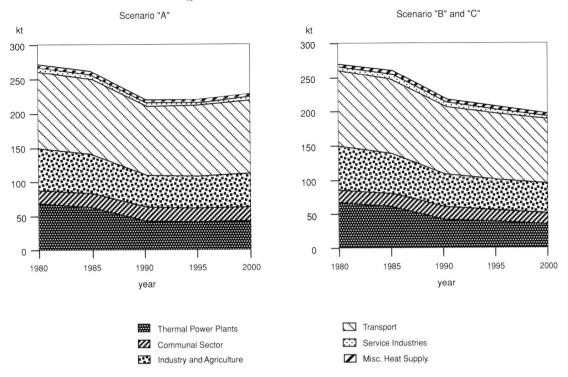

Scenario "A"   Scenario "B" and "C"

Thermal Power Plants   Transport
Communal Sector   Service Industries
Industry and Agriculture   Misc. Heat Supply.

Figure o
SO$_2$ EMISSIONS BY SECTOR, 1988

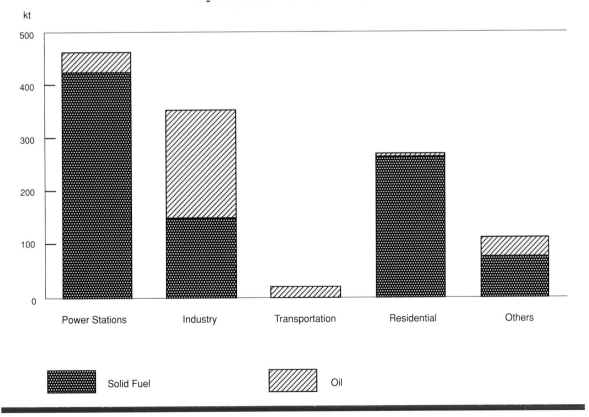

Solid Fuel   Oil

Figure p
SO$_2$ EMISSION TRENDS BY SOURCE

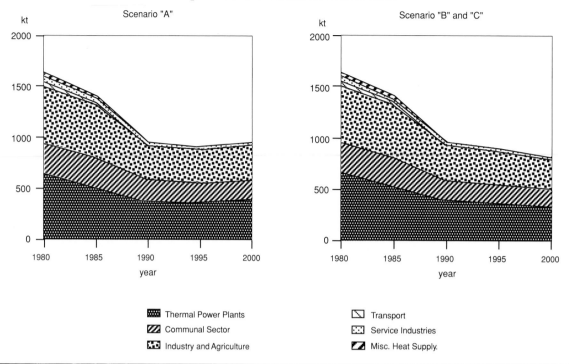

Thermal Power Plants

Communal Sector

Industry and Agriculture

Transport

Service Industries

Misc. Heat Supply.

ANNEX II

Statistical Appendix

Statistical Appendix

The Hungarian Government provided the following detailed energy balances for 1989 and 1990 and projected balances for 1995, 2000, 2005 and 2010 together with supporting energy and economic indicators. For the period after 2000 two variants are presented, one involving new nuclear power capacity, the other involving a new baseload lignite power station. The projections are based on the GDP growth assumptions shown in the following Table.

GDP Growth Rates and Population

	GDP Growth Rate*	Population in Millions
1988-1989	-0.2	10.6
1989-1995	-0.3	10.5
1995-2000	2.8	10.5
2000-2005	4.0	10.5
2005-2010	4.7	10.5

* Average annual growth rates

1989 Energy Balance (Mtoe)

	Coal+ Other Solids	Oil	Natural Gas	Nuclear Power	Hydro+ Others	Elec- tricity	Heat	TOTAL
Indigenous Production	5.62	2.72	4.72	3.62	0.01	-	-	16.69
Imports	2.20	8.08*	4.84	-	-	1.11	-	16.23
Exports	-0.06	-2.01*	-0.02	-	-	-0.16	-	-2.25
Stock Changes	-0.09	0.00	-0.18	-	-	-	-	-0.27
TPES	**7.67**	**8.79**	**9.36**	**3.62**	**0.01**	**0.95**	**0.00**	**30.40**
Transformation and Energy Sector	**-3.21**	**-1.37**	**-3.21**	**-3.62**	**-0.01**	**1.77**	**1.67**	**-7.98**
Electricity Generation	-2.26	-0.33	-0.97	-3.62	-0.01	2.31	-	-4.88
District Heating	-0.78	-0.28	-1.59	-	-	-	2.02	-0.63
CHP Plants	-0.18	-0.09	-0.23	-	-	0.24	0.16	-0.10
Petroleum Refineries	-	-0.15	-	-	-	-	-	-0.15
Own Use & Losses	0.01	-0.52	-0.42	-	-	-0.78	-0.51	-2.22
TFC	**4.46**	**7.42**	**6.15**	**-**	**-**	**2.72**	**1.67**	**22.42**
TOTAL INDUSTRY	**1.28**	**1.77**	**3.44**	**-**	**-**	**1.17**	**0.58**	**8.24**
Iron and Steel	0.62	0.08	0.48	-	-	0.17	0.15	1.50
Non-Ferrous Metals	0.26	0.09	0.14	-	-	0.17	0.06	0.72
Petrochemical & Chemical	0.00	0.83	0.94	-	-	0.28	0.33	2.38
(of which: Petrochem. Feedstocks)	-	0.77	0.74	-	-	-	-	1.51
Other Industries	0.40	0.77	1.88	-	-	0.55	0.04	3.64
TOTAL TRANSPORT	**0.00**	**3.11**	**0.00**	**-**	**-**	**0.10**	**0.00**	**3.21**
of which: Road	-	2.74	0.00	-	-	-	-	2.74
TOTAL OTHER SECTORS	**3.16**	**2.19**	**2.71**	**-**	**-**	**1.45**	**1.09**	**10.60**
of which: Residential	2.69	0.82	1.52	-	-	0.74	0.84	6.61
NON-ENERGY USE	**0.02**	**0.35**	**-**	**-**	**-**	**-**	**-**	**0.37**
MEMO ITEM								
Electricity Generated (TWh)	*9.29*	*1.36*	*4.90*	*13.89*	*0.16*	*-*	*-*	*29.60*

* Transit of oil included in 1989 figures but not in 1990 figures or in projections.

Source: AEEF.

1990 Energy Balance (Mtoe)

	Coal+ Other Solids	Oil	Natural Gas	Nuclear Power	Hydro+ Others	Elec- tricity	Heat	TOTAL
Indigenous Production	4.73	2.51	3.81	3.58	0.02	-	-	14.64
Imports	1.43	7.91	5.19	-	-	0.96	-	15.49
Exports	-0.04	-1.64	-0.02	-	-	-	-	-1.69
Stock Changes	0.49	-0.56	-0.07	-	-	-	-	-0.15
TPES	**6.61**	**8.21**	**8.92**	**3.58**	**0.02**	**0.96**	**-**	**28.29**
Transformation and Energy Sector	**-3.23**	**-1.12**	**-2.99**	**-3.58**	**-0.02**	**1.70**	**1.52**	**-7.72**
Electricity Generation	-2.25	-0.23	-0.82	-3.58	-0.02	2.22	-	-4.68
District Heating	-0.72	-0.31	-1.50	-	-	-	2.00	-0.54
CHP Plants	-0.16	-0.09	-0.21	-	-	0.23	0.15	-0.09
Petroleum Refineries	-	-0.04	-	-	-	-	-	-0.04
Own Use & Losses	-0.14	-0.34	-0.46	-	-	-0.75	-0.62	-2.30
TFC	**3.38**	**7.09**	**5.92**	**-**	**-**	**2.66**	**1.52**	**20.58**
TOTAL INDUSTRY	**0.88**	**1.60**	**3.17**	**-**	**-**	**1.13**	**0.41**	**7.18**
Iron and Steel	0.66	0.10	0.42	-	-	0.15	0.10	1.44
Non-Ferrous Metals	0.08	0.12	0.10	-	-	0.15	0.01	0.45
Petrochemical & Chemical	0.00	0.74	0.95	-	-	0.24	0.23	2.16
(of which: Petrochem. Feedstocks)	-	0.60	0.55	-	-	-	-	1.15
Other Industries	0.14	0.64	1.70	-	-	0.59	0.07	3.13
TOTAL TRANSPORT	**0.00**	**2.88**	**0.00**	**-**	**-**	**0.10**	**0.00**	**2.98**
of which: Road	-	2.55	0.00	-	-	-	-	2.55
TOTAL OTHER SECTORS	**2.50**	**2.38**	**2.76**	**-**	**-**	**1.43**	**1.12**	**10.19**
of which: Residential	2.18	1.16	1.58	-	-	0.79	0.83	6.54
NON-ENERGY USE	**-**	**0.23**	**-**	**-**	**-**	**-**	**-**	**0.23**
MEMO ITEM								
Electricity Generated (TWh)	*8.3*	*1.4*	*4.8*	*13.7*	*0.2*	*-*	*-*	*28.4*

Source: AEEF.

1995 Energy Balance (Mtoe)

	Coal+ Other Solids	Oil	Natural Gas	Nuclear Power	Hydro+ Others	Elec- tricity	Heat	TOTAL
Indigenous Production	4.07	2.45	4.20	3.52	0.01	-	-	14.25
Imports	1.82	6.39	5.45	-	-	0.61	-	14.27
Exports	0.00	-0.19	0.00	-	-	-0.07	-	-0.26
Stock Changes	0.00	0.00	0.00	-	-	-	-	0.00
TPES	**5.89**	**8.65**	**9.65**	**3.52**	**0.01**	**0.54**	**-**	**28.26**
Transformation and Energy Sector	**-2.68**	**-1.49**	**-4.39**	**-3.52**	**-0.01**	**2.15**	**1.42**	**-8.52**
Electricity Generation	-1.88	-0.50	-2.07	-3.52	-0.01	2.57	-	-5.41
District Heating	-0.68	-0.31	-1.44	-	-	-	1.83	-0.60
CHP Plants	-0.14	-0.07	-0.47	-	-	0.41	0.16	-0.11
Petroleum Refineries	-	-0.13	-	-	-	-	-	-0.13
Own Use & Losses	0.02	-0.48	-0.41	-	-	-0.83	-0.57	-2.27
TFC	**3.21**	**7.16**	**5.26**	**-**	**-**	**2.69**	**1.42**	**19.74**
TOTAL INDUSTRY	**0.57**	**1.27**	**2.07**	**-**	**-**	**0.86**	**0.37**	**5.14**
Iron and Steel	0.25	0.09	0.27	-	-	0.12	0.11	0.84
Non-Ferrous Metals	0.09	0.05	0.07	-	-	0.09	0.03	0.33
Petrochemical & Chemical	0.00	0.70	0.69	-	-	0.17	0.21	1.77
(of which: Petrochem. Feedstocks)	0.00	0.67	0.54	-	-	-	-	1.21
Other Industries	0.23	0.43	1.04	-	-	0.48	0.02	2.20
TOTAL TRANSPORT	**0.00**	**3.51**	**0.00**	**-**	**-**	**0.10**	**0.00**	**3.61**
of which: Road	-	3.15	0.00	-	-	-	-	3.15
TOTAL OTHER SECTORS	**2.62**	**2.02**	**3.19**	**-**	**-**	**1.73**	**1.05**	**10.61**
of which: Residential	2.42	1.08	2.13	-	-	0.89	0.87	7.39
NON-ENERGY USE	**0.02**	**0.36**	**-**	**-**	**-**	**-**	**-**	**0.38**
MEMO ITEM								
Electricity Generated (TWh)	*7.5*	*2.1*	*11.4*	*13.5*	*0.2*	*-*	*-*	*34.7*

Source: AEEF.

2000 Energy Balance (Mtoe)

	Coal+ Other Solids	Oil	Natural Gas	Nuclear Power	Hydro+ Others	Elec-tricity	Heat	TOTAL
Indigenous Production	4.18	1.86	3.21	3.52	0.01	-	-	12.78
Imports	1.71	7.96	6.96	-	-	0.61	-	17.24
Exports	0.00	-0.33	0.00	-	-	-0.07	-	-0.40
Stock Changes	0.00	0.00	0.00	-	-	-	-	0.00
TPES	**5.89**	**9.49**	**10.17**	**3.52**	**0.01**	**0.54**	**-**	**29.62**
Transformation and Energy Sector	**-2.85**	**-1.94**	**-4.34**	**-3.52**	**-0.01**	**2.37**	**1.41**	**-8.88**
Electricity Generation	-1.98	-0.89	-1.79	-3.52	-0.01	2.66	-	-5.53
District Heating	-0.75	-0.31	-1.47	-	-	-	1.85	-0.68
CHP Plants	-0.14	-0.07	-0.67	-	-	0.57	0.16	-0.15
Petroleum Refineries	-	-0.15	-	-	-	-	-	-0.15
Own Use & Losses	0.02	-0.52	-0.41	-	-	-0.86	-0.60	-2.37
TFC	**3.04**	**7.55**	**5.83**	**-**	**-**	**2.91**	**1.41**	**20.74**
TOTAL INDUSTRY	**0.55**	**1.30**	**2.18**	**-**	**-**	**0.88**	**0.36**	**5.27**
Iron and Steel	0.21	0.05	0.22	-	-	0.11	0.09	0.68
Non-Ferrous Metals	0.08	0.04	0.06	-	-	0.08	0.03	0.29
Petrochemical & Chemical	0.00	0.72	0.72	-	-	0.18	0.22	1.84
(of which: Petrochem. Feedstocks)	0.00	0.69	0.56	-	-	-	-	1.25
Other Industries	0.26	0.49	1.18	-	-	0.51	0.02	2.46
TOTAL TRANSPORT	**0.00**	**3.91**	**0.00**	**-**	**-**	**0.11**	**0.00**	**4.02**
of which: Road	-	3.55	0.00	-	-	-	-	3.55
TOTAL OTHER SECTORS	**2.47**	**1.95**	**3.65**	**-**	**-**	**1.92**	**1.05**	**11.04**
of which: Residential	2.30	1.02	2.41	-	-	0.98	0.85	7.56
NON-ENERGY USE	**0.02**	**0.39**	**-**	**-**	**-**	**-**	**-**	**0.41**
MEMO ITEM								
Electricity Generated (TWh)	*8.1*	*3.6*	*12.3*	*13.5*	*0.2*	*-*	*-*	*37.7*

Source: AEEF.

2005 Energy Balance - Nuclear Expansion Scenario (Mtoe)

	Coal+ Other Solids	Oil	Natural Gas	Nuclear Power	Hydro+ Others	Elec-tricity	Heat	TOTAL
Indigenous Production	2.76	1.45	2.85	7.30	0.01	-	-	14.37
Imports	1.79	7.82	6.67	-	-	0.61	-	16.89
Exports	0.00	-0.08	0.00	-	-	-0.07	-	-0.15
Stock Changes	0.00	0.00	0.00	-	-	-	-	0.00
TPES	**4.55**	**9.19**	**9.52**	**7.30**	**0.01**	**0.54**	**-**	**31.11**
Transformation and Energy Sector	**-1.58**	**-1.33**	**-3.14**	**-7.30**	**-0.01**	**2.72**	**1.38**	**-9.26**
Electricity Generation	-0.88	-0.31	-0.56	-7.30	-0.01	3.00	-	-6.06
District Heating	-0.60	-0.32	-1.46	-	-	-	1.85	-0.53
CHP Plants	-0.12	-0.08	-0.71	-	-	0.60	0.16	-0.15
Petroleum Refineries	-	-0.12	-	-	-	-	-	-0.12
Own Use & Losses	0.02	-0.50	-0.41	-	-	-0.88	-0.63	-2.40
TFC	**2.97**	**7.86**	**6.38**	**-**	**-**	**3.26**	**1.38**	**21.85**
TOTAL INDUSTRY	**0.53**	**1.40**	**2.33**	**-**	**-**	**0.99**	**0.35**	**5.60**
Iron and Steel	0.17	0.04	0.18	-	-	0.10	0.07	0.56
Non-Ferrous Metals	0.07	0.03	0.05	-	-	0.08	0.02	0.25
Petrochemical & Chemical	0.00	0.78	0.76	-	-	0.20	0.23	1.97
(of which: Petrochem. Feedstocks)	0.00	0.74	0.60	-	-	-	-	1.34
Other Industries	0.29	0.55	1.34	-	-	0.61	0.03	2.82
TOTAL TRANSPORT	**0.00**	**4.27**	**0.00**	**-**	**-**	**0.12**	**0.00**	**4.39**
of which: Road	-	3.90	0.00	-	-	-	-	3.90
TOTAL OTHER SECTORS	**2.44**	**1.81**	**4.05**	**-**	**-**	**2.15**	**1.03**	**11.48**
of which: Residential	2.28	0.86	2.65	-	-	1.09	0.85	7.73
NON-ENERGY USE	**0.00**	**0.38**	**-**	**-**	**-**	**-**	**-**	**0.38**
MEMO ITEM								
Electricity Generated (TWh)	*3.6*	*1.6*	*8.3*	*28.0*	*0.2*	*-*	*-*	*41.7*

Source: AEEF.

2005 Energy Balance - Lignite Expansion Scenario (Mtoe)

	Coal+ Other Solids	Oil	Natural Gas	Nuclear Power	Hydro+ Others	Elec- tricity	Heat	TOTAL
Indigenous Production	5.23	1.45	2.85	3.52	0.01	-	-	13.06
Imports	1.79	8.60	7.97	-	-	0.61	-	18.97
Exports	0.00	-0.43	0.00	-	-	-0.07	-	-0.50
Stock Changes	0.00	0.00	0.00	-	-	-	-	0.00
TPES	**7.02**	**9.62**	**10.82**	**3.52**	**0.01**	**0.54**	**-**	**31.53**
Transformation and Energy Sector	**-4.05**	**-1.76**	**-4.44**	**-3.52**	**-0.01**	**2.72**	**1.38**	**-9.68**
Electricity Generation	-3.35	-0.67	-1.90	-3.52	-0.01	3.00	-	-6.45
District Heating	-0.60	-0.32	-1.42	-	-	-	1.85	-0.49
CHP Plants	-0.12	-0.08	-0.71	-	-	0.60	0.16	-0.15
Petroleum Refineries	-	-0.15	-	-	-	-	-	-0.15
Own Use & Losses	0.02	-0.54	-0.41	-	-	-0.88	-0.63	-2.44
TFC	**2.97**	**7.86**	**6.38**	**-**	**-**	**3.26**	**1.38**	**21.85**
TOTAL INDUSTRY	**0.53**	**1.40**	**2.33**	**-**	**-**	**0.99**	**0.35**	**5.60**
Iron and Steel	0.17	0.04	0.18	-	-	0.10	0.07	0.56
Non-Ferrous Metals	0.07	0.03	0.05	-	-	0.08	0.02	0.25
Petrochemical & Chemical	0.00	0.78	0.76	-	-	0.20	0.23	1.97
(of which: Petrochem. Feedstocks)	0.00	0.74	0.60	-	-	-	-	1.34
Other Industries	0.29	0.55	1.34	-	-	0.61	0.03	2.82
TOTAL TRANSPORT	**0.00**	**4.27**	**0.00**	**-**	**-**	**0.12**	**0.00**	**4.39**
of which: Road	-	3.90	0.00	-	-	-	-	3.90
TOTAL OTHER SECTORS	**2.44**	**1.81**	**4.05**	**-**	**-**	**2.15**	**1.03**	**11.48**
of which: Residential	2.28	0.86	2.65	-	-	1.09	0.85	7.73
NON-ENERGY USE	**0.00**	**0.38**	**-**	**-**	**-**	**-**	**-**	**0.38**
MEMO ITEM								
Electricity Generated (TWh)	*12.4*	*2.8*	*12.8*	*13.5*	*0.2*	*-*	*-*	*41.7*

Source: AEEF.

2010 Energy Balance - Nuclear Expansion Scenario (Mtoe)

	Coal+ Other Solids	Oil	Natural Gas	Nuclear Power	Hydro+ Others	Elec-tricity	Heat	TOTAL
Indigenous Production	2.39	1.03	2.38	7.30	0.01	-	-	13.11
Imports	2.13	9.04	8.24	-	-	0.61	-	20.02
Exports	0.00	-0.25	0.00	-	-	-0.07	-	-0.32
Stock Changes	0.00	0.00	0.00	-	-	-	-	0.00
TPES	**4.52**	**9.82**	**10.62**	**7.30**	**0.01**	**0.54**	**-**	**32.81**
Transformation and Energy Sector	**-1.70**	**-1.63**	**-3.67**	**-7.30**	**-0.01**	**3.06**	**1.38**	**-9.87**
Electricity Generation	-1.12	-0.55	-0.82	-7.30	-0.01	3.23	-	-6.57
District Heating	-0.60	-0.32	-1.48	-	-	-	1.85	-0.55
CHP Plants	0.00	-0.08	-0.96	-	-	0.71	0.16	-0.17
Petroleum Refineries	-	-0.14	-	-	-	-	-	-0.14
Own Use & Losses	0.02	-0.54	-0.41	-	-	-0.88	-0.63	-2.44
TFC	**2.82**	**8.19**	**6.95**	**-**	**-**	**3.60**	**1.38**	**22.94**
TOTAL INDUSTRY	**0.52**	**1.48**	**2.47**	**-**	**-**	**1.13**	**0.35**	**5.95**
Iron and Steel	0.14	0.03	0.15	-	-	0.09	0.06	0.47
Non-Ferrous Metals	0.06	0.03	0.04	-	-	0.07	0.02	0.22
Petrochemical & Chemical	0.00	0.82	0.81	-	-	0.22	0.24	2.09
(of which: Petrochem. Feedstocks)	0.00	0.78	0.63	-	-	-	-	1.41
Other Industries	0.32	0.60	1.47	-	-	0.75	0.03	3.17
TOTAL TRANSPORT	**0.00**	**4.56**	**0.00**	**-**	**-**	**0.13**	**0.00**	**4.69**
of which: Road	-	4.21	0.00	-	-	-	-	4.21
TOTAL OTHER SECTORS	**2.30**	**1.75**	**4.48**	**-**	**-**	**2.34**	**1.03**	**11.90**
of which: Residential	2.18	0.78	2.90	-	-	1.15	0.85	7.86
NON-ENERGY USE	**0.00**	**0.40**	**-**	**-**	**-**	**-**	**-**	**0.40**
MEMO ITEM								
Electricity Generated (TWh)	*4.3*	*2.5*	*10.7*	*28.0*	*0.2*	*-*	*-*	*45.7*

Source: AEEF.

2010 Energy Balance - Lignite Expansion Scenario (Mtoe)

	Coal+ Other Solids	Oil	Natural Gas	Nuclear Power	Hydro+ Others	Elec-tricity	Heat	TOTAL
Indigenous Production	5.44	1.03	2.38	3.52	0.01	-	-	12.38
Imports	2.13	9.22	9.24	-	-	0.61	-	21.20
Exports	0.00	-0.31	0.00	-	-	-0.07	-	-0.38
Stock Changes	0.00	0.00	0.00	-	-	-	-	0.00
TPES	**7.57**	**9.94**	**11.62**	**3.52**	**0.01**	**0.54**	**-**	**33.20**
Transformation and Energy Sector	**-4.76**	**-1.75**	**-4.67**	**-3.52**	**-0.01**	**3.06**	**1.38**	**-10.27**
Electricity Generation	-4.18	-0.65	-1.94	-3.52	-0.01	3.23	-	-7.07
District Heating	-0.60	-0.32	-1.33	-	-	-	1.85	-0.40
CHP Plants	0.00	-0.08	-0.96	-	-	0.71	0.16	-0.20
Petroleum Refineries	-	-0.15	-	-	-	-	-	-0.15
Own Use & Losses	0.02	-0.55	-0.41	-	-	-0.88	-0.63	-2.45
TFC	**2.81**	**8.19**	**6.95**	**-**	**-**	**3.60**	**1.38**	**22.93**
TOTAL INDUSTRY	**0.52**	**1.48**	**2.47**	**-**	**-**	**1.13**	**0.35**	**5.95**
Iron and Steel	0.14	0.03	0.15	-	-	0.09	0.06	0.47
Non-Ferrous Metals	0.06	0.03	0.04	-	-	0.07	0.02	0.22
Petrochemical & Chemical	0.00	0.82	0.81	-	-	0.22	0.24	2.09
(of which: Petrochem. Feedstocks)	0.00	0.78	0.63	-	-	-	-	1.41
Other Industries	0.32	0.60	1.47	-	-	0.75	0.03	3.17
TOTAL TRANSPORT	**0.00**	**4.56**	**0.00**	**-**	**-**	**0.13**	**0.00**	**4.69**
of which: Road	-	4.21	0.00	-	-	-	-	4.21
TOTAL OTHER SECTORS	**2.29**	**1.75**	**4.48**	**-**	**-**	**2.34**	**1.03**	**11.89**
of which: Residential	2.18	0.78	2.90	-	-	1.15	0.85	7.86
NON-ENERGY USE	**0.00**	**0.40**	**-**	**-**	**-**	**-**	**-**	**0.40**
MEMO ITEM								
Electricity Generated (TWh)	*14.7*	*2.7*	*14.6*	*13.5*	*0.2*	*-*	*-*	*45.7*

Source: AEEF.

Status of Electricity Capacity - Nuclear Expansion Scenario (GW)

		Coal	Other Solid Fuels	Oil & Gas	Nuclear	Hydro	TOTAL
I.	**1989 (31st December)**	**2.05**	**0.02**	**3.29**	**1.76**	**0.05**	**7.17**
II.	**To be commissioned between 1st January 1990 and 31st December 1995**						
-	Capacity currently under construction	-	-	0.14	-	-	0.14
-	Capacity authorised and site confirmed	-	-	0.15	-	-	0.15
-	Other planned capacity	-	-	0.15	-	-	0.15
-	Conversion to other fuel	-	-	-	-	-	-
-	Operating capacity to be decommissioned 1990-1995	-	-	-	-	-	-
-	**Total operating capacity in 1995**	**2.05**	**0.02**	**3.73**	**1.76**	**0.05**	**7.61**
III.	**To be commissioned between 1st January 1996 and 31st December 2000**						
-	Capacity currently under construction	-	-	-	-	-	-
-	Capacity authorised and site confirmed	-	-	-	-	-	-
-	Other planned capacity	0.60	-	0.40	-	-	1.00
-	Conversion to other fuel	-	-	-	-	-	-
-	Operating capacity to be decommissioned 1996-2000	-0.35	-	-0.45	-	-	-0.80
-	**Total operating capacity in 2000**	**2.30**	**0.02**	**3.68**	**1.76**	**0.05**	**7.81**
IV.	**To be commissioned between 1st January 2001 and 31st December 2005**						
-	Capacity currently under construction	-	-	-	-	-	-
-	Capacity authorised and site confirmed	-	-	-	-	-	-
-	Other planned capacity	-	-	-	2.00	-	2.00
-	Conversion to other fuel	-	-	-	-	-	-
-	Operating capacity to be decommissioned 2001-2005	-0.30	-	-0.20	-	-	-0.50
-	**Total operating in 2005**	**2.00**	**0.02**	**3.48**	**3.76**	**0.05**	**9.31**
I.	Combined heat and power plant in 1989	-	-	2.83	-	-	2.83
II.	Combined heat and power plant in 1995	-	-	3.73	-	-	3.73
III.	Combined heat and power plant in 2000	-	-	3.73	-	-	3.73
IV.	Combined heat and power plant in 2005	-	-	3.73	-	-	3.73

Based on new baseload nuclear power plant between 2000-2005. Throughout the total period 110 MW of import capacity from the former USSR is assumed. Sould these imports fall below this level domestic generating capacity would be expanded.

Status of Electricity Capacity - Lignite Expansion Scenario (GW)

		Coal	Other Solid Fuels	Oil & Gas	Nuclear	Hydro	TOTAL
I.	**1989 (31st December)**	**2.05**	**0.02**	**3.29**	**1.76**	**0.05**	**7.17**
II.	**To be commissioned between 1st January 1990 and 31st December 1995**						
-	Capacity currently under construction	-	-	0.14	-	-	0.14
-	Capacity authorised and site confirmed	-	-	0.15	-	-	0.15
-	Other planned capacity	-	-	0.15	-	-	0.15
-	Conversion to other fuel	-	-	-	-	-	-
-	Operating capacity to be decommissioned 1990-1995	-	-	-	-	-	-
-	**Total operating in 1995**	**2.05**	**0.02**	**3.73**	**1.76**	**0.05**	**7.61**
III.	**To be commissioned between 1st January 1996 and 31st December 2000**						
-	Capacity currently under construction	-	-	-	-	-	-
-	Capacity authorised and site confirmed	-	-	-	-	-	-
-	Other planned capacity	0.60	-	0.40	-	-	1.00
-	Conversion to other fuel	-	-	-	-	-	-
-	Operating capacity to be decommissioned 1996-2000	-0.35	-	-0.45	-	-	-0.80
-	**Total operating in 2000**	**2.30**	**0.02**	**3.68**	**1.76**	**0.05**	**7.81**
IV.	**To be commissioned between 1st January 2001 and 31st December 2005**						
-	Capacity currently under construction	-	-	-	-	-	-
-	Capacity authorised and site confirmed	-	-	-	-	-	-
-	Other planned capacity	1.20	-	-	-	-	1.20
-	Conversion to other fuel	-	-	-	-	-	-
-	Operating capacity to be decommissioned 2001-2005	-0.30	-	-0.20	-	-	-0.50
-	**Total operating in 2005**	**3.20**	**0.02**	**3.48**	**1.76**	**0.05**	**8.51**
I.	Combined heat and power plant in 1989	-	-	2.83	-	-	2.83
II.	Combined heat and power plant in 1995	-	-	3.73	-	-	3.73
III.	Combined heat and power plant in 2000	-	-	3.73	-	-	3.73
IV.	Combined heat and power plant in 2005	-	-	3.73	-	-	3.73

Based on new baseload lignite fired power plant between 2000-2005. Throughout the period 110 MW of import capacity from the former USSR is assumed. Should these imports fall below this level domestic generating capacity would be expanded.

Coal Production, Imports and Exports
(Mtoe)

	1988	1989	1995	2000	2005	2010
PRODUCTION - Coal:	5.70	5.30	3.78	3.92	2.50-4.97	2.15-5.20
Coking coal	0.34	0.25	0.20	0.20	0.20	0.20
Other bituminous coal & anthracite	-	-	-	-	-	-
Sub-bituminous coal	0.56	0.60	0.50	0.45	0.40	0.40
Brown coal/lignite	4.80	4.45	3.08	3.27	1.90-4.37	1.55-4.60
IMPORTS - Coal and Coal Products	2.25	2.20	1.82	1.71	1.79	2.13
Coking coal	0.55	0.28	0.20	0.17	0.15	0.11
Other bituminous coal & anthracite	0.05	0.05	0.05	0.05	0.05	0.05
Sub-bituminous coal	0.71	0.90	0.55	0.49	0.60	1.02
Brown coal/lignite	0.02	0.02	0.02	0.02	0.02	0.02
Coal products	0.92	0.95	1.00	0.98	0.97	0.93
EXPORTS - Coal and Coal Products	0.00	0.03	-	-	-	-
Coking Coal	-	-	-	-	-	-
Other bituminous coal & anthracite	-	-	-	-	-	-
Sub-bituminous coal	-	-	-	-	-	-
Brown coal/lignite	0.00	0.00	-	-	-	-
Coal products	-	0.03	-	-	-	-

Imports and Exports of Natural Gas
(Mtoe)

		1989	1995	2000	2005	2010
Pipeline	Imports	4.84	5.45	6.96	6.67-7.97	8.24-9.24
	Exports	0.02	-	-	-	-
LNG	Imports	-	-	-	-	-
	Exports	-	-	-	-	-
Total	Imports	4.84	5.45	6.96	6.67-7.97	8.24-9.24
	Exports	0.02	-	-	-	-

Contribution to Energy Supply from Renewables
(Mtoe)

	1989	1995	2000	2005	2010
ELECTRICITY GENERATION					
Wood	-	-	-	-	-
Other Biomass	-	-	-	-	-
Wind	-	-	-	-	-
Solar Thermal	-	-	-	-	-
Photovoltaic	-	-	-	-	-
Hydro	0.01	0.01	0.01	0.01	0.01
Geothermal	-	-	-	-	-
Other (e.g. tidal)	-	-	-	-	-
TOTAL	**0.01**	**0.01**	**0.01**	**0.01**	**0.01**
DIRECT USE					
Wood	-	-	-	-	-
Other Biomass	0.32	0.26	0.26	0.26	0.24
Active Solar	-	-	-	-	-
Passive Solar	-	-	-	-	-
Agr./Ind. Process Heat from Solar	-	-	-	-	-
Geothermal	-	-	-	-	-
Wind	-	-	-	-	-
Photovoltaic	-	-	-	-	-
Other	-	-	-	-	-
TOTAL	**0.32**	**0.26**	**0.26**	**0.26**	**0.24**
TOTAL RENEWABLES	**0.33**	**0.27**	**0.27**	**0.27**	**0.25**

End-Use Efficiency Indicators

	1980	1985	1989	1995	2000
Transport - Passenger Cars					
Total Fleet (000's)	1 013	1 436	1 732	2 330	2 740
Gasoline	1 012	1 433	1 724	2 230	2 610
Diesel	1	3	8	100	130
Average distance driven (000/km/car/year)	12.4	11.3	9.0	10.4	13.5
Average fleet fuel efficiency (litres/100 km)	9.0	8.8	8.5	8.0	7.0
Industry (toe/ton of product)					
Iron	0.658	0.639	0.526	0.512	0.508
Steel	0.102	0.092	0.083	0.081	0.078
Alumina	0.339	0.339	0.325	0.286	0.276
Aluminium	1.441	1.367	1.362	1.200	1.152
Cement & Clinker	0.111	0.108	0.101	0.094	0.089
Ammonia	1.219	1.204	1.208	1.200	1.194
Residential					
By floor space (toe/m^2)	0.026	0.028	0.023	0.025	0.023
Total floor space (million m^2)	204	231	280	298	322
Commercial/Public					
By floor space (toe/m^2)	n.a.	n.a.	0.024	0.03	0.029
Total floor space (10^{6}m^2)	n.a.	n.a.	30.8	31.9	33.1

GLOSSARY

AEEF	Hungarian State Energy and Energy Safety Authority.
bcm	Billion cubic metres.
CHP	Combined heat and power.
CIF	Cost, insurance and freight.
CMEA	Council for Mutual Economic Assistance (COMECON).
CO_2	Carbon dioxide.
CSFR	Czech and Slovak Federal Republic.
DSM	Demand side management.
EC	European Community.
EGI	Hungarian Energy Management Institute.
EHI	Hungarian Energy Efficiency Office (part of AEEF).
FBB	Fluidised bed boiler.
FGD	Flue gas desulphurisation.
Ft	Hungarian Forint.
GDP	Gross domestic product.
GJ	Gigajoule, 10^9 joules.
GW	Gigawatt, 10^9 watts.
GWh	Gigawatt-hour.
IAEA	International Atomic Energy Agency.
IEA	International Energy Agency.
kg	Kilogramme.
kJ	Kilojoule.
km	Kilometre.
kV	Kilovolt.
kWh	Kilowatt-hour.
LNG	Liquified natural gas.
LPG	Liquid petroleum gas.
LRTAP	United Nations Convention on Long Range Trans-boundary Air Pollution.
mcm	Million cubic metres.
mg	Milligramme.
MJ	Megajoule.
mm	Millimetres.
MOIT	Hungarian Ministry of Industry and Trade.
MOL	Hungarian Oil and Gas Corporation (formerly OKGT).
mSv	Millisivert.
Mt	Million metric tons.
Mtoe	Million metric tons of oil equivalent.
MVA	Megavolt-ampere.
MVMT	Hungarian Electricity Board.
MW	Megawatt.
MW_e	Megawatt-electric.
MW_t	Megawatt-thermal.
NGLs	Natural gas liquids.

NO_X	Nitrogen oxides.
OECD	Organisation for Economic Co-operation and Development.
OKGT	Hungarian National Oil and Gas Trust (now MOL).
OMFB	Hungarian National Technical Development Committee.
ÖMV	ÖMV Ag., Austrian oil company.
OSART	Operational safety review team of the IAEA.
OVIT	Hungarian high voltage grid company, part of MVMT.
PJ	Petajoule, 10^{15} joules.
Q8	Q8, Kuwaiti oil company.
R&D	Research and development.
SO_2	Sulphur dioxide.
SPA	Hungarian State Property Agency.
SZÉSZEK	Hungarian Coal Mining Restructuring Centre.
TFC	Total final energy consumption.
TPES	Total primary energy supply.
TWh	Terawatt-hour.
UCPTE	Union for the Co-ordination of Production and Transmission of Electricity.
USSR	Former Union of Soviet Socialist Republics.
VAT	Value added tax.
VEIKI	Hungarian Institute for Electrical Power Research.
VOC	Volatile organic compound.
WHO	United Nations World Health Organisation.

MAIN SALES OUTLETS OF OECD PUBLICATIONS – PRINCIPAUX POINTS DE VENTE DES PUBLICATIONS DE L'OCDE

Argentina – Argentine
Carlos Hirsch S.R.L.
Galería Güemes, Florida 165, 4° Piso
1333 Buenos Aires   Tel. (1) 331.1787 y 331.2391
Telefax: (1) 331.1787

Australia – Australie
D.A. Book (Aust.) Pty. Ltd.
648 Whitehorse Road, P.O.B 163
Mitcham, Victoria 3132   Tel. (03) 873.4411
Telefax: (03) 873.5679

Austria – Autriche
OECD Publications and Information Centre
Schedestrasse 7
D-W 5300 Bonn 1 (Germany)   Tel. (49.228) 21.60.45
Telefax: (49.228) 26.11.04

Gerold & Co.
Graben 31
Wien I   Tel. (0222) 533.50.14

Belgium – Belgique
Jean De Lannoy
Avenue du Roi 202
B-1060 Bruxelles   Tel. (02) 538.51.69/538.08.41
Telefax: (02) 538.08.41

Canada
Renouf Publishing Company Ltd.
1294 Algoma Road
Ottawa, ON K1B 3W8   Tel. (613) 741.4333
Telefax: (613) 741.5439
Stores:
61 Sparks Street
Ottawa, ON K1P 5R1   Tel. (613) 238.8985
211 Yonge Street
Toronto, ON M5B 1M4   Tel. (416) 363.3171

Federal Publications
165 University Avenue
Toronto, ON M5H 3B8   Tel. (416) 581.1552
Telefax: (416)581.1743

Les Éditions La Liberté Inc.
3020 Chemin Sainte-Foy
Sainte-Foy, PQ G1X 3V6   Tel. (418) 658.3763
Telefax: (418) 658.3763

China – Chine
China National Publications Import
Export Corporation (CNPIEC)
P.O. Box 88
Beijing   Tel. 44.0731
Telefax: 401.5661

Denmark – Danemark
Munksgaard Export and Subscription Service
35, Nørre Søgade, P.O. Box 2148
DK-1016 København K   Tel. (33) 12.85.70
Telefax: (33) 12.93.87

Finland – Finlande
Akateeminen Kirjakauppa
Keskuskatu 1, P.O. Box 128
00100 Helsinki   Tel. (358 0) 12141
Telefax: (358 0) 121.4441

France
OECD/OCDE
Mail Orders/Commandes par correspondance:
2, rue André-Pascal
75775 Paris Cédex 16   Tel. (33-1) 45.24.82.00
Telefax: (33-1) 45.24.85.00
or (33-1) 45.24.81.76
Telex: 620 160 OCDE

Bookshop/Librairie:
33, rue Octave-Feuillet
75016 Paris   Tel. (33-1) 45.24.81.67
(33-1) 45.24.81.81

Librairie de l'Université
12a, rue Nazareth
13100 Aix-en-Provence   Tel. 42.26.18.08
Telefax: 42.26.63.26

Germany – Allemagne
OECD Publications and Information Centre
Schedestrasse 7
D-W 5300 Bonn 1   Tel. (0228) 21.60.45
Telefax: (0228) 26.11.04

Greece – Grèce
Librairie Kauffmann
Mavrokordatou 9
106 78 Athens   Tel. 322.21.60
Telefax: 363.39.67

Hong Kong
Swindon Book Co. Ltd.
13 - 15 Lock Road
Kowloon, Hong Kong   Tel. 366.80.31
Telefax: 739.49.75

Iceland – Islande
Mál Mog Menning
Laugavegi 18, Pósthólf 392
121 Reykjavik   Tel. 162.35.23

India – Inde
Oxford Book and Stationery Co.
Scindia House
New Delhi 110001   Tel.(11) 331.5896/5308
Telefax: (11) 332.5993

17 Park Street
Calcutta 700016   Tel. 240832

Indonesia – Indonésie
Pdii-Lipi
P.O. Box 269/JKSMG/88
Jakarta 12790   Tel. 583467
Telex: 62 875

Ireland – Irlande
TDC Publishers – Library Suppliers
12 North Frederick Street
Dublin 1   Tel. 74.48.35/74.96.77
Telefax: 74.84.16

Israel
Electronic Publications only
Publications électroniques seulement
Sophist Systems Ltd.
71 Allenby Street
Tel-Aviv 65134   Tel. 3-29.00.21
Telefax: 3-29.92.39

Italy – Italie
Libreria Commissionaria Sansoni
Via Duca di Calabria 1/1
50125 Firenze   Tel. (055) 64.54.15
Telefax: (055) 64.12.57

Via Bartolini 29
20155 Milano   Tel. (02) 36.50.83
Editrice e Libreria Herder
Piazza Montecitorio 120
00186 Roma   Tel. 679.46.28
Telex: NATEL I 621427

Libreria Hoepli
Via Hoepli 5
20121 Milano   Tel. (02) 86.54.46
Telefax: (02) 805.28.86

Libreria Scientifica
Dott. Lucio de Biasio 'Aeiou'
Via Meravigli 16
20123 Milano   Tel. (02) 805.68.98
Telefax: (02) 80.01.75

Japan – Japon
OECD Publications and Information Centre
Landic Akasaka Building
2-3-4 Akasaka, Minato-ku
Tokyo 107   Tel. (81.3) 3586.2016
Telefax: (81.3) 3584.7929

Korea – Corée
Kyobo Book Centre Co. Ltd.
P.O. Box 1658, Kwang Hwa Moon
Seoul   Tel. 730.78.91
Telefax: 735.00.30

Malaysia – Malaisie
Co-operative Bookshop Ltd.
University of Malaya
P.O. Box 1127, Jalan Pantai Baru
59700 Kuala Lumpur
Malaysia   Tel. 756.5000/756.5425
Telefax: 757.3661

Netherlands – Pays-Bas
SDU Uitgeverij
Christoffel Plantijnstraat 2
Postbus 20014
2500 EA's-Gravenhage   Tel. (070 3) 78.99.11
Voor bestellingen: Tel. (070 3) 78.98.80
Telefax: (070 3) 47.63.51

New Zealand – Nouvelle-Zélande
GP Publications Ltd.
Customer Services
33 The Esplanade - P.O. Box 38-900
Petone, Wellington   Tel. (04) 5685.555
Telefax: (04) 5685.333

Norway – Norvège
Narvesen Info Center - NIC
Bertrand Narvesens vei 2
P.O. Box 6125 Etterstad
0602 Oslo 6   Tel. (02) 57.33.00
Telefax: (02) 68.19.01

Pakistan
Mirza Book Agency
65 Shahrah Quaid-E-Azam
Lahore 3   Tel. 66.839
Telex: 44886 UBL PK. Attn: MIRZA BK

Portugal
Livraria Portugal
Rua do Carmo 70-74
Apart. 2681
1117 Lisboa Codex   Tel.: (01) 347.49.82/3/4/5
Telefax: (01) 347.02.64

Singapore – Singapour
Information Publications Pte. Ltd.
Pei-Fu Industrial Building
24 New Industrial Road No. 02-06
Singapore 1953   Tel. 283.1786/283.1798
Telefax: 284.8875

Spain – Espagne
Mundi-Prensa Libros S.A.
Castelló 37, Apartado 1223
Madrid 28001   Tel. (91) 431.33.99
Telefax: (91) 575.39.98

Libreria Internacional AEDOS
Consejo de Ciento 391
08009 - Barcelona   Tel. (93) 488.34.92
Telefax: (93) 487.76.59

Llibreria de la Generalitat
Palau Moja
Rambla dels Estudis, 118
08002 - Barcelona   Tel. (93) 318.80.12 (Subscripcions)
(93) 302.67.23 (Publicacions)
Telefax: (93) 412.18.54

Sri Lanka
Centre for Policy Research
c/o Colombo Agencies Ltd.
No. 300-304, Galle Road
Colombo 3   Tel. (1) 574240, 573551-2
Telefax: (1) 575394, 510711

Sweden – Suède
Fritzes Fackboksföretaget
Box 16356
Regeringsgatan 12
103 27 Stockholm   Tel. (08) 23.89.00
Telefax: (08) 20.50.21

Subscription Agency/Abonnements:
Wennergren-Williams AB
Nordenflychtsvägen 74
Box 30004
104 25 Stockholm   Tel. (08) 13.67.00
Telefax: (08) 618.62.32

Switzerland – Suisse
OECD Publications and Information Centre
Schedestrasse 7
D-W 5300 Bonn 1 (Germany)   Tel. (49.228) 21.60.45
Telefax: (49.228) 26.11.04

Suisse romande
Maditec S.A.
Chemin des Palettes 4
1020 Renens/Lausanne   Tel. (021) 635.08.65
Telefax: (021) 635.07.80

Librairie Payot
6 rue Grenus
1211 Genève 11   Tel. (022) 731.89.50
Telex: 28356

Subscription Agency – Service des Abonnements
Naville S.A.
7, rue Lévrier
1201 Genève   Tél.: (022) 732.24.00
Telefax: (022) 738.87.13

Taiwan – Formose
Good Faith Worldwide Int'l. Co. Ltd.
9th Floor, No. 118, Sec. 2
Chung Hsiao E. Road
Taipei   Tel. (02) 391.7396/391.7397
Telefax: (02) 394.9176

Thailand – Thaïlande
Suksit Siam Co. Ltd.
113, 115 Fuang Nakhon Rd.
Opp. Wat Rajbopith
Bangkok 10200   Tel. (662) 251.1630
Telefax: (662) 236.7783

Turkey – Turquie
Kültur Yayinlari Is-Türk Ltd. Sti.
Atatürk Bulvari No. 191/Kat. 21
Kavaklidere/Ankara   Tel. 25.07.60
Dolmabahce Cad. No. 29
Besiktas/Istanbul   Tel. 160.71.88
Telex: 43482B

United Kingdom – Royaume-Uni
HMSO
Gen. enquiries   Tel. (071) 873 0011
Postal orders only:
P.O. Box 276, London SW8 5DT
Personal Callers HMSO Bookshop
49 High Holborn, London WC1V 6HB
Telefax: 071 873 2000
Branches at: Belfast, Birmingham, Bristol, Edinburgh,
Manchester

United States – États-Unis
OECD Publications and Information Centre
2001 L Street N.W., Suite 700
Washington, D.C. 20036-4910   Tel. (202) 785.6323
Telefax: (202) 785.0350

Venezuela
Libreria del Este
Avda F. Miranda 52, Aptdo. 60337
Edificio Galipán
Caracas 106   Tel. 951.1705/951.2307/951.1297
Telegram: Libreste Caracas

Yugoslavia – Yougoslavie
Jugoslovenska Knjiga
Knez Mihajlova 2, P.O. Box 36
Beograd   Tel. (011) 621.992
Telefax: (011) 625.970

Orders and inquiries from countries where Distributors have not yet been appointed should be sent to: OECD Publications Service, 2 rue André-Pascal, 75775 Paris Cédex 16, France.

Les commandes provenant de pays où l'OCDE n'a pas encore désigné de distributeur devraient être adressées à : OCDE, Service des Publications, 2, rue André-Pascal, 75775 Paris Cédex 16, France.